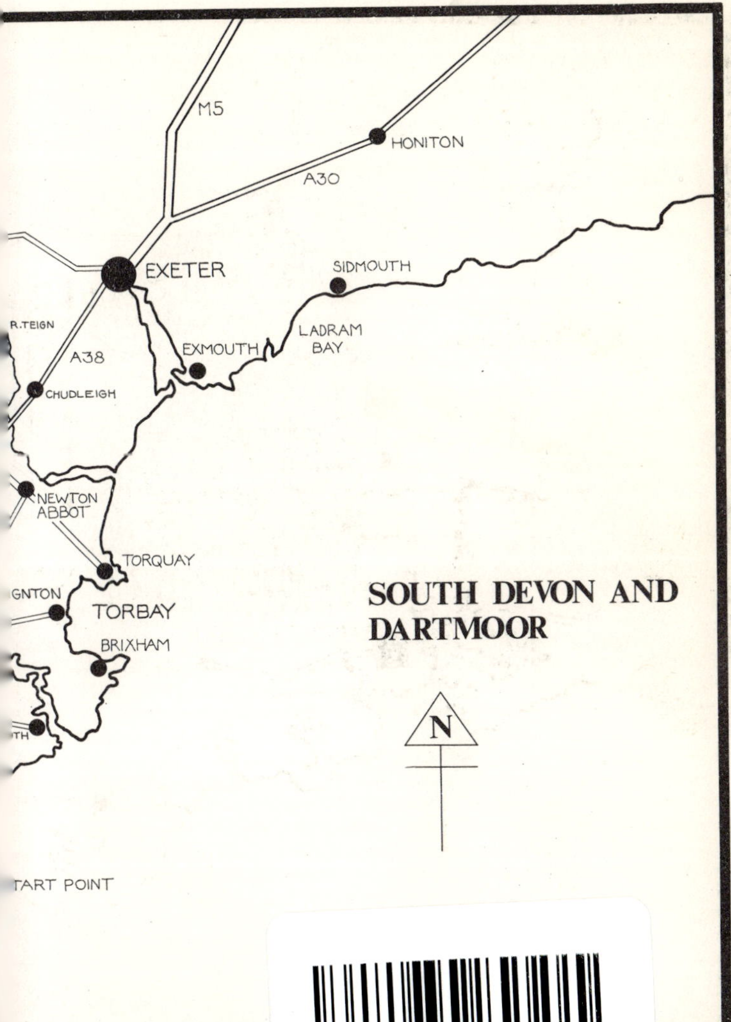

M5
HONITON
A30
EXETER
SIDMOUTH
R.TEIGN
A38
EXMOUTH
LADRAM
BAY
CHUDLEIGH
NEWTON
ABBOT
TORQUAY
GNTON
TORBAY
BRIXHAM
TH
TART POINT
SOUTH DEVON AND
DARTMOOR
N

Rock Climbs in the
South West

SOUTH DEVON AND DARTMOOR

By Pat Littlejohn and Pete O'Sullivan

Maps by Pete O'Sullivan

Photodiagrams prepared by Don Sargeant

Cover photographs by Mick Fowler and Don Sargeant

Published by **CORDEE** Leicester

Climbing Guide to Dartmoor and South West Devon, by K.M. Lawder, 1957 (RNSMC)

Rock Climbing in Devonshire, edited by R.D. Moulton, 1966 (RNSMC)

First Edition (South Devon), by P.R. Littlejohn and P.H. Biven, 1971 (West Col)

Devon Rock Climbs, edited by R.D. Moulton, (1978 RN & RMMC)

Second Edition (South Devon and Dartmoor), by P.R. Littlejohn and P. O'Sullivan, 1985 (Cordee)

Littlejohn, Pat

South Devon and Dartmoor — 2nd ed.
1. Rock climbing — England — Devon
I. Title   II. O'Sullivan, Pete
796.5'223'094235   GV199.44.G72D4

ISBN   0-904405-97-4

Produced by the Ernest Press, Glasgow G44 5QD.

Prepared for printing by Microset, Cartmel, Cumbria.

Front cover: Caveman, Berry Head, Andy Meyers
              Photo: Mick Fowler
Back cover: Interrogation, Haytor Low Man, Charlie Heard
              Photo: Don Sargeant

          This guide-book is available from all specialist climbing shops and book shops within the area, or direct from the publishers **CORDEE** 3a De Montfort Street, Leicester, LE1 7HD

CONTENTS

ACKNOWLEDGEMENTS

We would like to thank Polly Biven and Nick Biven for allowing free use of material from this book's predecessor, South Devon, which was written in association with the late Peter Biven.

Also vital was information, advice and criticism from some of the current 'hardcore' of Devon climbing, particularly Andy Gallagher, Andy Grieve, Nick Hancock, Iain Peters, Nick White, Brian Wilkinson and Bruce Woodley.

Don Sargeant has once again produced a fine set of photodiagrams (from photographs by himself and Pat Littlejohn), which will make life much easier for those using this book. Special thanks must go to Bob Moulton, whose editorial expertise has made the task of producing this guide much easier.

PRL, PO'S 1985

Introduction

Renowned for its picturesque countryside and spectacular coastline, Devon is a climbing area of great charm and enduring appeal.

The region covered by this guide-book is rich in variety and the cliffs echo this, from the sheltered sea-cliffs, of Torbay to the almost surreal offshore formations of Ladram Bay. Acting as a foil to the coastal areas are the many inland crags, ranging from the pleasantly situated Dewerstone and Chudleigh cliffs to the bleaker tors of the high moor, such as Haytor and Low Man.

The diversity of rock types encountered in this book is probably wider than in any other guide-book in the country, with climbs on sandstone, granite, limestone, shale and various metamorphosed rocks. Each of these imparts its own peculiar pleasures, and each requires a different approach and method of handling.

In terms of future development there is no doubt that Torbay still has an enormous amount of unclimbed rock and will continue to yield fine climbs to those bold enough to accept the challenge.

The fact that Dartmoor is a National Park does not necessarily imply a right of access to every area inside it. Most of the moor is in fact owned by someone, mainly farmers. At present it is possible to climb without hinderance on all the crags on the moor, though specific advice on access to the Dewerstone and Vixen Tor is given in the introductory paragraphs for those cliffs. Details of the access arrangements for Morwell Rocks and of the important seasonal restrictions at Berry Head are given in those sections.

Each cliff is given a grid reference, which relates to one of the following 1:50,000 series OS maps:

191 for Central and Eastern Dartmoor, and Chudleigh
192 for the South Coast east of Torbay
201 for Western Dartmoor, The Dewerstone, Morwell Rocks and Plymouth
202 for Torbay and the South Coast west of Torbay

It has been considered that some routes, for reasons of length or quality do not justify the space of a fully detailed description and such routes are referred to in the general description to a cliff or section of a cliff.

Left and right are always as the climber faces the cliff unless otherwise stated.

Please send details of any new routes and of inaccuracies in this book to the British Mountaineering Council, Crawford House, Precinct Centre, Booth Street East, Manchester M13 9RZ. The BMC will forward such information to authors/editors for use in future editions.

Historical

DARTMOOR AND MORWELL

Although the first reference to climbing on Dartmoor was by Hasket Smith in his book 'Climbing in the British Isles', published in 1894, no specific details of 'ascents on some of the Dartmoor tors' were made. Amazingly, the first recorded routes were the *Climbers' Club* routes on the Dewerstone climbed by David Cox, Rene Bere and Robin Hodgkin in 1935 and '36. Even though these lines have been adjusted to provide the best combinations of pitches, in their original state they remained the hardest routes on Dartmoor for the next 20 years.

As with the rest of the country the Depression and the Second World War effectively stifled development and it was not until 1946 when Tony Moulam climbed *Aramis* at Haytor that the potential of the area began to be realized. In 1948 Jim Moulton, the C.O. of the Royal Marine Commando School at Bickleigh, soloed *Colonel's Arête* at the Dewerstone while reconnoitering the crag as a training ground. Shortly after this members of the infant Royal Navy Ski Mountaineering Club, spearheaded by Admiral Keith Lawder and Bob Higgins, began a fruitful period of exploration at the Dewerstone and on the tors. This resulted in a fine crop of routes in the lower grades, taking obvious features, but it was left to Jim Simpson to climb the most obvious line on the Dewerstone with his ascent of *Central Groove*. On the same day he made the first ascent of *Needle Arête*, solo.

Development on the eastern side of the moors was left to a civilian group from Exeter. In 1949 the Higgins brothers climbed the classic Raven Gully on Low Man, and this was followed in 1952 by the ascent of *Canis* on the main tor by Moulam. Without a doubt the hardest routes of this period were the ascents of *Ann* at Haytor and *Kistvaen Corner* at Hound Tor. A certain amount of confusion surrounds the latter, which had been recorded in the two previous guide books as Hard Very Severe but has repulsed all recent attempts to lead it. It had been assumed that Geoff Sutton had led this route, but on checking it has been discovered that in fact the route had only been top-roped some time in the early to middle fifties with no record of the climber(s) involved. This is not to belittle the achievement as the route is now considered to be the hardest on Dartmoor at E3, 6a and has still to be led!

In 1957 Admiral Lawder documented all this exploration in a guide-book published by the R.N.S.M.C., thus beginning this Club's involvement with guide-books for the county which lasted until 1978. The publication of the guide-book coincided with the first appearance of Tom Patey, who was serving as a Naval Doctor with the Royal Marines. He opened his account with the superb *Leviathan* at the Dewerstone and followed this with routes on the Upper Buttresses, the finest being *Spider's Web*. His partner on the latter climb was

Barry Page who had himself, in the previous year, 1957, led the technical *Super Direct Start* to the Climbers' Club routes. Patey was also active on the tors but in 1958 he turned his attention to the shale cliffs at Morwell. These cliffs had first been inspected by G. Whittaker in 1949 and were included in the 1957 guide-book. It was left to Patey to climb the lines, which he did, even drafting in Zeke Deacon and Vivian Stevenson for the ascent of *Ultramontane*, which for its time was an astonishing route. Deacon and Stevenson then added *Globe and Laurel* to the Dewerstone, finishing up the unclimbed crack which is now the final pitch of Climbers' Club Direct. Patey's last route on Dartmoor was predictably bold taking a line through the overhangs left of Raven Gully at Haytor to produce *Outward Bound*.

The sixties saw the emergence of local climbers who began to dominate climbing in Devon. In 1961 instructors at the Ashburton Outward Bound School made a number of first ascents on Haytor including *Haggis* and *Hangover*. However, it was Dave Basset and Harry Cornish who made the great breakthrough on Low Man with their ascent of *Aviation*, which set a new standard of difficulty for climbing in Devon. On the Dewerstone, Brian Shackleton and Mike Rabley climbed *Valhalla Wall* in 1962, and later that year Rabley and John Jones made the first ascent of *Gideon*. This latter route had seen a number of attempts, most of them failing at the then artificial section. Rabley was killed in an accident at the Dewerstone in 1963, and his death dealt a severe blow to the small band of climbers then operating in the area.

However standards continued to rise, and in 1964 Frank Cannings climbed two characteristically difficult routes on Haytor, *Interrogation* and the *Low Man Girdle*. He also turned his attention towards the Dewerstone and with Shackleton climbed *Cyclops*. Shackleton continued to be active on the Dewerstone, producing *Vala* and, with John Jones, *Yogi*, whilst also making forays to King's Tor Quarry. The next few years were quiet, mainly because the predominant Exeter climbers were involved in developing the limestone sea-cliffs at Torbay. Pat Littlejohn, during a visit to the Dewerstone in 1968, led *Scimitar*, a typically bold and steep route. At Haytor in 1971, he advanced standards by climbing a direct start to Interrogation, which was, in terms of difficulty and seriousness, years ahead of its time. Another tenuous line of weakness gave him *Rhinoceros*, still one of the hardest routes on Dartmoor. Ranging across the moor, Littlejohn also climbed *Plektron* at Vixen Tor and *Hostile Witness* on Bench Tor.

The late sixties saw a strong local team from Plymouth climb the obvious remaining lines at the Dewerstone. Len Benstead, an ex-Marine, was in the forefront of this group, producing *Dangler* and *Imperialist*. Benstead crowned his activities with a free ascent of *Gideon* to give the crag its hardest route. At the same time Andrew

McFarlane and Deryck Ball, both schoolboys, added *Fruitflancase* and *Tarantula*, both steep and impressive routes of quality, and if the stories are true the ascents had their fair share of thrills and spills.

The mid-seventies were relatively quiet with activity being confined to Bench Tor, which was re-discovered and developed by the ageing Iain Peters, and the ascents of routes at Foggintor, including *Rockface* and *Fogginard*, by Littlejohn. Keith Darbyshire climbed the isolated block at Chinkwell Tor to give *Widecombe Wall*. This, sadly, was his only contribution to Dartmoor.

In 1976 Pete O'Sullivan and Tony Pearson girdled the Upper Raven Buttress at the Dewerstone with *Nibeling*. O'Sullivan followed this in 1977 with a number of aid eliminations on the same crag.

In 1978 O'Sullivan and Pip George solved two long standing problems with their ascents of *Energy Crisis* at the Dewerstone and *Feasibility Study* at Vixen Tor. Morwell was also re-visited and the fine *Vacancy at the Vatican* was climbed by O'Sullivan and Tim Carter. The early part of 1979 saw frantic activity by Plymouth-based climbers, who produced 13 new routes at Morwell, most of these in just one month. The outstanding routes of this period were *Palace of Skulls* and *Cold Grief*. During 1979 more routes were added to the Dewerstone, the best being *Extendable Arms* by O'Sullivan and *Dragon Song* by Steve Bell, the latter being a long standing 'last great problem'. On Vixen Tor 'Nipper' Harrison climbed the often-tried *Torture* on the North Face. During a brief visit Pat Littlejohn added *Rough Diamond* to the main tor at Haytor, thus maintaining his, by now, long distance involvement with the area.

The latest phase of development has tended to be in the quarries on either side of the moor. Iain Peters has added two routes at King's Tor Quarry, while Bruce Woodley and Chris Nicholson have climbed three steep lines in Holwell Quarry near Haytor. Besides this, Paul Dawson climbed the middle of the blank slab at Vixen Tor to give *Docker's Dilemma*, a serious, unlikely-looking route. At Eagle Rock, O'Sullivan climbed the obvious arête to give *The Eyrie*, probably the last remaining line on this cliff. Mick Fowler free climbed the *Low Man Girdle* and in the process eliminated the aid point on the Direct Start to *Interrogation*.

To come right up to date, the shallow cracks on the left of *Rough Diamond* at Haytor have been climbed by Pete Bull to give Rough Justice. The route was top-roped prior to its ascent, which has caused some controversy, and originally had a peg for protection, which has subsequently disappeared. However, this ascent does point to the future of Dartmoor climbing: short, technically hard climbs with sparse protection. This is illustrated by Bruce Woodley's routes at Chinkwell Tor: *The Fair* and *Scrumpy Special*. Many short lines of this nature exist and are bound to be the focus of attention for activists in the latter part of the eighties.

SOUTH DEVON

Limestone climbing in Devon began at the remarkable date of 1923, when I.B. Prowse ascended Wogs at Chudleigh Rocks. Following this no routes were recorded until 1960, when Tom Patey climbed *Sarcophagus, Chudleigh Overhang* and *Barn Owl Crack* with friends from the Royal Marines base at Lympstone. Servicemen were also responsible for the next batch of climbs at Chudleigh. The classic lines of *Lute, Slot, Inkerman Groove* and *Great Western* were completed throughout 1961 by N. Hannaby and E. Rayson and established Chudleigh as a major crag and the forcing ground for standards in Devon. The same year saw the first recorded climbing in Torbay, where Dave Bassett explored the friendly Coastguard Cliffs at Berry Head.

1962 marked the arrival on the Devon scene of Pete Biven, an accomplished climber who had made his name on gritstone and pioneered a brilliant series of routes on Cornish granite. After climbing *Combined Ops* at Chudleigh he attacked the highest part of the cliff and produced *The Fly*, the first route to take the 'western tower'.

Exeter-born Frank Cannings was next to make his mark with a series of climbs on the eastern end of Chudleigh North Face, and soon afterwards the Garden Wall was opened up by Biven with his fine trilogy of routes: *Nexus, Sexus* and *Plexus*. Later in 1964 Cannings and Biven teamed up to climb *The Spider*, then the most difficult and for a long time the most prestigious climb in Devon, and throughout 1965 Cannings established himself at the forefront of Devon climbing with a series of fine leads, including *Nimrod* and *The Track*. Around this time Biven visited the cliffs at Long Quarry and climbed *The Grey Tower*, but he explored no further in Torbay at this stage.

With the emergence of more strong teams from Exeter, 1966 was a productive year at Chudleigh. Denver Rainford produced the aid routes *Obstreperous* and *Black Death*, Ian McMorrin climbed the difficult *Panga* and the last major line on the Garden Wall, *Perseus*, and Andy Powling led *Bolero* accompanied by a 15-year old Pat Littlejohn.

New Crags On The Coast

The development of Torbay gave Devon climbing a new importance and provided local climbers with the skills and experience to tackle the big, serious crags on the North Coast of Devon and Cornwall in subsequent years. The first tentative steps were taken by Steve Dawson and John Hammond, who ventured onto Daddyhole Main Cliff to climb *Gates of Eden* in May 1967. Within days Biven had added *Last Exit* and *Triton*, and throughout that summer routes at Daddyhole fell thick and fast to Biven, Cannings and Littlejohn, of particular note being the difficult and serious *Pantagruel*.

In July Littlejohn climbed the first route on the big slabs at Long Quarry, *Coup de Grâce*, then climbing in Torbay entered a new phase with the discovery of The Old Redoubt. The ascent of *Moonraker* by Biven and Littlejohn was a real adventure. Sharing leads, they climbed the route in five pitches, starting up the corner now taken by Goddess of Gloom. Now Torbay had a route to compare with the classics of Cornwall or Anglesey — Biven loved it so much that he made the first five ascents! Obviously the cliff had much more to offer, and within a month Biven had pointed Cannings at the awe-inspiring line of Dreadnought. The attempt ended at the top of the hanging groove on pitch 3, and the pair exited rightwards to produce *Barbican*, still a major achievement. The year closed with a visit by John Cleare and Rusty Baillie, who traversed the base of The Old Redoubt to produce *Magical Mystery Tour*, a new phenomenon on the South Devon coast. The sea-traversing craze was taken up by Biven, who created nearly all the Torbay traverses over the next couple of years.

The Long Quarry area began to yield some worthwhile climbs in 1968. While Biven and Littlejohn attacked the imposing groove of *Incubus*, Cannings forged the intricate and technical line of *The Mitre*. Until this point all first ascents in Torbay had been made on sight, but in June Littlejohn and John Hammond spent 16 man-hours gardening the line of *Grip Type Thynne*. An ascent on immaculately clean rock followed and the route was judged 'magnificent', however the vegetation soon crept back and the climb lost its original stature, a fate shared by most routes on these slabs.

While Torbay was the arena for big intimidating routes, Chudleigh remained a forcing ground for technical standards. Littlejohn climbed *Penny Lane* and *The Spy* with John Hammond, then *The Equation* was pieced together with Charles Wand-Tetley. Paul Leedell managed a free ascent of *Smoke Gets in Your Eyes*, *Combat* fell to Littlejohn and Steve Jones, then there was a lull in new route activity until the late seventies.

New Faces

Exeter University had always had an active climbing club, but 1969 saw the emergence of a particularly strong group headed by Ed Grindley. They developed Daddyhole Upper Cliff and added climbs at Anstey's Cove and Meadfoot Quarry, culminating in the ascent of the *Meadfoot Girdle* by Grindley.

April '69 was a boom month in Torbay. Littlejohn and Cannings, both climbing with daemonic enthusiasm, teamed up to climb *Dreadnought*, *The Hood* and *The Seventh Circle* on The Old Redoubt, all of which proved memorable ascents. On the hanging stance of Dreadnought most of the belay fell away and the pair were left swinging from one peg. So great was the rush of adrenalin that

Cannings dispensed with the next pitch in five minutes and placed only two runners! Littlejohn then added the powerful *Neophron* on the Babbacombe Crags and the month was rounded off when, after a week of repeating Drummond's routes in the Avon Gorge, he returned to a scene of previous failure and completed *The Pinch*, perhaps the 'most extending and hair raising' lead in the South West at the time.

Hammond made the first probes on Quarry Wall and produced the surprisingly worthwhile *Gilded Turd*. Others soon got a taste for the cliff and a batch of climbs appeared, including the fine *Steppenwolf* by Grindley. This focussed attention on the quarried limestone, and in 1970 Berry Head Quarry was opened up with on-sight ascents of *Booh-bah Plost* by Hammond and Littlejohn, and *Dust Devil* by Biven. Subsequent routes on the face were gardened beforehand, which greatly improved the quality of the climbing on such routes as *Yellow Rurties* and *Paranoid*. The latter was perhaps Grindley's finest route on Torbay, but his involvement with the quarry continued in 1971 when he created the mammoth girdle of *Opus Dei*.

Aid routes were in vogue during the Winter of 1971. *Iron Butterfly* gave Wand-Tetley and Ben Goodman several days' fine sport, while Royal Marine team Martin Chambers, Frank Hayton and Nigel Gifford made their epic ascent of *The Curse* over several weekends, little dreaming that above the initial roof it would be climbed free only a decade later.

1972 was quiet apart from a dramatic, on-sight ascent of *The Quaker* by Littlejohn and Jones, then 1973 saw activity by several different teams. The superb *Black Ice* fell to Littlejohn and Keith Darbyshire, then the Slabs found more devotees in the form of K. Bentham and C. Gimblett, who laboured hard to clean and climb four big lines, including *Ruby in the Dust*. Darbyshire added the fierce *Man Bites Dog* in a rare foray from the North Coast, and the first major input by a Plymouth team took place when Andy MacFarlane and Derek Ball embarked on the magnificent *Rainbow Bridge*.

For the next couple of years Torbay was forgotten as attention was focussed on the North Coast, then in 1976 Littlejohn revisited the area. He climbed *Snakecharmer*, *Fear of Flying* and *The Wake*, and nearly made it up Call to Arms, where a retreat sling hung enticingly near the stance for several years. A year later he discovered the instantly classic *Yardarm* and climbed the superb arête of *Zuma*, a long-standing ambition.

Local Talent and New Megaroutes

1978 saw the re-emergence of local talent, with Andy Gallagher and Brian Wilkinson to the fore. For the next two years they discovered worthwhile routes all over Torbay, especially on the Coastguard Cliffs at Berry Head. Another local lad, Steve Bell, hit the scene in 1979. He was Devon's first 'modern rock athlete' and concentrated on aid eliminations on the limestone crags, notable successes being *The Mitre* and *Neophron* in Torbay, and *Penny Lane* and *Panga* at Chudleigh. Torbay's main event that year however was the ascent by Arnis Strapcans and Mick Fowler of a formidable line which had repulsed several strong teams — *Depth Charge*. This was soon sequelled when Fowler and Andy Meyers climbed *Lip Trip*, thus becoming more acclimatized to the nightmare of overhanging rock above the Great Cave and preparing the way for Caveman.

1980 saw the solution to another long-standing problem, when Steve Monks and Ed Hart (who had done second ascents of many of the South West's hardest climbs in the latter seventies) completed *Call to Arms*. At the same time Pete O'Sullivan began to make his presence felt in South Devon by exploring the remoter part of The Old Redoubt, one result being the spectacular *False Alarms*. Another local man, Chris Nicholson, made a significant contribution when he and Gallagher climbed the excellent *Buzby* at Telegraph Hole, but three years were to pass before Nicholson showed his real potential in Torbay.

1982 — the year of *Caveman*. After many attempts Fowler and Meyers succeeded on this incredible line. It is the true successor to Dreadnought, having the special Torbay blend of desperate climbing in awe-inspiring situations. A route in almost the same class appeared a year later, when Littlejohn returned to Torbay to settle some old scores accompanied by South Wales ace Tony Penning. *Madness* was a mind-blowing, on-sight lead of a soaring traverse line which had defeated him twice before, and *Blonde Bombshell* gave the area its first 6b pitch. *The Pinch* went free, giving a magnificent wall climb, and two excellent, high-standard slab routes were created in Telegraph Hole — *Flashdance* and *Blinding Flash*.

In 1983, several important routes were achieved by Nicholson and Bruce Woodley, Devon residents who have raised local standards to their highest level (relative to the rest of U.K.) since Steve Bell left the area.. Woodley transformed Berry Head Quarry with four very impressive lines — *Burning Bridges, Sunset Boulevard, Dirt Eater* and *Desparête* — and added the fierce *Mukdah's Wall* at Daddyhole. Nicholson grabbed one of the best and boldest lines at Anstey's Cove with *Devonshire Cream*, and left the desperate test piece of *American Express* as a companion to Blonde Bombshell.

There is and always will be, much scope for first ascents on South Devon limestone. Chudleigh will become ever more popular and polished; Torbay will provide the area's major challenges which, though they may not have mass appeal, will confer special rewards upon those with sufficient expertise and taste for adventure to enjoy them.

The Dewerstone   GR 538 638

The heavily wooded valley of the River Plym, above Shaugh Bridge provides the backdrop to some of the best middle-grade climbing on Dartmoor. The Dewerstone cliffs are situated on the hillside above the Plym roughly half a mile upstream from the car-park at the bridge. The land is owned by the National Trust, who are seriously concerned with levels of erosion both in the woodlands and at the base of the cliff. At the time of writing they have just completed extensive path building activities. Due to the serious erosion problems which have manifested themselves in the last few years, all visitors are asked to use the designated approach path. It is probably fair to say that the ground below Devil's Rock constitutes an ecological disaster area. In the light of this it is not an unreasonable request to ask anyone who uses the crag to be responsible for removing their litter and to refrain from ripping up stones. Large groups under instruction appear to be the main culprits in this abuse.

The Main Area of the crag is unmistakable, with the 170-foot high face of Devil's Rock rising almost from the river. On the right of this in the trees lie the Needle Buttress to the left, and the Upper and Lower Raven Buttresses to the right. These are clearly seen from the summit of Devil's Rock.

The crag is approached from Shaugh Bridge by crossing the wooden footbridge near the car-park and then following the wide track which leads gradually up the hillside. After a few hundred yards an obvious subsidiary path forks right and leads through the woods to the bottom of Devil's Rock.

THE WESTERN ROCKS
From the approach path the first rocks which one sees on the left are the Western Rocks, with the Tower being the most westerly of these:

THE TOWER
This is the prominent rock tower, some 50 feet high on its front side. The easiest ascent and descent is by starting on the left of the front face and climbing a slanting slab to the right, **Tower Stairs** (50ft Moderate)

Tower Crack   30ft   Hard Severe
A great little route taking the obvious crack in the west face.
1   30ft   4b.   Climb the crack to a difficult move out left at its top.

Windowsill   40ft   Severe   1958
This takes the obvious wide crack in the nose of The Tower. Start below a tree under the nose.

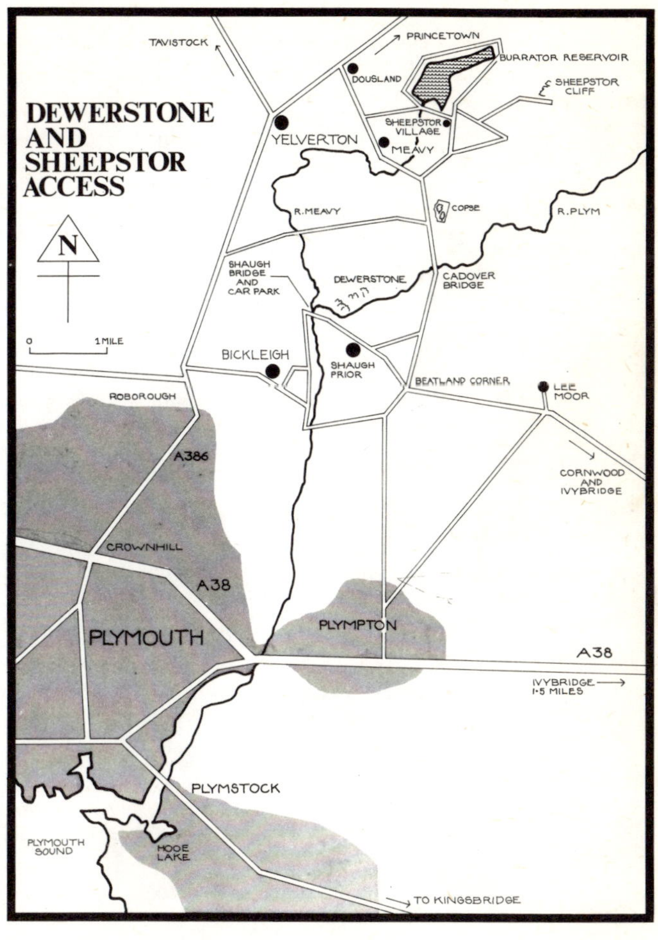

DEWERSTONE AND SHEEPSTOR ACCESS
N
0   1 MILE
TAVISTOCK
PRINCETOWN
BURRATOR RESERVOIR
DOUSLAND
SHEEPSTOR CLIFF
SHEEPSTOR VILLAGE
YELVERTON
MEAVY
R.MEAVY
COPSE
R.PLYM
SHAUGH BRIDGE AND CAR PARK
DEWERSTONE
CADOVER BRIDGE
BICKLEIGH
SHAUGH PRIOR
BEATLAND CORNER
LEE MOOR
ROBOROUGH
A386
CORNWOOD AND IVYBRIDGE
CROWNHILL
A38
PLYMOUTH
PLYMPTON
A38
IVYBRIDGE
1·5 MILES
PLYMSTOCK
PLYMOUTH SOUND
HOOE LAKE
TO KINGSBRIDGE

1   40ft   Use the branch to enter the crack, which is followed to the top.

Window Slit   60ft   Very Difficult
For troglodytes and general deviants only. Start at the foot of the slanting slab of Tower Stairs.
1   60ft   Climb the slab and then move into the narrow cleft; squirm up this to exit via a narrow hole. Follow the arête to the top.

PENNY BAY
This is a strange bay of rock to the right of The Tower. At the back of the bay is a hole which leads upwards under an overhanging block. This is named, rather unfortunately, The Admiral's Hole. The chimney outside of this is climbed by **Circle Climb** (Severe).

Wobbling Wall   45ft   E1   1979
1   45ft   5b.   Climb the wall left of Twittering Crack and finish directly over the overhang.

Twittering Crack   40ft   Hard Very Severe
This is the prominent crack in the right wall of the bay, left of the obvious niche. Harder than it looks!
1   40ft   5a.   Climb the crack until near its top, then move right to the arête and finish up the slab.

Saint's Niche   40ft   Severe
Start beneath the obvious niche.
1   40ft   4a.   Climb into the obvious niche until it is possible to move right to join Agag's Slab.

Agag's Slab   40ft   Difficult   1950
A good introductory climb, starting below the slab.
1   40ft   Move up left and then back right to a tree. Step up left and then go direct to the top.

Agag's Direct   40ft   Severe
1   40ft   Climb the obvious line up the left side of the slab over a tricky bulge near the top.

Mambo Slab   50ft   Very Difficult
1   50ft   This climbs the slab right of Agag's with a problematic start.

Noddy   45ft   Very Severe   1980
Start as for Mambo Slab.
1   45ft   4c.   Climb over the initial bulge as for Mambo Slab, then make some difficult moves up the nose to gain easier-angled rock, which leads to the top.

Goblin   50ft   Very Severe   1969
Start midway between Mambo Slab and Ceasar's Nose, below a shallow groove.
1 50ft 4c.   Climb to the overhang, then traverse left, using holds above the roof, to a rib. Continue easily to the top.

Ceasar's Nose   40ft   Severe
A very pleasant route taking the prominent nose at the extreme end of the flanking wall of Penny Bay.
1 40ft 4a.   Climb up until it is possible to step right onto the nose. Climb to a crack, which leads to the right and follow this to the top.

THE MAIN AREA
The most obvious feature is the very steep face of Devil's Rock. Left of this is the Main Gully, which is wide and vegetated. Left again are the buttresses of Colonel's Arête and Pinnacle Buttress, with Mucky Gully separating them. Left of Pinnacle Buttress on its flank is a short 40-foot wall, which gives some interesting routes. The short chimney is Pinnacle Chimney.

Holly Tree Wall   40ft   Difficult
Start just left of Pinnacle Chimney.
1 40ft   Climb the slab on the left to a tree. Move past this and climb the chimney on the right to the top.

Holly Tree Wall Direct   35ft   Hard Very Severe
1 35ft 5a.   Climb straight up to the tree, then climb the nasty crack above with difficulty.

Pinnacle Chimney   30ft   Very Difficult   1949
A pleasant pitch.
1   30ft   Climb the chimney to the pinnacle then the steep left-hand wall to the top.

Pinnacle Buttress Direct   110ft   Severe
A series of variants on the parent route giving good climbing. Start left of the tree beneath the block at the foot of the buttress.
1 85ft 4a.   Climb the face of the block and move round the right arête. Scramble up to some rock steps, which lead to a steep crack. Climb this with difficulty, to a wide ledge.
2 25ft 4a.   Climb the crack behind the ledge to the top of the pinnacle. Cross from this to the rock behind.

Variation   Hard Severe
2a 25ft   Move out left from the ledge and climb direct to a ledge, from which the summit block is easily reached.

Pinnacle Buttress   120ft   Difficult   1949   ★
A good introductory climb, escapable throughout, but with a finely
positioned last pitch. Start below a chimney at the foot of the buttress.
1   40ft   Climb the chimney, then scramble to block belays.
2   20ft   Climb just right of the arête to a large ledge on the left.
3   30ft   Step off the wobbly block and climb the exposed wall to a
ledge below the Pinnacle.
4   30ft   Move right above an overhang, then move up to a small
ledge on the arête of the Pinnacle and follow this to the summit. Either
jump or climb across onto the final wall.

Variation   Hard Severe
4a   30ft   4a.   Move right below the overhang and take this at its
widest point to join the original route on the arête.

Mucky Gully   110ft   Difficult   ★
It does not deserve its name as it is a good clean line taking the gully
between Pinnacle Buttress and Colonel's Arête.
1   40ft   Follow the corner of the gully or the right wall to a nut and
flake belay on a narrow ledge.
2   70ft   Follow the gully to a large chockstone, up over this and then
take the right-hand wall to finish.

Reverse Cleft   50ft   Severe   1949
A good exposed crack climb. Start at the belay 40 feet up Mucky Gully.
1   50ft   4a.   Move up to the prominent crack on the right and follow
this with difficulty to the top pitch of Colonel's Arête.

Colonel's Cavort   125ft   Hard Severe
A series of variations on Colonel's Arête. Start beneath a wide crack
formed by a detached block right of the foot of Mucky Gully.
1   50ft   Climb the crack and traverse right to the ledge above pitch
two of Colonel's Arête.
2   45ft   4a.   Climb up just left of the arête to a ledge. Climb the
off-width crack above to the ledge.
3   30ft   The best finish is to climb the outside of the block above,
stepping across the gap to finish.

Colonel's Arête   130ft   Hard Very Difficult   1948   ★
A good climb. Start below an earthy wall just left of Main Gully.
1   30ft   Climb the earthy wall and scramble to belay at a crack.
2   25ft   Move left and gain a ledge on the arête, which is followed to
a large ledge and block belay.
3   45ft   Climb up past the tree to the foot of a short crack. Climb this,
moving right at the top. Climb over a rocking stone on the arête to
gain a tree belay.

4   30ft   Climb the outside of the block to its summit and cross the gap to the top.

MAIN GULLY
This is the wide gully which is almost totally overgrown. Care should be taken in the middle section of the gully due to loose rock and, when wet, dangerous muddy slopes. The left wall gives a few short climbs.

The Echo   45ft   Hard Very Severe   1977
This is almost totally overgrown with slime and moss and would need cleaning prior to an ascent.
1   45ft   5a.   Climb the obvious finger crack left of Dark Cleft to a ledge, then layback the edge on the right to the top.

Dark Cleft   40ft   Very Difficult
Start three-quarters of the way up the gully below a large chimney on the left wall.
1   40ft   Climb the chimney and traverse right at half-height. Move up and back left into the chimney and step onto the top of pitch three of Colonel's Arête.

Kernow   40ft   Severe
Start as for Dark Cleft.
1   40ft   Climb the deceptively easy-looking wall up to the overhang, then move left and make a difficult move over the overhang to finish.

The Tunnel   25ft   Difficult   1949
Start at the top of the gully.
1   25ft   Climb past an overhanging block and crawl into the natural tunnel behind to emerge 15 feet higher up.

The next climbs are on Devil's Rock but are approached from Main Gully.

The High Traverse   45ft   Very Difficult   1949
An exposed pitch which makes a good continuation to Colonel's Arête1   45ft   Step right and climb a short groove. Traverse delicately right
until clear of the overhang, then climb direct to the top passing a tree.

Inkspots Hangover   40ft   Hard Very Severe   1962
A strenuous route taking the overhang above High Traverse. Start as for that route.
1   40ft   4c.   As for High Traverse to a large flake, then step left and climb over the roof on black flake holds. Scramble right to finish.

DEVIL'S ROCK

The main area of the Dewerstone. The most obvious feature is the clean cut corner of Central Groove. The large rambling terrace at the top left-hand section of the Devil's Rock is known as the Meadow. To the right of Central Groove is the steep wall taken by Gideon and the Climbers' Club routes. The obvious hand-jamming crack is taken by the Direct route and leads to the overhung niche, which is also gained, though from the right, by the Ordinary route.

As a general rule the top pitches of the climbs on Devil's Rock are not an integral part of the climbs and they can be interchanged at will. The exceptions are Extendable Arms, Climbers' Club Direct and Route B, whose top pitches are very much the climaxes of the routes.

Vineyard   135ft   Hard Severe   1952
A pleasant route with some interesting positions. Start just right of Main Gully.
1 50ft 4a.   Climb the steep wall to a niche at half height and then follow a crack to a tree belay. The left-hand groove can also be climbed to reach the same point.
2 55ft 4b.   Move up, then traverse left along a sloping ledge to a groove. Follow this, turning the overhang above on the left. Move back right to a tree belay.
3 30ft   Move back left and then up over a dead tree until beneath a roof. Move left to the edge and then up to a tree and the top.

Cretin's Cavort   60ft   Hard Very Severe   1962
Interesting, open climbing. Start on the ledge just below the steep wall left of Leviathan.
1 60ft 4c.   Climb the wall on widely-spaced holds direct to the tree belay of Leviathan.

Leviathan   160ft   Very Severe   1957   ★★
A good route with a magnificent first pitch which takes the groove in the blunt arête right of Vineyard. Start beneath the blocks at the foot of the groove.
1 75ft 4c.   Take any line to the ledge below the groove and follow this to where it fades. Move up right below an overhang, then traverse right around the arête and climb the wall to a ledge and tree belay. The overhang can be climbed direct at a slight increase in the grade.
2 60ft   Move right and climb to broken rock above Central Groove. Follow a ramp rightwards to a ledge below a slabby corner.
3 25ft 4a.   Climb the corner to the top.

Extendable Arms   155ft   E1   1979
A very steep eliminate line between Leviathan and Vala. The second pitch climbs the large bulge above the Meadow.

1   75ft   5c.   From the bottom of the groove of Leviathan swing right onto the arête and follow this to a ledge. Continue over a roof to the left end of Vala's roof and then follow the arête to the tree belay.
2   80ft   5b.   As for Leviathan until broken rock is gained below the roof. Go straight over the overhang to gain a crack, which leads more easily to the top.

Vala   160ft   Hard Very Severe   1963
A route with exhilarating climbing over the overhangs left of Central Groove. Low in its grade.
1   75ft   4c.   Climb to the bollard of Central Groove, then layback onto the steep wall beneath the roof. Surmount the roof and follow huge holds to the tree belay and ledge above (shared with Leviathan).
2   60ft   4a.   Walk down left behind a flake until beneath a small overhang. Climb over this to the Meadow. Tree belay high on the right.
3   25ft   5a.   Climb the problematic wall between the two chimneys, finishing up the slab.

Central Groove   160ft   Hard Severe   1949   ★★
The classic route of the cliff, taking the steep corner on large holds. Start below the 20-foot wall which leads to the corner.
1   80ft   4b.   Climb the wall to the foot of the groove. Follow this to the capping overhang, then traverse right on black flakes to a belay ledge on the arête.
2   80ft   4b.   Climb up left until below an overhang. Move left below the roof to the Meadow and scramble up to a chimney just left of a tree, which leads awkwardly to the top. A better finish is to climb to the roof and then to follow a ramp rightwards and then the slabby groove, as for Leviathan.

Scimitar   170ft   Hard Very Severe   1968   ★
A steep and intimidating route which breaks out left from the slab of Gideon to gain the right wall of Central Groove.
1   90ft   5a.   Follow Gideon to beneath the overhang. Traverse left under the roof until a hard layback move can be made to gain the wall above. Climb directly up the right wall of Central Groove and move right to the belay ledge at the top of the arête.
2   80ft   Finish up Central Groove.

Variation E1, 5b
1a.   From the move around the roof, traverse immediately right to the arête and follow this direct to the belay of Central Groove.

Fruitflancase   150ft   E1   1969   ★★
A superb jamming pitch taking the obvious crack above the narrow slab of Gideon.

1 85ft 5a. Follow Gideon to the top of the narrow slab and move awkwardly into the crack immediately right of the overhang. Follow this and the one on the left to a resting place below a small bulge. Surmount this and climb up left to the belay of Central Groove.
2 40ft 4c. Climb up to the left on broken rock to a short rounded crack right of the easy rake taken by Leviathan. Climb the crack to the belay below the final pitch of C.C. Ordinary.
3 25ft 5a. Just left of the belay a rounded crack breaks through the overhanging wall. Climb this direct and finish up the slab above.

Gideon   155ft   E1   *1962/1969*   ★
A well protected and technical route whose difficulties are short-lived. Start below the short wall at the bottom of Central Groove.
1 85ft 5b. Climb the short wall, then move right onto the slab. Follow this to the roof, then swing right above this to a large flake. Climb the shallow groove directly to better holds above. Continue direct to the ledge and bollard belay of C.C. Ordinary.
2 70ft 4c. Climb the narrow crack above the bollard to the ledge below the corner of Leviathan. Finish up this.

Energy Crisis   80ft   E3   1978
A hard problem taking the roof and thin crack left of CC Direct. Start as for that route. It will probably require cleaning before an ascent.
1 80ft 6a. Climb directly over the roof using the small flake. Follow the thin crack and the edge of the slab to the spike of Gideon, continue as for that route.

Climbers' Club Direct   160ft   Hard Very Severe   1936   ★★★
An impressive line with a well positioned final pitch. Start beneath a short corner leading up to an overhang some 20ft right of Central Groove.
1 70ft 5a. Climb up to and over the roof strenuously using the obvious crack. Follow this past a tree into a niche. Climb up and exit out left on large holds above the overhang to a large bollard belay.
2 90ft 4c. Climb the V-chimney to the overhang and pull over this to a crack leading to a large niche. Move left slightly and follow the continuation crack steeply to the top.

Super Direct Start   40ft   E1   *1957*
Often wet.
1 40ft 5b. Climb the wall right of the Direct to the overhanging flake.

Climbers' Club Ordinary   170ft   Very Severe   1935   ★
A good, varied climb which maintains its interest throughout its length. The first pitch is poorly protected but the route is not

technically difficult. Start in an earthy gully on the right-hand edge of the main face.
1   75ft   4b.   Climb up to gain a line of footholds leading out left to a flake. Move under an overhang into the large niche. Move up the groove and swing right into a smaller groove, which leads to the large bollard belay on the left.
2   70ft   4a.   Climb the V-chimney to the overhang. Move right and then back left to the continuation crack, which leads to a shallow niche. Traverse left on good holds to a large ledge below the slabby corner of Leviathan.
3   25ft   Climb the overhanging crack on the left and then to the top.

The Original Finish   70ft   Very Difficult
Not worthwhile except as an escape in rain or impending darkness.
2a   70ft   From the bollard belay move over brambles to the left to the stance of Central Groove. Move up left and then back right along the ramp to the belay below pitch 3 of the parent route.

Globe and Laurel   145ft   Hard Very Severe   1959
A rather disjointed climb taking the rounded cracks right of CC Ordinary. Start in the niche just left of the earthy gully.
1   80ft   4c.   Climb out of the niche to join CC Ordinary and follow this to the large flake. Move right under the overhang to a groove. Swing left on reluctant holds and move left over ribs and grooves to the bollard belay of the CC routes. It is possible to climb straight over the roof above the large flake at no increase in grade.
2   65ft   5a.   From the ledge below the bollard tiptoe right into a groove and layback up this to a ledge on the right. Move up to easier rock, which leads to a belay on Route B. Various ways off.

Bee Line   100ft   Hard Very Severe   1965
A route of little merit apart from an airy second pitch. Start in the muddy gully as for CC Ordinary.
1   50ft   4a.   Climb an earthy crack left of Route B to the stance above the second pitch of that climb.
2   50ft   5a.   Step left and follow the cracks in the rounded arête until level with the top of the chimney on the right. Traverse left to a ledge on the main face. Easier climbing leads to the ledge below the top pitch of Route B. Various ways off.

Route B   150ft   Hard Very Difficult   1949
After a scrappy start the climbing becomes good with the final pitch being pleasantly exposed. Start right of the earthy gully, beneath the centre of a large block.
1   30ft   Climb over a bulge and move left into a short groove and follow this to the top of the block.
2   25ft   Climb over blocks to a tree.

3   45ft   Move left along a ledge and climb into a shallow chimney, exit out right. Climb the wall above to a large ledge. Belay on the right.
4   50ft   Step around onto the main face and move into a niche. Climb the groove above and step right onto a nose. Go up left from this and so to the top.

Variations
1a   40ft   4b.   Climb over the bulge, but then move right beneath the overhang to climb a short groove.
4a   40ft   Climb the flake behind the belay until it is possible to move left to join the parent route on the nose.

Knucklecracker   100ft   Hard Severe   1964
A route which is harder to find than climb! In the trees to the right of Route B is a buttress. Start just left of a crack, below a mossy groove.
1   50ft   4a.   Climb the groove and the slab above to a tree belay.
2   50ft   4a.   Walk down left until beneath a crack. Climb this and move left onto a narrow slab. Follow this and the slabs above to the top.

GIRDLE TRAVERSES
There are three main lines, but others are possible.

The Admiral's Traverse   300ft   Very Difficult   1949
A route which takes an impressive line across the top of Devil's Rock. Start as for Holly Tree Wall.
1   40ft   Climb the slab of Holly Tree Wall and cross to Pinnacle Chimney. Belay on the large chockstone.
2   40ft   Move out right across the wall to the belay on Colonel's Arête beneath the last pitch of that route.
3   20ft   Descend a few feet and cross the top of Dark Cleft to belay in Main Gully.
4   30ft   Descend Main Gully to a holly tree belay level with the ledge at the top of Vineyard pitch 1.
5   30ft   Traverse right along the ledge of Vineyard and then climb up to the right to another large ledge and tree belay as for Leviathan.
6   60ft   Traverse up and right on broken rock above Central Groove until a rake leads up right to a belay below the final crack of CC Ordinary.
7   40ft   Move down to the right until it is possible to make a short exposed traverse to a crack (CC Ordinary reversed). Continue right to the edge and belay as for Route B.
8   40ft   Climb the flake on the right as for the variation finish to Route B.

Cornish Reprieve   290ft   Hard Very Severe   1963
A good exposed line with a fine crux pitch. Start as for Vineyard.
1   50ft   4b.   As for pitch 1 of Vineyard.
2   80ft   4b.   Climb across the wall to the arête of Leviathan, round this and down into Central Groove. Reverse this to the thread belay.
3   70ft   5a.   Traverse across the right wall to a ledge on the arête (manky peg). Make some difficult moves into a crack on the right and climb this to a diagonal break. Move right along this break until below the bollard belay of the CC routes. Climb up onto this.
4   50ft   4a.   Climb the V-chimney of CC Ordinary, then go right and up to the belay ledge of Route B on the right of the face.
5   40ft   Finish as for Route B pitch 4.

Lateral Thinking   175ft   E1   1978   ★
A fine airy route, better than it looks. Start as for CC Ordinary.
1   45ft   4b.   As for CC Ordinary, to belay in the niche above the tree.
2   60ft   5c.   Climb down below the tree, then move with difficulty into Energy Crisis and climb to the spike. Traverse left, just above the lip of the overhang, and belay on the thread in Central Groove.
3   70ft   4c.   Climb up to the roof on Vala, then traverse into Leviathan. Continue across the wall of Cretin's Cavort to the tree belay above pitch 1 of Vineyard. Various ways off.

THE UPPER BUTTRESSES
Right of Devil's Rock and high in the trees are two buttresses, separated by a wide tree-filled gully. The left-hand one is Needle Buttress and is distinguished by a clean narrow buttress topped by the Needle. Raven Buttress to the right is much larger, but is split by the Saddle at half-height. At the top of the wide, dividing gully is a small bluff of rock which is often wet.

NEEDLE BUTTRESS
The cracks just left of the arête are taken by Needle Arête, whilst Camel follows the arête more closely. The front face is taken by Cyclops, whilst the crack right of this gives the upper pitch of Scorpion. The gully wall gives a number of climbs but they are usually wet and overgrown. Below the Needle is a short layback crack which leads to a ledge with trees below the buttress proper.

Cleopatra   100ft   Very Severe   1981
Start 15 feet left of Portal.
1   100ft   4c.   Climb the slab and scramble to the steeper rock above. Follow cracks through the overhangs above to finish.

Portal   120ft   Severe
Start just left of the layback crack.
1   40ft   Climb the mossy slab to the ledge above.
2   80ft   Move up to gain an overhung recess. Move out of this on the right and climb the slabs to finish up twin cracks.

Needle Arête   120ft   Very Difficult   1949   ★★
A good, clean open route with a good second pitch. Start below the layback crack.
1   30ft   Climb the crack to the ledge above.
2   60ft   Climb the easy slab above to where it steepens, then climb the crack just left of the arête until it is possible to move out right at a spike to a tree belay.
3   30ft   Move up and back left around the corner. Follow the groove to the top.

The Camel   100ft   Hard Severe   1964
A somewhat artificial route with some good climbing. Start above the layback crack, on a ledge by a tree.
1   60ft   4a.   Climb the slab by a rounded rib to the arête below the steep section. Move up and right onto a small slab, which is followed to the tree belay of Needle Arête.
2   40ft   4a.   Climb up above the tree to a thin crack and use this to move left onto the nose. Finish up the edge of the Needle.

The Stitch   90ft   E1   1976
An eliminate line between Camel and Cyclops. The first pitch is poorly protected. Start as for Cyclops.
1   60ft   5b.   Climb the slab until the wall steepens, then climb a line of weakness right of Camel to a horizontal break. Move right then up and back left onto the slab of Camel. Follow this to the tree belay.
2   30ft   5a.   Climb the crack of Cyclops but continue direct to the narrow overhang. Surmount this and move left to the summit of the Needle.

Cyclops   100ft   Hard Very Severe   1964   ★
A very good route up the steep front face of the buttress. Start at the foot of the arête just right of Camel.
1   70ft   4c.   Climb the slab and then hand-traverse right to a block. From the top of this step left onto rounded holds and then climb direct via a flared crack to the tree belay.
2   30ft   5a.   Climb the rounded crack above, peg runner, and using layback holds step right onto a good foothold. Move up and right into Scorpion, which leads to the top.

Scorpion   100ft   Hard Severe   1958
A route which is not as good as it looks. Start at a group of oak trees
below a short earthy crack.
1 70ft 4b.   Climb the crack to below a short wall and then move
right delicately to a grassy recess. Climb left up a rake and move back
right to a tree belay.
2 30ft 4b.   Climb the grooves, making a difficult exit left near the
top.

Final Touch   100ft   E1   1979
This route climbs the blunt arête right of Scorpion. Start as for that
route.
1 100ft 5b/c.   Follow Scorpion to the grassy recess. Move right and
follow the curving line of cracks to a horizontal break. Pull onto the
ledge with a large flake. Climb directly up the wall to the right arête.
Move left and surmount the bulge on good holds to reach the top.

The next routes have become somewhat overgrown and it would be
advisable to clean them from an abseil prior to an ascent:

Exaltation   70ft   Hard Very Severe   1968
This climbs the long crack right of Scorpion, large nut runners
recommended.
1 70ft 5a.   Climb the crack to a small niche and then move into the
higher crack. Follow this to exit over grass and grot to tree belays.

Babylon   60ft   Severe   1960
The mossy groove right of Exaltation.
1 60ft 4a.   Climb into the groove, move left and follow it with
difficulty to the hanging gardens above.

The Winnet   40ft   Hard Very Severe   1976
This lies on the shorter wall at the extreme right end of the gully wall.
Start at the foot of the vague crack some 5 feet left of a tree.
1 40ft 4c.   Move up to the obvious flake, then follow the crack to
finish on dubious earth ledges.

Shades of Green   165ft   Hard Very Severe   1978
A girdle of Needle Buttress. Start as for The Stitch.
1 75ft 5b.   As for The Stitch. Climb the slab to the break. Move
right and continue traversing until it is possible to climb up to the tree
belay of Scorpion.
2 90ft 5a.   Step around the corner to a flake, step down onto a
horizontal break and follow this to Babylon. Descend a few feet, then
hand-traverse to the bottom of The Winnet.

ROCK BETWEEN THE UPPER BUTTRESS

Just behind the summit of Needle Buttress, there is a small bluff of rock. There are three routes on this. The chimney in the middle needs no explanation, being **Left Chimney** (20ft Difficult).

In Extremis   30ft   Very Severe   1958
Worth doing if only as a grim reminder of one's unfitness. Start below the slightly overhanging groove left of the chimney.
1   30ft   5a.   Climb the groove to exit, by a strange jamming move, to the right.

La Bête Noir   45ft   Hard Very Severe   1960/*1977*
A difficult, unattractive climb. Start right of the chimney, below a slabby corner.
1   45ft   5a/b   Climb the slab to the overhang. Move left and follow the groove, exiting right at the top.

Opposite the bluff, on the right side of the gully, is another short chimney: **Right Chimney** (20ft Difficult).

LOWER RAVEN BUTTRESS

The front of the buttress is characterized by three tiers of slabs and overhangs, which give the line of Spider's Web. The next two climbs lie on the steep left wall of the buttress, which is capped by a slanting line of overhangs.

Fly on the Wall   100ft   Hard Severe   ★
A good route taking the curving line of weakness at the left-hand end of the wall. Start left of the frontal slabs, below a small tree in a corner.
1   50ft   4b.   Climb past the tree into the groove and follow this to the slab and thence to the tree belay of Valhalla Wall.
2   50ft   From the flake move left onto a ramp, which leads to the overhang. Move diagonally right beneath the overhang to the edge. Follow the slabs to the top.

Valhalla Wall   100ft   Hard Very Severe   1962
The second pitch climbs the middle of the left wall and is well worthwhile. Start below a short lichenous wall left of the start of Fly on the Wall.
1   40ft   4b.   Climb the short wall and cross a mossy slab. Move diagonally right to a rounded flake. Follow the slab to a tree belay by a flake.
2   60ft   5a.   From the top of the flake move up right on a line of footholds to a horizontal break, peg runner. Traverse right to the edge and climb slabs to the top. Alternatively one can climb direct from the peg up the steep wall to the top (harder).

Imperialist   110ft   Hard Very Severe   1969   ★
A fine route which follows the vague arête right of Valhalla Wall. Start in the recess just left of the frontal slabs.
1   40ft   5a.   Climb the corner for 10 feet, then swing onto the right wall and pull over onto the slab beneath the overhang. Move left and then climb a short wall onto another slab. Move right and belay at the peg of Spider's Web.
2   70ft   4c.   Move back left into the overhung niche and climb this moving left onto the arête which is followed to easier ground and the easy finishing slabs.

Black Widow   110ft   E1   1979
A strenuous route initially taking the obvious overhanging crack above Silken Thread.
1   50ft   5b. Climb the arête left of Silken Thread to gain a niche below the crack. Follow the crack, strenuously, to the slab above and a nut belay.
2   60ft   5a.   Climb the crack above, which leads out right from the niche to join Spider's Web, finish as for that route.

Silken Thread   60ft   Very Severe   1958
A deceptively easy looking route which can be used to start Valhalla Wall or Fly on the Wall. Start below a line of weakness just left of the centre of the slab.
1   60ft   5a.   Follow the obvious crackline to the overhang. Traverse left and turn the overhangs by an awkward move to gain the slab leading to the tree belay of Valhalla Wall.

Tarantula   50ft   Hard Very Severe   1969   ★
An impressive direct start to Spider's Web, starting as for Silken Thread.
1   65ft   5a.   As for Silken Thread to the overhang, then move right and up to the overhang, pulling over onto a narrow ledge on the slab above.

Spider's Web   150ft   Hard Very Severe   1959   ★★
One of the classic routes of the crag, involving some intricate route finding and a delicate final pitch. Start by a tree right of Silken Thread.
1   60ft   5a.   Climb the slab to the overhang. Enter the groove on the right, tricky, and follow this for 10 feet. Swing left via a rounded flake onto a slab. Continue left to a peg belay.
2   90ft   5a.   Climb straight up behind the belay to a small slab. Step delicately right onto another slab and move right again until it is possible to climb up to the roof. Traverse left under this to the left edge and then follow slabs to the top.

Direct Start 4c
1a   Climb the cleaned buttress right of the normal start direct to the smooth groove of the parent route.

Shelob   130ft   Hard Very Severe   1981
A direct line up the buttress finishing directly over the final roof. Start as for Spider's Web.
1   50ft   5b.   Climb as for Spider's Web to the roof and surmount this on dubious-sounding holds. Move up and then left to the belay of Spider's Web.
2   80ft   5a.   Move back right and gain a groove leading up to a tree below the roof. Surmount the overhang, using a crack, and belay on a tree above.

Mango Corner   90ft   Very Severe   1964
A better route than it looks. Right of Spider's Web is a square-cut corner. Start beneath this.
1   90ft   4c.   Straight up the doubtful rock to below a slab. Move onto this and climb up to the large roof above. Step up and left onto a slab and tree belay.

Boris   80ft   Very Severe   1981
Start just right of Mango Corner,
1   80ft   4c.   Climb the wall and groove above to the roof. Move left and surmount this by a long reach.

UPPER RAVEN BUTTRESS
The Saddle is reached from the wide tree-filled gully, via a line of ledges and flakes. The large overhang is skirted by Raven Face and the large nose right of this provides the crux of Randy.

Sloppy Gully   130ft   Difficult   1950
From the bottom of the easy access route to the Saddle a vague groove can be seen disappearing into vegetation. Follow this with various diversions (birds' nests etc.) to the top.

Yogi   130ft   Hard Very Severe   1964/*1977*
A cunning, though worthwhile line up the wall right of Sloppy Gully. Start at the top of the easy access route to the Saddle.
1   80ft   5b.   Surmount the bulge above and then move up to a bollard on the right (huge bird's nest). Move left until it is possible to climb steeply to a tree.
2   50ft   5a.   Move left to a small ledge on the steep wall and climb up to the crack, which leads past a sapling to the top.

Back to Nature   45ft   Very Severe   1981
Start as for Raven Wall.
1   45ft   4c.   Gain cracks in the arête left of Raven Wall and follow
them to the easier-angled rock above.

Raven Wall   65ft   Very Difficult   1949
An enjoyable route with some delicate climbing. Start at the highest
part of the Saddle.
1   65ft   Climb over bulges to beneath the overhang. Traverse right
below this to a groove, which leads to the top.

Randy   80ft   Very Severe   1969
A delicate and somewhat unprotected route, which starts in an
obvious groove just right of Raven Wall.
1   50ft   4c.   Follow the groove, moving delicately out right at the
top, to belay on Raven Face to the left of the prominent nose of rock.
2   30ft   4c.   Climb awkwardly onto the nose and then follow a
slanting groove to the top.

Armada   110ft   Hard Severe   1952
An interesting route up the vague corner about 30 feet right of Raven
Face. The second pitch is a rather brutal chimney. Start below the
groove, some way down the path from the Saddle.
1   60ft   4a.   Climb into the groove and follow it, over an overhang,
to a tree. Move up and right to a large ledge and tree belay.
2   50ft   4a.   Follow the constricted chimney to the top.

Bolshevik   110ft   Hard Very Severe   1969
Start below the buttress between Armada and Corner Chimney.
1   70ft   5b.   Climb the buttress for 20 feet to a slab on the right and
go up this to the overhang. Step left and climb the V-groove in the
overhang to a tree. Climb the short wall to a tree on the terrace.
2   40ft   4a.   Climb the wall right of the chimney of Armada, starting
at the square cut corner on the right.

Corner Chimney   95ft   Hard Very Severe   1957
This route climbs the obvious chimney right of Armada. Start at the
lowest part of the buttress, below a tree 15 feet above the ground.
1   95ft   5a.   Climb to the tree and move up behind this into a
chimney, move right and then go up to the V-groove. Move into this
from the left awkwardly and climb the crack above to a ledge. Either
climb direct to a tree (difficult) or scramble easily off to the right.

Diagonal Start
This avoids the unpleasant wall below the tree.
1a   30ft   4c.   Climb the obvious diagonal line of holds which lead
up left into the corner.

Dragon Song   90ft   E2   1979   ★
A very hard route up the wall just left of the Dangler. Start below an overhang just to the right of Corner Chimney.
1   90ft   5c.   Pull right out of the overhang and climb to the diagonal break. Move up and right to a horizontal break (peg removed). Make difficult moves to gain better holds. Step right and gain the V-groove and follow this finishing by a leftwards diagonal line on the slab above.

Dangler   70ft   Hard Very Severe   1969   ★
A rather bold route taking a devious line on the right of the wall. Start in the shallow corner 30 feet right of Corner Chimney.
1   70ft   5b.   Climb up to a niche below an overhang. Move out left and climb through the V-groove to the niche above. Exit out left from the niche and climb the slab to the terrace.

The Apparition   70ft   Hard Very Severe   1979
This takes a direct line from the first roof on Dangler. Start as for that route.
1   70ft   5b.   As for Dangler to the first niche. Climb straight up cracks to a leftward-slanting crack. Follow this to a roof and surmount this, finishing directly up the slab above.

Nibelung   150ft   E1   1976/*1979*
A good diagonal line, starting at the foot of Dangler and finishing as for Randy.
1   40ft   5b.   Follow Dangler to the horizontal break, which is followed leftwards into Corner Chimney. Belay in the groove below the roof.
2   60ft   5b.   Step down and across into Bolshevik and descend to a steep slab below a roof. Cross to the bottom left corner of the slab, then swing around into Armada. Belay on the small tree.
3   50ft   4c.   Climb the chimney of Armada for 6 feet, then use a sloping ledge on the left wall to gain the nose of Randy.

CROW BUTTRESS

This lies about a quarter of a mile upstream from the Main Area and can be seen from the top of Devil's Rock as a pinnacle of rock protruding from the trees. The buttress is rather overgrown and the climbing is characterless and the best reason for visiting the area is that a superb pool exists just upriver, which can take the sting out of a very hot day's climbing.

   The obvious crack-line just left of the left arête of the steep east-facing wall gives **Semiramis** (45ft, Very Difficult), the arête itself gives **Moral Fibre** (45ft, Very Severe). The wide crack just right of the arête is **Cracking Plant** (40ft, Very Severe) and right of this are two Very Severe routes and finally a Very Difficult crack.

The Dartmoor Tors

Tors are the eroded granite rocks which often form the summits of the Dartmoor hills. Apart from the Dewerstone most of the climbing on Dartmoor is on these rocky outcrops. The exceptions to this are Bench Tor and Eagle Rock, which are lower lying and more akin to the close grained granite of the Dewerstone than the rough, hand-grinding rock of cliffs such as Haytor.

Without a doubt, the finest climbing on the tors is found at Haytor with the routes on Low Man being exceptional both in quality and length. Both Haytor and Sheepstor are popular tourist spots so expect crowds, especially at Haytor, which has steps cut into the main tor to facilitate an ascent. By far the most esoteric routes lie in the granite quarries such as Foggintor and King's Tor. The granite in the quarries is highly kaolinized, not having the weathered exterior surface of the natural tors. Many of the tors provide ideal areas for an evening's climbing or a diversion during a day's walking on Dartmoor. Bonehill, near Widecombe, provides some of the best bouldering in the south-west, with a strategically placed pub in the valley below.

With minor exceptions the tors are described in west-to-east sequence across the Moor.

Vixen Tor   GR 543 743

The prominent rock formation of Vixen Tor lies half a mile south of the Tavistock to Princetown Road, just before the road descends to Merrivale. Cars can be left at a car-park at the nearest point to the tor. The rocks lie in private ground in a walled enclosure and can be approached by a stile on the western side of the enclosure. Visitors are asked to use this approach and to avoid clambering over the stone wall at other points.

The obvious prominent narrow chimney, when seen from the north, gives the line of the easiest route, **The Ordinary Route** (60ft, Moderate), this is also the easiest descent. Many routes have been climbed but the easiest tend to be severely overgrown, due, no doubt, to lack of traffic. Due to this they have not been described but are left to the enterprise of the individual climber.

The south face boasts a 100-foot high slab, which is split at mid-height by a horizontal break, The Stomach Traverse. On the left of the slab is a prominent crack, the lower section of which is grassy and often wet.

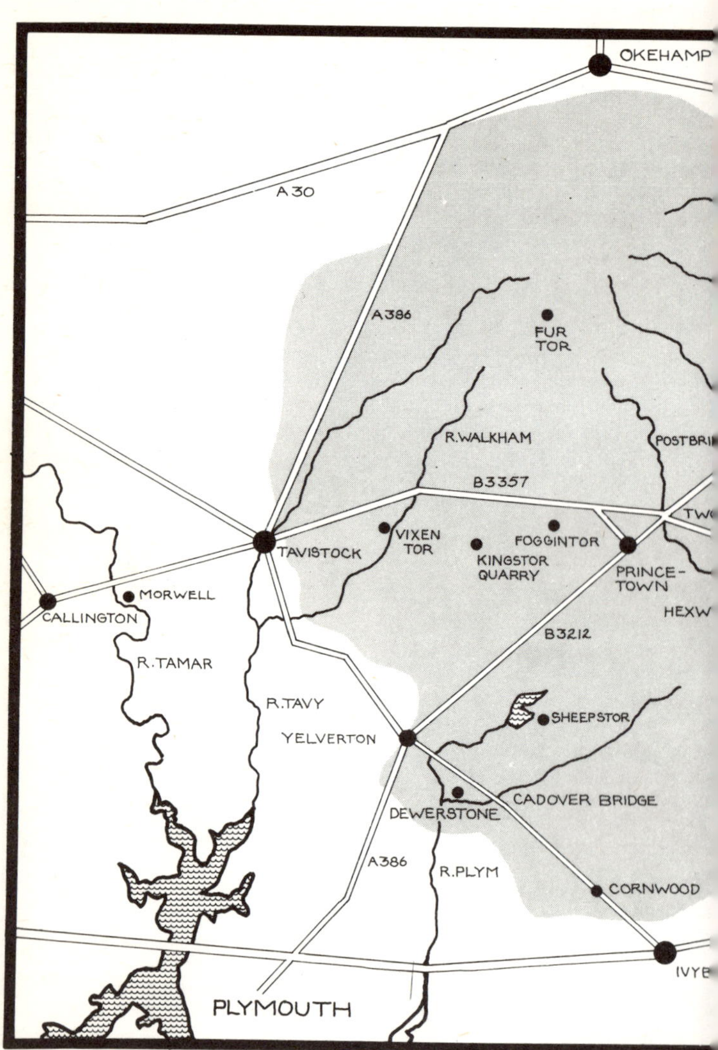

OKEHAMP
A 30
A 386
FUR
TOR
R.WALKHAM
POSTBRI
B 3357
TWO
VIXEN
TOR
FOGGINTOR
KINGSTOR
QUARRY
PRINCE-
TOWN
TAVISTOCK
HEXW
MORWELL
CALLINGTON
B 3212
R.TAMAR
R.TAVY
SHEEPSTOR
YELVERTON
CADOVER BRIDGE
DEWERSTONE
A 386
R.PLYM
CORNWOOD
IVYB
PLYMOUTH

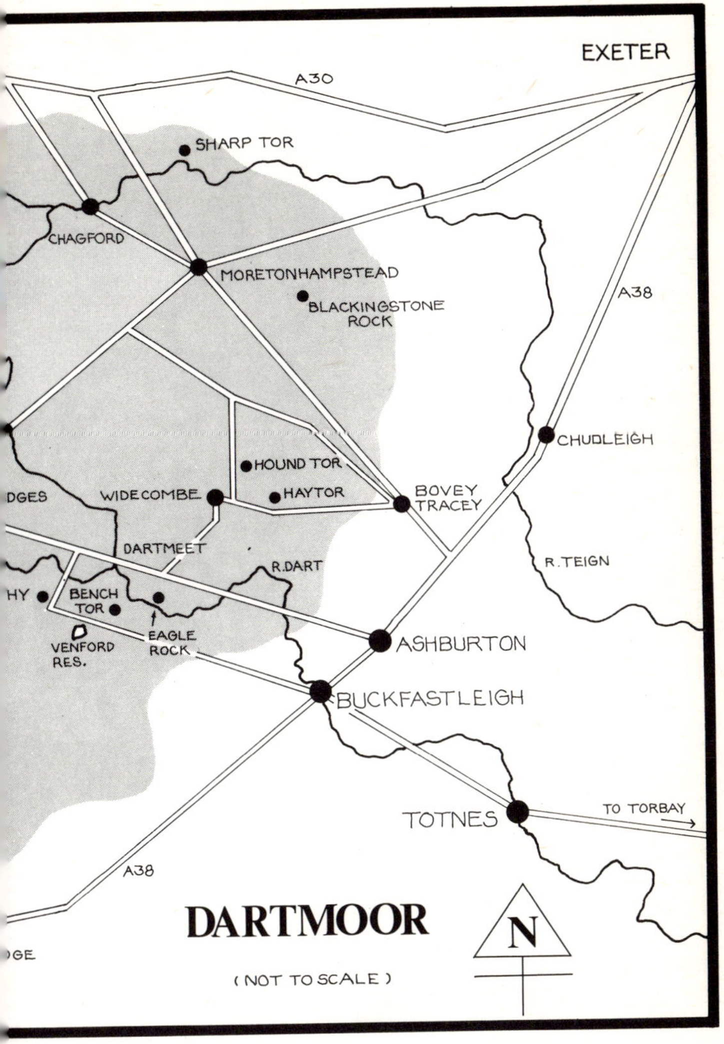

EXETER
A30
SHARP TOR
CHAGFORD
MORETONHAMPSTEAD
BLACKINGSTONE ROCK
A38
CHUDLEIGH
HOUND TOR
HAYTOR
WIDECOMBE
BOVEY TRACEY
DGES
DARTMEET
R.DART
R.TEIGN
HY
BENCH TOR
VENFORD RES.
EAGLE ROCK
ASHBURTON
BUCKFASTLEIGH
TOTNES
TO TORBAY
A38
DARTMOOR
(NOT TO SCALE)
N
DGE

Commando Crack   90ft   Very Severe   1959
The top pitch is worth doing on its own if the lower crack is wet. Start below the chimney near the left-hand side of the face.
1   50ft   4c.   Enter the chimney by the slabs on the right and climb it strenuously to the grass terrace above.
2   40ft   4c.   Climb the overhang and follow the crack above to bulges, which are surmounted to reach the top.

Docker's Dilemma   100ft   E4   1980   ★
A very bold and sparsely protected route following the white streak on the left side of the bald slab.
1   100ft   6a.   Climb the easy-angled slab to where it steepens, then make tenuous moves onto small crystals just left of the highest horizontal crack. Improving holds lead to the wider break (Friend No 3 runner). The wall above is followed on surprisingly good holds to The Stomach Traverse. Follow pitch 2 of Feasibility Study to the summit.

Feasibility Study   120ft   E2   1978   ★★
A fine climb offering the easiest way up the long slab. Friends are very useful.
1   90ft   5b.   Move up to a horizontal break, then go right to a vertical crack. Follow this to the next break and make difficult moves to stand in this. Traverse left to reach a flake, then climb directly up to the grassy terrace.
2   30ft   6a.   Traverse right along the fault for 10 feet, then pull over the bulge to another bulge (thread runner). Make a series of very tenuous moves over the bulge direct until better holds lead to the top. It is possible to move right above the thread runner at 5c standard.

Green Beret   100ft   Hard Very Severe   1958/*1979*
This climbs the right edge of the slab and the edge of the main block above.
1   60ft   5a.   As for Feasibility Study to the second horizontal break, then move right and climb a shallow groove to easy-angled rock above.
1   40ft   4c.   Climb the arête of the main block above with a difficult start.

Babylon   100ft   Very Difficult
A pleasant but rambling route. Start beneath a vegetated corner on the right-hand side of the face.
1   35ft   Climb the corner to a ledge and then move left into a chimney, which leads to easy ground to the right of the top part of the face.
2   25ft   Follow The Stomach Traverse left across the face to the grassy bay.

3   40ft   Climb the undercut chimney at the back of the bay to the summit.

Plektron   60ft   E1   1969   ★
A somewhat brutal route with an awkward traverse to finish. Start beneath the obvious rightward-slanting crack.
1   60ft   5b.   Move up and climb the crack, then continue diagonally right and make a hard move to stand on a rounded flake. Traverse left with difficulty to the glacis, then climb easily to the top.

Direct Finish E1, 5b
From the rounded flake move right slightly, then take the bulge direct and so to the top.

Crunchy Toad   60ft   E1   1982
Start just right of Plektron.
1   60ft   5b.   Climb the wall, passing horizontal breaks, until it is possible to move left slightly to gain the Direct Finish to Plektron. Finish up this.

Two Way Stretch   60ft   E3   1985
A strenuous and exciting climb over the roof left of Torture, well protected with Friends.
1   60ft   5c.   Climb the initial undercut layback of Torture to the roof, and make a long reach to a good shelf. Traverse this rightwards and pull over the roof to gain a standing position. Finish over the bulge above.

Torture   60ft   E3   1979   ★
This takes the obvious overhanging groove on the north face, moving right to surmount the roof. Start just left of the bottom of the groove.
1   60ft   5c.   Climb up to the right to gain the groove and follow this to the obvious undercut. Step right onto the slab and climb through the roof via the obvious crack.

On the west face of the main block there is one route, which follows the obvious rounded cracks and breaks:

Solus   45ft   Hard Very Severe   1979
The most natural line on the face.
1   45ft   5b   Step onto the wall, then climb past horizontal breaks and move right below a diagonal one. Follow this to below the final block. Take the obvious slanting ramp to the top.

Great Links Tor   GR 551 867

A rather remote tor which offers a number of boulder problems and short pitches.

Kings Tor Quarry   GR 560 733

This is the prominent quarry which can be seen from the Yelverton to Princetown road. It can be approached by walking from this road via the old railway track or more easily by the track to Foggintor Quarry. The rock tends to be greasy in all but the driest weather.

The quarry takes the form of an amphitheatre with its entrance facing south. A descent can be made into the back of the amphitheatre from the north via a series of ledges. In the back of the quarry and opposite the entrance is a steep smooth slab with a curious vertical line of scoops. This is taken by Three Steps, the oldest climb here.

Lime Street   40ft   Severe   1965
Left of and separate from Three Steps is a buttress stained by bird droppings. Start left of an overhang pierced by a large drill hole.
1   40ft   Climb to the overhang and move out right onto the face of the buttress to a ledge. Continue up by a series of mantelshelves moving left to finish.

Three Steps   30ft   Hard Severe   1965
A short but very delicate route starting at the base of the slab.
1   30ft   4b.   Climb up to the right and make a long stride to gain the lowest scoop. Continue delicately up the slab, passing a slight overhang with difficulty. Belay well back on the right.

Oblomov   80ft   Very Severe   1965
To the right of Three Steps is a saddle, the wall right of this is taken by this route. Start beneath the wall on a ledge by a sapling.
1   80ft   Climb cracks on the right to a small ledge. Traverse left to an iron spike and climb to a ledge, peg runner. Climb the short overhanging corner above and traverse left along a ledge. A difficult mantelshelf onto a grassy ledge leads to the saddle.

Tenterhooks   80ft   Hard Severe   1967   ★
A good route but with a poorly protected crux. It follows the diagonal line of steps on the 70-foot slab right of Oblomov. Start in the corner on the left of the slab.

1   80ft   4a.   Climb the corner to a large downward-pointing flake, then step right onto a grassy ledge. Mantelshelf onto a ledge on the right and then follow the line of steps to a blank section. Make a committing swing onto a high right foothold and continue, via another strenuous mantelshelf, to the top.

Republican   80ft   E2   1985
A fine bold route taking a line up the slab between Tenterhooks and Monarchist.
1   80ft   5b/c.   Climb a short wall to a ledge and then continue boldly to the second borehole. Move right to two peg runners, then follow the obvious line up to join Tenterhooks

The following two routes lie on the steep slabs right of Tenterhooks:

Monarchist   70ft   Hard Very Severe   1981
Start beneath the niche in the shallow groove in the centre of the slab.
1   70ft   5a.   Climb to the niche and then up to the crack above. Continue steeply past a block and from the ledge above climb the wall above to a heathery mantelshelf. Block belays 45 feet back.

Anarchist   80ft   E2   1981   ★
A serious route which starts beneath the right-hand arête of the slab.
1   80ft   5c.   Pull onto a sloping ledge, then move up and right to gain a rib. Follow cracks to an earthy ledge at 40 feet, peg runner removed. Step left and make steep moves to reach a slight rib on the left, poor peg runner. Follow the obvious line to finish, and belay on a spike.

Foggintor Quarry   GR 566 735

A secluded amphitheatre whose central feature is a clear pool, which gives a refreshing swim after a hot and worrying day on the rock. The best approach is by taking the road from Two Bridges to Tavistock; about half a mile after it is joined by the Princetown Road is a track on the left. Cars must be left in the small layby at the beginning of the track. The quarry is in the form of a large amphitheatre with two entrances. The most usual entrance is on the northerly side of the quarry near a ruined building. The path wends its way through a narrow defile and leads to the edge of the lake. The first route is on a speckled wall of reasonably good rock about 100 yards from the entrance and about 30 yards from the pool.

Rockface   50ft   Hard Very Severe   1976   ★
A fine pitch with serious climbing in the first 30 feet, which is followed by a hard but solidly protected finish. Start in the middle of the wall beneath a large iron spike at 35 feet.
1 50ft 5b.   Climb to a small ledge and poor protection peg at 20 feet. Climb straight up to a good ledge below the iron spike and then continue up the wall on the right to the top.

Further along is a small amphitheatre opposite the entrance to the quarry and well back from the pool. The left-hand wall facing the entrance to the quarry is characterized by a slightly overhanging wall split by a thin crack. This is taken by **Wicker** (45ft A1); various attempts have been made to free climb this over the years but little progress has been made.

Wicked   45ft   Hard Very Severe   1976
A rather serious route, essentially taking the right arête of Wicker Buttress. Start at the foot of the arête.
1 45ft 5b.   Climb the arête for 10 feet, then move right and climb the steep fragile crack to gain the other edge of the buttress. Step up to a line of handholds leading back left, peg runner
(removed), then traverse left to the true arête and climb it to the top. Nut belay.

Just right of Wicked is an eroded bay with a small overhang on its right side. A route called Fogginard (1976) has been climbed from here up the obvious line leading up right. Unfortunately the route does not seem possible any more due to a large rockfall which has destroyed the initial crack. The arête opposite Wicker Buttress has been climbed at Hard Severe, 4a/b.

Stepladder   60ft   Hard Severe   1976   ★
In the amphitheatre behind Wicker Buttress is a stepped wall of solid orange granite with a prominent iron ring at half-height.
1 60ft   Climb to a broad ledge and then follow a shallow groove for 15 feet to a horizontal crack on the left, nut runners. Move diagonally left to encounter the iron ring at waist level and then climb straight up the wall above on perfect holds, keeping just right of the grassy ledge.

Swan Lake   35ft   Hard Severe   1967   ★
A very pleasant pitch, which takes the left arête of the blank wall that rises out of the south side of the lake. Start on a ledge 15ft above the lake.
1 35ft 4a.   Climb the arête and pull over the small overhang to gain a niche. Step left and make an awkward move to gain good holds and the top. Iron spike belays well back.

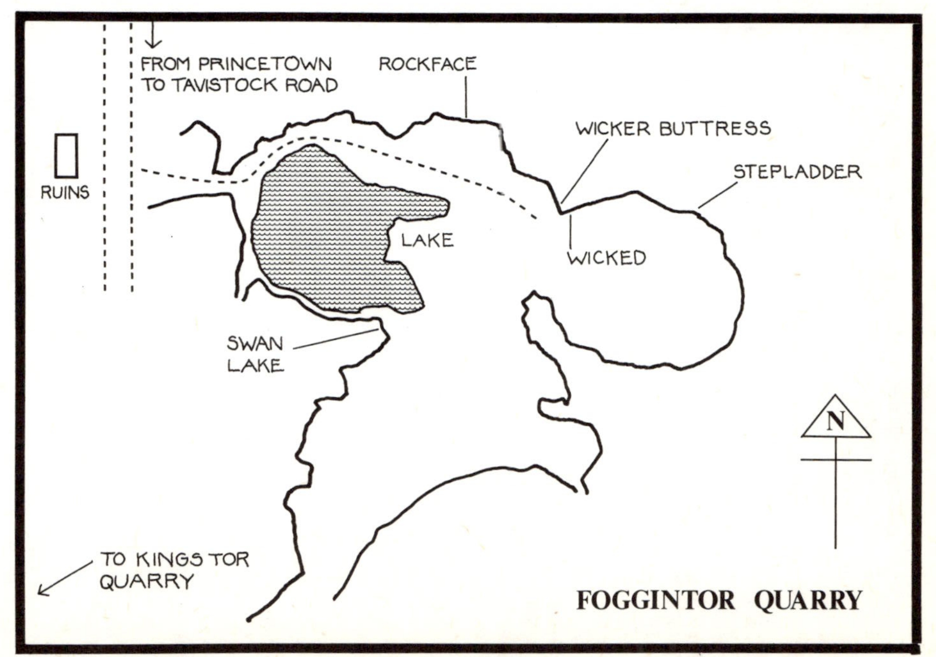
FROM PRINCETOWN
TO TAVISTOCK ROAD
ROCKFACE
WICKER BUTTRESS
STEPLADDER
RUINS
LAKE
WICKED
SWAN
LAKE
N
TO KINGS TOR
QUARRY
FOGGINTOR QUARRY

Saturday Night Finger   40ft   Very Severe   1983
This lies on the black wall a little to the left of Swan Lake.
1   40ft   5a.   Climb up and slightly left to a ledge. Climb a groove on the left to a foothold, then surmount the impending wall with difficulty to the top.

Leather Tor   GR 567 682

This tor is approached from the Yelverton to Princetown Road and is immediately north of Burrator Reservoir.

All of the climbs lie on the east face and tend to hold water, making them rather unpleasant except during the summer months. On the left of the face is a small wall which leads to a subsidiary summit; two short routes of Very Difficult standard go up this. The obvious open groove on the left side of the main face is **Ivy Bend** (25ft, Very Difficult). **Dies Irae** (40ft, Very Severe, 4c) starts 10 feet left of the lowest point of the face and climbs to the overhang to finish up a strenuous overhanging crack. **Vae Victus** (40ft, Severe) climbs a groove and then the arête to finish. On the right-hand side of the face is a small cave. **Troglodyte** (30ft, Severe) goes left out of the cave and then moves delicately right above it to finish up a groove.

Left of the east face are several boulders, which give some entertainment; as also does the ridge which runs down to the reservoir.

Sheepstor   GR 567 682

A pleasantly-situated outcrop, which is ideal for an evening's entertainment. It is approached by the road to Sheepstor Village, above which a road leads to within a few hundred yards of the tor itself.

The climbing lies on the 30-foot high east face and gives routes of all grades, most of which are suitable for soloing or top-roping. Because of the shortness of the climbs only a brief description has been thought necessary, most of the lines are self-explanatory.

On approaching from the road the most obvious feature of the face is the triangular slab of **Slab Route** (Difficult). The deep crack just left of this gives **Crack and Chimney** (Severe). The crack left of this is **Workers' Wall** (Very Difficult). The thin crack between Workers' Wall and Crack and Chimney gives **Fingerin'** (Hard Very Severe, 5b.). The crack in the wall right of Crack and Chimney is **Wind Wall** (Very Severe, 4c), a good exercise. Right of Slab Route are firstly a narrow wall taken by **Slanting Crack** (Severe) and **Mushroom Wall** (Very Severe, 4c). The rounded arête right of this gives a gymnastic problem at 5b standard. **Omega Crack** (Very Difficult) takes the crack just right of the arête

Coombeshead Tor   GR 587 688

This tor can be approached directly from Sheepstor or from the road which goes around Burrator Reservoir. Two or three hundred yards south of the summit of the tor is a large isolated pinnacle, Cuckoo Rock, which gives a 25-foot climb on its east face at Very Difficult standard. There is a box with a stamp in it on the summit to record the ascent.

Fur Tor   GR 588 831

An isolated tor which lies directly in the centre of the moor between Princetown and Okehampton. There are a number of short climbs among the boulders and blocks that form the summit of the tor.

West Mill Tor   GR 588 910

This provides a long low wall of good clean rock. There are a number of 20-foot climbs of Moderate to Very Difficult standard and also a 100-foot long girdle traverse at Severe standard. A good place for a light-hearted afternoon or evening.

Eagle Rock   GR 685 721

A superbly situated crag which overlooks the River Dart. Although only a short cliff, at its highest point it is barely 50 feet high, it provides some athletic climbing.

The cliff lies on the north side of the Dart and can be approached by a long scenic walk from Dartmeet. A quicker approach, with permission from the farmer, is from Rowbrook Farm. From here a number of tracks lead through the undergrowth down to the river. The main feature of the cliff is the line of overhangs through which Eagle's Nest finds its way. Left of this the crag merges into the hillside; just before it does the left-hand bounding gully gives **Main Gully** (30ft, Difficult, 1960), which is best climbed by large holds on the right wall.

Ivy Wall   40ft   Very Severe   1961
Start just left of the arête bounding the front face.
1   40ft   4c.   Climb the steep wall, via an overhung niche, to the top. It is possible to traverse right above the overhangs on rounded holds and then climb to the top.

The Eyrie   50ft   E2   1980   ★
A good route taking a line up the arête. Start as for Ivy Wall.
1   50ft   5b.   Move right and climb the steep wall just right of the arête to ledges below the roof. Move left and pull up into a short crack, which leads to a ledge. From here climb over bulges to the top.

Eagle's Nest   50ft   Severe   1961   ★
An impressive route for its grade, taking the obvious break in the highest point of the overhangs in the left half of the front face.
1   50ft   Climb the twin cracks up to the overhang and then out of the overhung niche by swinging on huge chockstones.

The Original Route   40ft   Severe   1960
Start up the shallow corner leading up to the right-hand end of the ledge in the centre of the face. Move delicately right from the ledge and climb up to finish by a gorse bush.

Bloodshot   35ft   Hard Very Severe   1984
This climbs the roof-crack 12 feet left of Black Jam Crack.
1   35ft   5b.   Climb easily up the large blocks to a ledge, then surmount the roof by difficult jamming and laybacking.

Black Jam Arête   30ft   Hard Very Severe   1980
1   30ft   5a.   Climb the left-hand arête of Black Jam Crack.

Black Jam Crack   25ft   Very Severe   1961
The narrow crack on the extreme right of the main face.
1   25ft   4c.   Climb the narrow black groove and the crack above to the top.

Right of the main face are several cracks and chimneys. On the far right the biggest chimney is **Right-Hand Chimney** (40ft, Difficult, 1969).

Bench Tor   GR 691 717

A short but impressive little cliff which is situated just below the top of a spur which runs down to the River Dart. The tor is best approached by taking the Holne to Hexworthy road and parking in the car-park just south of Venford Reservoir. Walk north to join a ridge and follow this northwards over a number of short outcrops until the 40-foot high south-facing wall of Bench Tor is seen down to the right. The wall slants down to the right and is about 50 feet high at its highest, where the slanting groove of Oak Tree Zig Zag runs up from right to left.

Central Buttress   30ft   Very Difficult   1959
The obvious narrow face at the left-hand end of the main crag. Start on a boulder below the bottom left corner of the face.
1   30ft   4a.   Step up to the right to gain large holds, which lead steeply to the top.

Senior's Wall   30ft   Very Severe   1974
Start 5 yards left of the central groove of Oak Tree Zig Zag, by a block.
1   30ft   4c.   Climb the overhang right of the block and then the broken crack above to finish. The hard moves over the roof can be avoided by taking the arête above the block and then moving right into the crack.

Oak Tree Zig Zag   50ft   Very Difficult   1959   ★★
A route of considerable character for its length, taking the obvious leftward-slanting groove left of the overhang. Start from a block beneath the centre of this overhang.
1   50ft   Step up and gain a traverse line beneath the overhang and follow this leftwards to the groove line, which is followed to the top. The groove below the oak tree can be climbed direct at Severe standard.

Hostile Witness   50ft   Hard Very Severe   1976   ★★
A power-packed route which takes the main face of the tor after surmounting the overhangs from the left. Start as for Oak Tree Zig Zag.
1   50ft   5b.   Climb into the main groove until level with the lip of the overhangs, then move right along the shelf to gain a flake on the face. Make a hard move off the flake and follow a crack to just below the top, then move right to finish using an excellent jug.

The obvious line through the overhang has been climbed using aid, but awaits a free ascent.

Trembling Wall   40ft   Very Severe   1974
This climbs the slab right of the central overhangs. Start 20 feet right of Oak Tree Zig Zag, at a break at the right-hand end of the low overhangs and below an obvious dead tree.
1 40ft 5a.   Climb onto the slab and then up it, bearing right to an obvious break in the overlap. Take this and continue to the top.

Ash Chimney   30ft   Very Difficult   1974
This climbs the obvious chimney at the right-hand end of the main face.

Legal Aid   115ft   Hard Very Severe   1980
An interesting girdle of the cliff. Start right of Trembling Wall, below a crack which runs up left of a chossy groove.
1 40ft 5a.   Climb up to gain the crack, which is climbed to a bulge. Traverse left across the wall to the dead tree on Trembling Wall.
2 40ft 5a/b.   Climb to the break in the overlap and go through this to a line which leads left across the central wall. Traverse delicately across to the flake on Hostile Witness, then move up and swing around the corner to a belay in Oak Tree Zig Zag.
3 35ft 4a.   Follow the obvious line left to join Central Buttress and finish up this.

Sharp Tor GR 728 898

A rambling cliff which is unusual for Dartmoor in that the rock is shale. The best approach is from the Mortenhampstead to Whiddon Down road (the A382). At the bridge over the River Teign by Mill End Hotel there are two signposted footpaths running east. The lower of these is the Fisherman's Path and provides a tedious approach. It is best to approach via the higher Hunter's Path and then descend the Main Scree Chute.

There are three main buttresses which give a number of routes up to 80 feet in length. Although these have been named and described in the past the nature of the cliff is such that one can wander at will and the choice of line has been left to the individual.

Chinkwell Tor Area GR 729 783

The three tors which lie in close proximity to one another, Bell Tor, Chinkwell Tor and Honeybag Tor, offer a multitude of boulder problems and short pitches. However, a more substantial buttress of rock lies on the west flank of Chinkwell Tor and is a prominent feature of the hillside above Widecombe appearing to be a large, leaning square tower.

A rather vegetated climb is given by the break in its south-west face, **The Sphinx** (60ft, Very Difficult). The next climb lies on the north-west face of the buttress.

Widecombe Wall   70ft   E1   1974   ★
Although short this is an impressive and awkward route. Start below the wall which leads up to the wide horizontal break.
1 70ft 5b/c.   Climb a line of flakes to the break then traverse left to a short blind crack. Climb this and move left to finish up a jamming crack.

The Fair   50ft   E3   1984   ★
A good route that bisects the line of Widecombe Wall. Start below the vague crackline 10 feet left of the start of that route.
1 50ft 5c/6a.   Climb the crack to the break, then move slightly right to gain the flared crack. Follow this to a bulge and surmount this before trending rightwards to finish easily up the arête.

Scrumpy Special   30ft   E1   1984
This takes the square wall higher up the slope and some 30ft rightwards of Widecombe Wall (the wall facing Widecombe village).
1 30ft 5b/c.   Climb the centre of the wall on small crystal holds, passing an obvious black 'chicken head', which provides a hold and a wire placement.

Bonehill Rocks   GR 732 775

These rocks lie just next to the road which runs down into the valley to Widecombe. An ideal place to wind up a day's climbing in the Haytor area. The boulders give a multitude of problems of all grades and on the south side of the tor there is a 30-foot high slab, which gives a number of good routes. The crack on the left gives a route of Very Difficult standard.

Hound Tor   GR 732 775

Cars can be left at the National Trust car-park, from where a short walk leads to the tor. As one approaches, it will be noticed that the summit mass is divided by a grassy valley, the Avenue. The isolated drum-shaped block on the right is the Perched Block. From here the face on the left of the Avenue is Hound Face which is characterized by its two hound's head, which are most noticeable from the north. Opposite Hound Face is the Central Block, which provides the highest point of the tor.

THE PERCHED BLOCK
Although only short the climbs have rather more bite than one would expect. The short wall facing Hound Face is split by a wide crack.

Cantilever Crack   30ft   Very Severe   1954
Start at the large block at the left end of the ledge at the foot of the crack.
1   30ft   4c.   Move up and follow a rising traverse, which leads into the crack. Make a delicate step into the crack and climb it to the top.

Cantilever Direct   25ft   Hard Severe   1954
1   25ft   4b.   Climb the crack direct from its foot with an awkward move from the ledge to gain the crack proper.

Suspension Flake   30ft   Very Severe   1954   ★★
A fine, dynamic little route.
1   30ft   4c.   Climb up to the ledge on Cantilever Direct and then follow the slanting diagonal line to the right, finishing by a hard move into a vertical crack.

Hob Hound   30ft   E2   1983
A serious route with its crux right at the top.
1   30ft   5c.   Climb the rounded crack system on the wall right of Suspension Flake.

The obvious chimney in the north face is **Perched Block Chimney** (25ft, Moderate). Continuing further round the front face is reached and this is characterized by a series of slanting fault lines:

Sheep May Safely Graze   35ft   Severe   1954
A number of lines are possible to reach the final overhang which provides the point of the climb.

Kistvaen Corner   40ft   E3
A difficult route which has probably never been led. It takes the obvious folded groove that slants up to the left. The final moves are extremely difficult. Start just right of the front face.
1   40ft   6a.   Move up and traverse left to gain the folded groove, which is followed with difficulty to a hard finish over the final overhang.

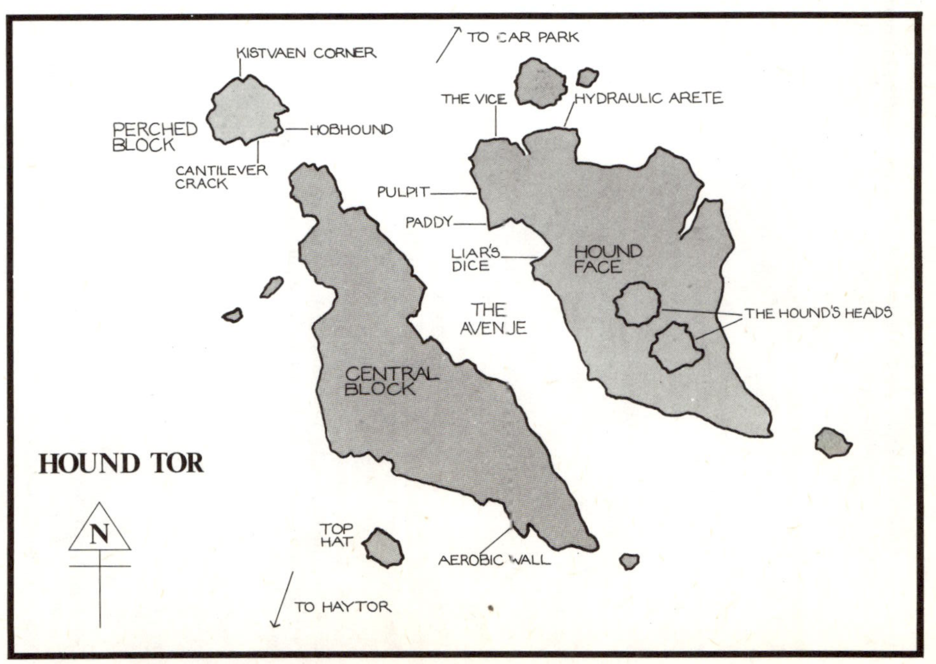
TO CAR PARK
KISTVAEN CORNER
THE VICE
HYDRAULIC ARETE
PERCHED BLOCK
HOBHOUND
CANTILEVER CRACK
PULPIT
PADDY
LIAR'S DICE
HOUND FACE
THE AVENJE
THE HOUND'S HEADS
CENTRAL BLOCK
HOUND TOR
TOP HAT
AEROBIC WALL
TO HAYTOR
N

HOUND FACE

The most continuous climbing is given by the buttress at the left end of the face, the one facing the Perched Block. The most prominent feature is a large projecting block, The Pulpit.

Hydraulic Arête   65ft   Hard Very Severe   1984   ★

This takes the rounded arête, left of The Vice, which overlooks the car-park.

1   65ft   5b.   Start from a ledge a few feet off the ground and climb the overhanging crack to a ledge on the right. Continue straight up passing two roofs en route.

The Vice   65ft   Very Difficult

This lies on the other side of the buttress from The Pulpit, on the left side of the nose that faces the car-park. Start below a wide winding crack-line.

1   25ft   Climb the slab on the left of the crack, and make an awkward move right into the crack. Follow this to a large ledge.

2   40ft   Climb the crack formed by the large block behind the belay and then step up to gain the summit of the buttress. Move across to the higher block and so gain its top.

The Pulpit   60ft   Difficult

Start at the foot of the slab beneath The Pulpit.

1   20ft   Climb the slab and traverse left to a large ledge.

2   40ft   Traverse right and make a steep move up to gain the left end of The Pulpit. Finish up the wall above on rounded holds or up the easier chimney on the left.

Paddy   50ft   Moderate

Start right of the corner leading up to the right end of The Pulpit.

1   30ft   Climb up to the left of a small overhang to a ledge.

2   20ft   Finish up the broken crack above.

Some 20 yards right of The Pulpit is a square bay. The right wall of this has a steep crack splitting it, this is taken by **Liars Dice** (20ft, Severe). Further right the wall loses height and a number of shorter pitches and problems are possible.

THE CENTRAL BLOCK

The face opposite Hound Face gives a number of pleasant pitches up to Very Difficult standard. An isolated boulder behind the Central Block gives a hard problem on a short vertical wall.

Just beyond the south-eastern corner of the Central Block is an isolated standing pillar of rock called The Top Hat which gives a number of short pitches, the cracked wall on the northern side being particularly worth noting. Just opposite this, on the Central Block, is a 30-foot wall split by an overhang at half-height. This gives the line of the next route.

Aerobic Wall   30ft   E2   1984   ★
A fine gymnastic problem, protection is with Friends.
1   30ft   5c.   Climb the lower wall, then move right and climb the line of weakness past horizontal cracks to the top.

Continuing right around the Central Block a small bay is reached with a prominent prow on its right side:

Little Prow   20ft   E1   5c   1984
Climb the prow direct, finishing steeply past two horizontal breaks.

The parallel cracks left of this are climbed at Hard Very Severe, 5b and are gained from the previous climb.

Old Friends   30ft   E2   1985
The overhanging tower opposite Paddy.
1   30ft   5c.   Climb the tower steeply with a spectacular finish over a roof.

Greator Rocks   GR 748 785

These rocks lie a quarter of a mile south-east of Hound Tor. They are clearly seen from Haytor, from where they look quite impressive but on closer inspection they are rather disappointing. Some good short pitches can be made on various walls on the south side of the ridge. The ridge itself, which runs from east to west, gives an interesting scramble.

Saddle Tor   GR 750 763

This tor lies just off the Haytor to Widecombe road. On the face overlooking the road there is one climb:

Firing Squad   25ft   Severe
Climb up under a small overhang, then move left into a crack to finish.

On the east face there is a wide slanting crack:

Verdigris Cleft   40ft   Very Severe
1   40ft   4c.   Climb up and move left to gain the crack, which is followed to a finish through bulges.

On the south-west face is **The Funnel** (20ft, Severe), which climbs a holdless chimney after an extremely awkward overhanging start.

Haytor

GR 758 771

Without a doubt the best climbing on Dartmoor Tors is found on Haytor itself and Low Man. The Main Tor is the distinctive rock mass which can be seen just north of the Bovey Tracey to Widecombe road. In fact, Haytor is a prominent landmark from the south and east and from its summit it is possible to see both Chudleigh and Berry Head on a clear day.
   The Main Tor gives a good selection of climbs up to about 90 feet but has a tendency to be crowded with tourists during high summer. The insignificant rock mass just to the south-west is in fact the summit dome of Low Man, the most impressive face on Dartmoor, giving routes up to 150 feet, mostly in the upper grades.

MAIN TOR
The climbing is on the East, North and West faces of the tor itself.

EAST FACE
This is comprised of a featureless slab which becomes very easy-angled near the top.

Corner Slab   80ft   Very Difficult
At the left of the slab is a chimney groove, start here.
1   80ft   Climb the chimney for 10 feet, then move right onto the slab, which is climbed via an overhang to the top.

Superdirect   80ft   Severe   1964
Climb directly up the middle of the slab.

Chimney and Direct   100ft   Difficult   c.1950
Start at the bottom of a chimney on the north-east corner.
1   25ft   Climb the chimney to easy ground beneath the East Face.
2   75ft   Walk left and then climb via a glacis to obvious flakes, which lead to the summit slabs.

Variation **Half Nelson**   70ft   Severe
2a   70ft   From the top of the chimney move left and climb direct to the flakes.

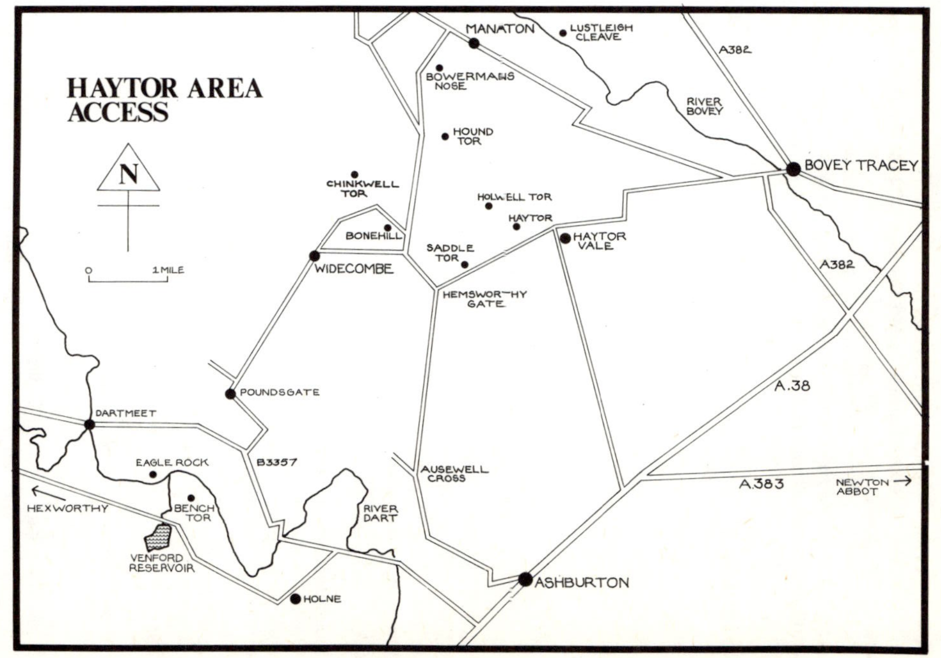

HAYTOR AREA ACCESS
N
0   1 MILE
MANATON
LUSTLEIGH CLEAVE
A382
BOWERMANS NOSE
RIVER BOVEY
HOUND TOR
BOVEY TRACEY
CHINKWELL TOR
HOLWELL TOR
HAYTOR
BONEHILL
HAYTOR VALE
SADDLE TOR
A382
WIDECOMBE
HEMSWORTHY GATE
A.38
POUNDSGATE
DARTMEET
EAGLE ROCK
B3357
AUSEWELL CROSS
A.383
NEWTON ABBOT
HEXWORTHY
BENCH TOR
RIVER DART
VENFORD RESERVOIR
HOLNE
ASHBURTON

Canis   100ft   Very Severe   1952   ★
A bold route of some character. Start below a fang on the north-east arête of the main block.
1 100ft 4b. Climb up onto the fang then onto a flake in the right-hand of the twin cracks above the fang. Follow the crack to a ledge and then move up and over the overhang above onto a slab, which leads delicately to the top.

NORTH FACE
The obvious feature of the left-hand part of the face is a 40-foot high flake. A number of climbs end on this and descent is then made either by abseil or by an easy way down right of Bridle Piton Slab, which is the short slab right of the flake. The Chimney above the slab is North Face Chimney, which is bounded on the right by the very intimidating and mean-looking wall taken by Rough Diamond.

East Chimney   40ft   Moderate
A pleasant pitch up the left-hand chimney.

The Diamond Sky   80ft   E2   1983
A very eliminate line.
1 80ft 5b/c   Climb the rounded arête left of Vandal, starting from the right, to the top of the flake. Then take the break 10 feet left of Ann and step left before finishing direct.

Vandal and Ann   80ft   Hard Very Severe   1955/*1959*   ★★
Originally two separate climbs but the combination gives a delicate and fairly serious route of quality. The route can be adequately protected with Friends. Start in the centre of the slab.
1 40ft 5b.   Climb the slab, passing the iron spike, direct to the top of the flake.
2 40ft 5a.   The groove above is entered awkwardly and climbed direct to a delicate exit onto the summit slabs.

Central Chimney   40ft   Difficult
The obvious chimney.

Bridle Piton Slab   40ft   Difficult
A number of lines are possible on the short, polished slab right of Central Chimney.

North Face Chimney   90ft   Hard Severe   1954
Not a route to underestimate, being both strenuous and somewhat exposed.
1 40ft As for Bridle Piton Slab.

2   50ft   4b.   From the glacis enter the chimney awkwardly and climb it to a rounded ledge on the left. Finish by an awkward move up to the left to gain the summit slabs.

West Chimney   40ft   Difficult
The outside of the chimney that bounds the flake on the right.

The steep wall right of North Face Chimney is characterized by a number of shallow uncompromising cracks. The first route takes the left-hand of these and is gained from the chimney.

Rough Justice   5c
A serious and sustained technical climb on which protection is almost non-existent. Abseil inspection is recommended. Start as for West Chimney.
1   60ft   5c.   Climb West Chimney until it is possible to traverse right about 10 feet above the glacis, and gain a line of weakness. Follow this to where it peters out, then climb in the same line to the top, passing a short groove. Note: on the first ascent a peg was placed by abseil at about half height, but this has since been removed.

Direct Justice   60ft   E4   1983   ★
Start as for Rough Diamond and climb direct to join Rough Justice.

Rough Diamond   60ft   E3   1979   ★
A fierce technical pitch on which Friends give vital protection. Start at a thin crack below and left of the deepest vertical cracks in the wall.
1   60ft   6a.   Move up and right to obvious sideholds, then make hard moves to gain the crack. Climb this and where it ends make more hard moves to gain a rounded crack above. Move up and exit right to easier ground.

Glass Bead Game   60ft   E4   1985
Sustained and bold. Two peg runners removed.
1   60ft   6a.   Climb the obvious crack right of Rough Diamond.

WEST FACE
The large recess at half-height at the left-hand edge of the face is The Meadow. Right of this the face is comprised of a series of buttresses split by vertical breaks, the two left-hand buttresses are quite wide whereas the right-hand two are considerably narrower.

Cobleigh's Chimney   70ft   Very Difficult
Start below the left-hand chimney leading up to The Meadow.
1   35ft   The Chimney is climbed to The Meadow.
2   35ft   Climb the steep chimney on the left, finishing up the wall above.

Grey Mare's Groove   60ft   Difficult
Start below the right-hand side of The Meadow.
1   60ft   Various lines lead to The Meadow. Climb up over blocks in the break on the right.

Letterbox Wall   60ft   Very Severe   1955
A disjointed route combining two boulder problem type pitches. Start below the middle of the overhanging buttress right of The Meadow.
1   35ft   5a/b.   Make a near desperate move onto the Letterbox, then climb more easily to the overhang. Move left to The Meadow.
2   25ft   4b.   Climb directly up the wall above the centre of The Meadow.

The buttress right of The Meadow is split by a horizontal crack which gives **Stomach Crack** (35ft, Very Difficult).

Don't Stop Now   50ft   E1   1980
1   50ft   5c.   Climb the disappearing crack right of the Letterbox, and then finish direct up the bulging wall above to finish.

Hangover   60ft   Hard Very Severe   1961
A bold route. Start at the short crack on the right.
1   60ft   5a.   Climb the crack to the overhang, then traverse left for 10 feet until it is possible to climb on good flake holds onto the steeper upper wall. A long reach enables better holds and the top to be gained.

Zig Zag   50ft   Difficult
A pleasant route on the right-hand side of the larger buttresses. Start by the break on the left.
1   50ft   Climb a rounded crack, which leads out right onto the buttress to large holds which lead to the top.

Bulging Wall   50ft   Very Difficult
The wall right of Zig Zag offers a number of lines and variations on the theme of this climb. Start near the right edge of the buttress.
1   50ft   Climb up and left to a ledge and climb the wall above to the top. A direct variation to this route is possible at a slightly harder grade by climbing the middle of the wall direct.

The gap between the buttress of Zig Zag and the left-hand of the narrow buttress is split by a 20-foot high wide triangular slab. The cracks bounding this on the left and right are climbed at Difficult standard.

The Step Across   50ft   Difficult
An artificial climb which wends its way up the break between the buttresses.
1   50ft   Climb the slab to a recess and chimney up the gap above, moving onto the right wall. Make a long stride across onto the left wall, then move out onto the face of the buttress and climb to the top.

Haggis   40ft   Hard Very Severe   1961   ★
A good gymnastic climb taking the centre of the left-hand buttress.
1   40ft   5a.   Climb up the centre of the wall to the overhang and surmount this using small flakes. Continue over another smaller overhang to the top.

Athos   30ft   Very Difficult
1   30ft   Climb the crack between the two narrow buttresses, moving out right to the top.

D'Artagnan   30ft   Hard Very Severe   1976
A dynamic little number.
1   30ft   5b.   Climb the centre of the buttress right of Athos to join Aramis near the top.

Aramis   30ft   Hard Severe   1946
This is the steep narrow crack at the right-hand edge of the buttress.
1   30ft   4a.   Climb the crack to an awkward exit left to finish as for Athos.

The lower wall of the West Face provides a multitude of boulder problems, the landing area below the face being clear of boulders. The low walls right of the face give some very fierce problems.

LOW MAN
Looking south-west from the main tor, a dome-shaped rock mass is seen, the summit of Low Man. Although seemingly insignificant from this viewpoint, when seen from the west it is a very impressive, brooding face which is the highest face on the tors.

A characteristic feature of the face is the undercut nature of the base which is due to the erosion of the finer-grained granite upon which the main granite mass rests. Because of this, the cruxes of many of the routes are in the first 30 feet before cracks and flakes are gained on the vertical walls above. At about two-thirds height the angle drops off and more gentle slabs lead to the summit.

The face is split by the obvious overhung break of Raven Gully. Left of this are the prominent overhangs that mark Outward Bound and The Flier. Right of the gully, the face is broken by a series of subtle cracks and horizontal breaks before it starts to lose height.

When approaching from the left, the most obvious approach from the main tor, the face begins at a short steep wall, the right edge of which forms an undercut arête:

Screw   50ft   Very Severe   1970
A delicate pitch which starts at a detached block to the left of the arête, protection is rather poor at the start.
1   50ft   5a.   Move onto the block, then ascend diagonally right to gain the rib above the overhang. Follow the rib over bulges, small thread runner, to the top.

Right of the Screw there is a wide slightly overgrown crack and right again is a big overhang which forms an obvious corner:

Honeymoon Corner   60ft   Severe   1955
Start below a pedestal at the foot of the corner.
1   60ft   4a.   From the pedestal climb up and enter the corner and follow this awkwardly to a large ledge (belay possible). Climb up, then move left round a bulge and follow easier rock direct to the top.

Outward Bound   70ft   Hard Very Severe   1960   ★
A spectacular route which breaks through the roof 10 feet right of Honeymoon Corner at a surprisingly low standard.
1   70ft   4c.   Climb up to the overhang, then move out right and pull over on superb flakes to a ledge. Move slightly right, then climb up and right to a sloping terrace (the first belay of Raven Gully).

The Flier   70ft   Hard Very Severe   1971
A well protected but somewhat brutal route through the break in the overhang 10 feet right of Outward Bound.
1   70ft   5b.   Climb up to and over the roof with difficulty. Continue up for 10 feet, then move right and follow Raven Wing to the terrace.

Raven Wing   70ft   Very Severe   1967
Start in the corner 10 feet right of the start of Raven Gully.
1   70ft   4b.   Climb for 10 feet, then swing left to gain the arête. Follow this to a horizontal break, then move left and climb to the terrace of Raven Gully.

Raven Gully   100ft   Severe   1949   ★★
One of the finest routes on Dartmoor, taking the obvious overhung gully which bounds the smooth main wall of Low Man. Start below the crack on the right-hand side of the gully.
1   70ft   Climb the crack or the slab to a niche and then either climb the steeper crack, or move left and follow the slab, to the narrowing chimney. Some awkward moves lead onto a sloping terrace.

2   30ft   Climb the easy chimney above, or traverse left and climb the slab on the outside of the block.

Direct Finish   30ft   Very Severe
A worthwhile pitch which is both delicate and exposed.
3   30ft   4c.   From the top of the chimney on pitch 2 of the parent route climb the wall of the main face past a good nut runner until beneath some bulges. Move right, then climb over bulges on small holds to gain easier-angled slabs which lead to the top.

Interrogation   150ft   E3   1964/*1975*   ★★★
A superb but uncompromising route which traces a tenuous line up the steep wall just right of Raven Gully. Start 6 feet right of that route.
1   75ft   6a.   Climb onto a rounded flake (peg runner), continue with difficulty to the obvious horizontal fault. Make some very hard moves past a peg runner on the left to gain a shallow groove. Follow this, past another peg runner, until it curves sharply to the left. Move left to gain the projecting holds, then easier ground leads to the terrace belay of Raven Gully.
2   75ft   5b/c.   Traverse back right and move up to gain the obvious narrow ledge by a difficult mantelshelf. Traverse delicately right and move up to gain easier slabs leading to the top.

Original Start
1a   30ft   5b/c.   Follow Raven Gully until it is possible to move right to gain the shallow groove.

Aviation   130ft   Hard Very Severe   1961   ★★★
A classic climb which takes the easiest line up the main face, giving sustained and varied interest. Start 30 feet right of Raven Gully, below a rib leading to an obvious bulging crack.
1   40ft   5a.   Climb the rib and enter the crack strenuously. Follow the groove above until just below the horizontal break, then move right and traverse delicately to the prominent flake on the right, nut belays.
2   90ft   5a.   Step right and climb the bulges into the shallow rounded groove above. Follow this with difficulty until the angle eases and pleasant slabs lead up left to the summit.

Igneous Pig   120ft   E3   1979
This takes the overhang between Aviation and Rhinoceros direct and then the wall left of the second pitch of Aviation. Start 10 feet right of Aviation below a short groove.
1   40ft   5c.   Climb to the overhang and move right beneath it to good undercuts. Pull over the roof using flake holds above to gain the sloping ledge by a hard move. Continue direct to the stance of Aviation.

2   80ft   5b.   Move slightly left to a layback flake. Follow this, then step left and climb the wall direct to the final bulge of Rhinoceros. Follow this to the top.

Rhinoceros   140ft   E2   1971   ★★
A fine, strenuous route which takes a counter-diagonal line to Aviation. Start 30 feet right of Aviation, at a pod-shaped crack.
1   40ft   5c.   Climb to the bulge and pull over it with difficulty to a leftward-slanting edge. Move left to a ledge, then climb direct to the belay of Aviation.
2   100ft   5b.   Traverse left, reversing Aviation and pull into the leftward-slanting groove. Follow this to its capping bulge, then move right for 10 feet (poor peg runner) and surmount the bulge by a long reach. Climb the slab, with diminishing difficulties, to the top.

Blood Lust   100ft   E3   1985
A fine climb taking the overhanging crack right of Rhinoceros.
1   100ft   6b.   Start the crack with a hard move and gain a suspect flake. Continue up the crack, then step right and climb up to the Girdle. Pull directly over the bulge and continue up grooves and bulges until the angle eases.

Levitation   90ft   Hard Severe   1967
A pleasant, open climb taking the shorter wall on the right of the main face where the initial overhangs end and some slanting cracks descend to the ground. Start by the cracks.
1   90ft   4b.   Climb up left to a ledge and continue leftwards to a flake. Climb straight up over the bulges on flakes and bear left to finish up easy ground.

Direct Start   25ft   Hard Very Severe   1968
A brutal pitch. Start 20 feet left of the parent route, below an obvious flake above a bulge.
1   25ft   5b.   Climb a small buttress, then make an unlikely move to reach the flake, from which a pull-up joins the parent route.

Nameless   60ft   Severe
A poor route, often damp. Start as for Levitation.
1   60ft   Climb up left to a ledge, then move right and climb the mossy slabs above until they ease.

The Capstan   40ft   Very Difficult
A pleasant pitch on the far right slabs. Start at a line of weakness left of a large block which abuts the cliff.
1   40ft   Climb the slab to the 'capstan' and continue to the top, via a short groove.

The Low Man Girdle   200ft   E3   1964/*1980*   ★
Two fine pitches make this a thoroughly worthwhile expedition. The second pitch is both technical and strenuous. Start as for Levitation.
1   70ft   5a.   Climb up left to a ledge. Continue leftwards to a flake, then traverse along the horizontal break to the flake and belay of Aviation.
2   50ft   6a.   Reverse the traverse of Aviation to beneath the leftward-slanting crack. Traverse along the rounded break with difficulty (poor peg runner) to gain the groove of Interrogation. Make more difficult moves past the peg to reach good holds. Move down left into Raven Gully and belay below the constricted chimney.
3   80ft   4c.   Follow Raven Gully to the sloping terrace. Move up slightly and continue the traverse until the crag peters out.

Dehydration   150ft   E2   1982
A high level girdle taking the upper traverse line, parts of which are already climbed by Rhinoceros and Interrogation. Start below the cleft just right of Levitation Direct.
1   75ft   5a/b.   Climb up to join Levitation and follow this leftwards until it is possible to belay at the level of the upper traverse line.
2   75ft   5c.   Traverse leftwards, crossing Aviation, to reach the poor peg on Rhinoceros. Continue left past the groove of that route until it is possible to gain the flakes at the top of the first pitch of Interrogation. Follow this to the belay in Raven Gully and finish up this route.

Holwell Quarry   GR 751 778

This lies a short distance from Haytor and is reached by following the line of the old granite railway west until the mouth of the quarry is reached.

Xmandifer   60ft   Hard Severe   1979
This takes the obvious stepped buttress. Start at the slab below a downward-pointing rock spike.
1   60ft   4a.   Climb direct to a ledge below the final overhanging wall, passing a borehole into which a long peg can be dropped for protection. Move left just around the arête and finish steeply on improving holds.

Direct Finish   Hard Very Severe, 5a   *1983*
From the ledge below the final overhanging wall, place a peg, and take the impending wall direct to the finishing platform.

Spear of Destiny   50 feet   Hard Very Severe   1984
The obvious corner right of Xmandifer.
1   50ft   5b.   Start up an arête, which leads to the bottom of the corner. Climb the corner.

The bay right of Xmandifer offers some very good short climbs. A period of dry weather is needed for these routes to come into condition. The left and right corners of the bay are taken by Brief Encounter and Jazoo respectively.

A Fall of Moondust   70ft   E2   1983
1   70ft   5c.   The ramp and crack-line left of Saversnake. The start requires a bold lead.

The Saversnake   75ft   E2/3   1983
1   70ft   5c.   The fine crack-line on the wall left of Brief Encounter, the rock is somewhat fragile and usually somewhat damp.

Le Dernier Cri   75ft   E3   1983
A great little climb between Saversnake and Brief Encounter, starting as for the latter route.
1   75ft   5c.   Climb leftwards to a peg runner then up the wall past two small bulges to a second peg. Move left and use a sapling to reach good holds. Finish up a thin crack between two overlaps.

Brief Encounter   60ft   Very Severe   1978
A good line which takes the left-hand corner.
1   60ft   4c.   Climb the corner to a steep finish.

Jazoo   40ft   Hard Very Severe   1983
A poor route.
1   40ft   5a/b.   Climb the right-hand corner at the back of the bay.

Lusteigh Cleave   GR 772 815

This consists of a number of boulders and buttresses overlooking the River Bovey. The rock is heavily vegetated in places and is only really suitable for a light-hearted evening's bouldering. The old railway bridges in the area offer better bouldering; these can be found adjacent to the Bovey Tracey road just south of Moretenhampstead.

Blackingstone Rock

GR 785 855

An impressive tor which on closer inspection is found to be somewhat disappointing.

The long northern slab is over 100 feet long and provides two lines of Very Difficult standard up to the final overhang. This is usually skirted either to the left or right as the two lines of weakness through the bulge are both Hard Very Severe. To the right of the slab is a deep, green chimney, which has been climbed at Very Severe standard.

The south side of the Rock is shorter, but much steeper and gives a number of pitches and problems.

Hel Tor

GR 800 872

One of the lowest tors on the moors, set in beautiful rural surroundings. The climbing lies on the west side of the tor, but it offers no real lines as such as the walls are broken by ledges that cross the face. To the left of the dividing gully the easier lines provide three 40-foot climbs at Very Difficult standard, while the walls in between give two climbs of Very Severe standard. The face to the right of the gully gives a 30-foot Difficult climb.

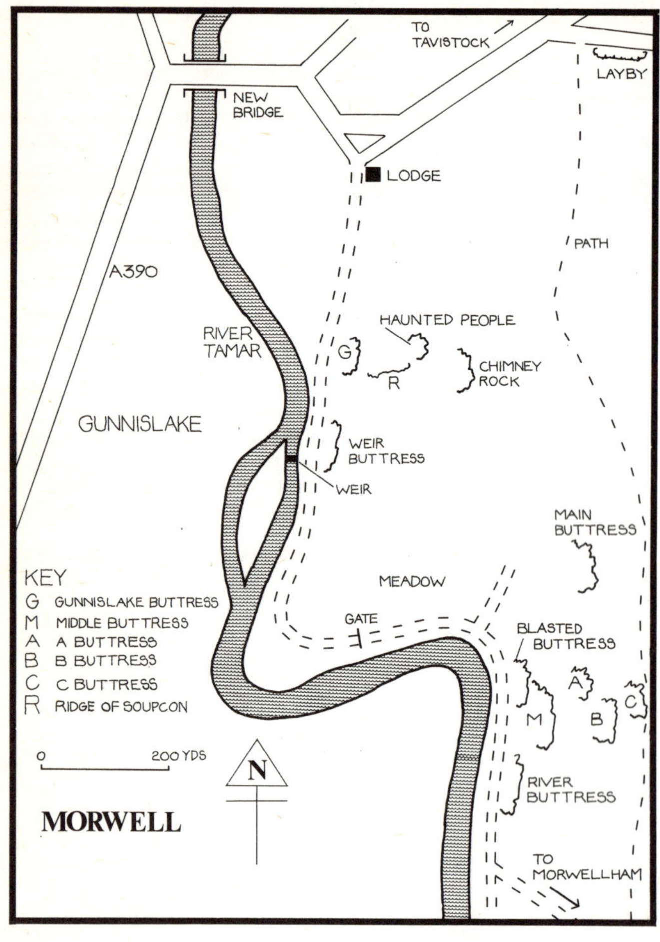

NEW BRIDGE
TO TAVISTOCK
LAYBY
LODGE
PATH
A390
RIVER TAMAR
HAUNTED PEOPLE
CHIMNEY ROCK
G
R
GUNNISLAKE
WEIR BUTTRESS
WEIR
MAIN BUTTRESS
MEADOW
KEY
G   GUNNISLAKE BUTTRESS
M   MIDDLE BUTTRESS
A   A BUTTRESS
B   B BUTTRESS
C   C BUTTRESS
R   RIDGE OF SOUPCON
GATE
BLASTED BUTTRESS
A
C
M
B
RIVER BUTTRESS
0   200 YDS
N
MORWELL
TO MORWELLHAM

Morwell Rocks

GR 435 717 to 440 702

This section deals with the various walls and buttresses which lie on the heavily wooded hillside above the eastern bank of the River Tamar below Gunnislake. The access situation at Morwell is sensitive, due, for the most part, to the serious fire risk which exists in the dense woodlands during dry spells. The land itself is private and run by a company called Tavistock Woodlands, and permission to climb should be sought from their office on the A 390 at the top of the hill which leads down to Gunnislake Bridge (approximately half a mile). The owners are sympathetic to climbers and will usually give permission to climb.

Due to the heavily vegetated nature of the hillsides and the loose appearance of the cliffs themselves many people may be deterred. In fact the quality of the climbing is higher than it first appears and the rock is mostly sound.

There is a track which follows the river and leaves the main A 390 at a sharp bend 100 yards on the Devon side of Gunnislake (New) Bridge by a lodge. If one approaches from this side, it is best to leave cars in a lay-by quarter of a mile further up the hill. One can reach the River Buttress area by entering at Morwellham and employing some stealth to avoid paying an entrance fee.

The first buttresses are directly opposite Gunnislake Village. From the gate lodge on the A 390 the track dips down for 400 yards to join the riverside. The first sizable crag is Gunnislake Buttress, which starts a few yards up in the trees from the level of the track. Much higher up and further right is Chimney Rock, which is a prominent feature from the other side of the river but not easily seen from the track.

GUNNISLAKE BUTTRESS

Cerebus   120ft   Very Difficult   1958
A poor route with some vegetation. Start just up to the right of the lowest rocks and to the left of a large bramble patch.
1   60ft   Climb for 25 feet, then step right into a shallow recess above the brambles. Go left and then up to an oak tree.
2   60ft   Traverse left and up over a projecting ledge, and move right into a chimney. Climb this to the top.

The Quickening Pulse   110ft   Hard Very Severe   1979
A fine route which takes the crest of the overhanging buttress to the left of Thor. Scramble to a ledge in an overhung bay, in-situ peg belay.
1   110ft   4c.   Climb straight up, then bear right to an overhang with ivy below it. Move left to gain an arête and follow this, stepping right into a shallow groove to finish.

Thor   80ft   Very Severe   1958/*1979*
This climbs the obvious inset corner and gives a good but somewhat shortlived route. Start by scrambling up to a tree on the right of the crack.
1   80ft   4c.   Climb the corner and overcome the bulge to gain easy ground.

Damaged Goods   70ft   Hard Very Severe   1979
On the wall right of Thor is a crack. Start below this.
1   70ft   5a.   Climb the crack to the roof and surmount this to gain good holds. Trend left and back right to finish.

Odin Your Tea's Ready   100ft   Hard Very Severe   1979
An intimidating route up the wall which forms the right-hand flanking wall of the buttress.
1   100ft   4c.   Climb straight to a sapling, then continue up the wall and take a short overhanging groove to gain a large ledge. Step left onto the arête to finish.

UPPER CLIFF
Between the top of Gunnislake Buttress and Chimney Rock is an isolated face with an overhanging groove line.

Haunted People   85ft   Hard Very Severe   1979   ★
A fine route. Start below the groove.
1   85ft   5a.   Gain the bottom of the groove via some friable rock and follow this to the capping roof. Now step right and traverse to the arête, and follow this to finish.

CHIMNEY ROCK
The broken west face of the tower gives a number of lines at Difficult standard on huge holds. The exact lines are left to the individual. The summit affords superb views of the Tamar Valley.
   The ridge which can be seen in the trees someway downriver from Gunnislake Buttress gives a heavily overgrown route. **Soupçon** (200ft, Very Difficult) which follows the ridge until it peters out.

Overhanging Crack   50ft   Severe   1958
Higher up in the trees above the previous climb is a small crag split by a central chimney. This gives a good, strenuous pitch if taken direct.

WEIR BUTTRESS
This is the impressive crag directly above the weir. The belay ledge of Vacancy at the Vatican is situated in the centre of the front face and is reached by a desperate scramble from the track.

Limping Home   130ft   Very Severe   1978
A girdle of the buttress. Start at a tree on the left of the cliff at the left end of the overhang.
1   100ft   4b.   Move up and out right onto the wall above the roof at a prominent loose block. Traverse right across the wall, then gain height to reach a tree belay.
2   30ft   4b.   Continue horizontally right to finish above grass slopes.

Palace of Skulls   100ft   E3   1979   ★★
A serious and powerful route. Start as for Vacancy at the Vatican.
1   100ft   5b.   Climb up to the left to the steepening wall. Move straight up and make a long reach left to a good hold. Using this pull up onto the wall and climb directly to the top.

Vacancy at the Vatican   100ft   Hard Very Severe   1978   ★★★
A tremendous route in a fine position. Scramble to a small ledge below a roof, nut belay.
1   100ft   4c.   Move up to the left, then step right and climb to a break. Step left and surmount the bulge to reach a groove, which leads to a tree. Step left and climb past another tree to the top.

Love is like Anthrax   130ft   Very Severe   1979
A bold route with some dubious rock. Start as for the previous route.
1   130ft   4c.   Step right onto the rampline and follow this to an exit out right to a pile of rocks on a ledge. Step up and gain the groove of Tiptoe but go straight over the roof on the right to finish.

Tiptoe   120ft   Hard Severe   1958
This takes a line up the right edge of the buttress. Start right of the right edge of the face.
1   120ft   Scramble up the available rock until below the overhangs at the top, and force an exit left through a tree.

The track continues through a cutting to a fork. The lower track passes through a gate into a meadow, from where the buttresses in the wooded slopes can be seen quite clearly.

High up in the trees on the left is Pinnacle Buttress, which is only a scramble. Directly ahead and in line with the track is Main Buttress, which is the largest face seen. Above this, on the skyline, is Summit Buttress. Beyond the bend in the river and rising from the track are two buttresses, firstly Blasted and then River Buttress. Just to the right above Blasted Buttress is Middle Buttress. A heavily vegetated approach from Middle Buttress leads to three smaller buttresses at the top of the hillside, A, B and C Buttresses. These can be reached more easily from a forestry track which contours along the top of the hillside, which can be reached easily from Morwellham, or by following a path which leads directly into the woods from the lay-by on the A 390.

MAIN BUTTRESS

Spinal Column   200ft   Severe   1958
The only good line on the face. Start from the lowest rocks in the trees.
1   20ft   Climb a short wall on the right edge to the top of a detached block.
2   80ft   Climb the rib slightly to the right and then straight up on good holds. This fine pitch is spoilt if any deviation to the left is made.
3   50ft   Scramble up heather to the foot of a steep tower.
4   50ft   Turn the overhang above on the left to climb the tower. A short ridge then leads to the hillside.

SUMMIT BUTTRESS
This is split into two by a ledge at half-height. The lower face gives a number of short scrappy climbs at Difficult to Severe standard. The upper face gives:

Fern Chimney   40ft   Difficult
This is the deep vegetated cleft that faces up the valley. Move out of the chimney onto the half-way ledge and then climb the wall above.

The Cleaver   80ft   Severe   1959
The prominent crack starting from the lowest rocks.
1   80ft   Make an awkward move into the crack from the left and follow the crack more easily to the top.

BLASTED BUTTRESS

Perfecto   100ft   Very Severe   1958   ★
A very good pitch which is lacking in protection on its initial section. Start from the track beneath the centre of the clean vertical wall.
1   100ft   4b.   Climb on good but hollow-sounding holds, moving rightwards to an oak tree in a groove. Traverse left for 10 feet to a crack and follow this to the top. The best descent is to abseil from the tree which provides the belay.

MIDDLE BUTTRESS

Continuation Wall   95ft   Severe
Start a few yards above the top of Blasted Buttress. Pegs recommended as runners.

1   95ft   Make a horizontal traverse right to a bramble ledge, then climb straight up to a ledge. Finish up the wall above.

Pine Top   120ft   Very Severe   1958
An unpleasant-looking climb taking a slightly diagonal line from right to left up the obvious fault that merges into the vertical face near the top. Pegs should be carried. Start by scrambling up from the track to a good stance and peg belay (not in place).
1   80ft   Climb the steep narrow shelf that leads up to the left for 70 feet. Where the face steepens step around to a small platform and peg belay on the left.
2   40ft   Climb the left-hand corner above the platform, which is hard and loose, and continue to the top.

Impertinent Robin   140ft   Very Severe   1979
A girdle of the cliff at two-thirds height, not technically difficult but a serious undertaking. Start as for Continuation Wall.
1   140ft   4b.   Step right onto a grassy ledge, then climb diagonally right to another ledge. Descend a ramp to gain an open groove and follow this to exit out right. Scramble to belays.

A BUTTRESS
Above Middle Buttress are three crags at varying heights ascending the hillside. The first of these is A Buttress and is clearly seen on the left.

Aerial Ballet   100ft   E2   1979
A superb, serious route following the clean arête in the centre of the cliff.
1   70ft   5b.   Climb a thin crack on the right of the arête, then step left onto a small foothold. Go straight up and exit out left over a roof. Belay on the grass ledge.
2   30ft   4c.   Climb the obvious crack to finish.

Daylight Saving   80ft   Hard Very Severe   1979
A poor route taking the arête some 20 feet right of the last route.
1   80ft   4c.   Climb the groove and exit onto the wall on the right. Move diagonally right to the arête, then climb overhanging rock to an unpleasant finish on grass.

B BUTTRESS
This lies above and to the right of the last crag. There is an obvious overlap at half-height and a ledge with a tree at the bottom right-hand corner. The next route starts here.

Quiet River   70ft   Very Severe   1979
A good climb with reliable protection.
1   70ft   4c.   Climb straight up a thin crack to the wall below the overlap. Climb up to the left-hand end of this and exit right onto the final slab.

C BUTTRESS
This lies just above and left of the last cliff.

Maybe Tomorrow   80ft   Hard Very Severe   1979
A good route. Start below the obvious groove.
1   80ft   5a.   Climb the obvious groove to a tree. Move right and climb the final wall direct.

Cold Grief   100ft   E1   1979   ★
This climb takes the overhanging left arête, giving very exciting climbing and positions. Start 10 feet to the left of the last route.
1   100ft   5b.   Climb steeply to a ledge, then traverse left to below the slanting groove, peg runner in situ. Climb directly to a resting place at the left-hand end of the roof. Surmount this to gain good holds and move up to a ledge below a steep crack. Climb the wall right of this, stepping into the crack to finish.

RIVER BUTTRESS
The last cliff on the track beside the river is the most impressive cliff in the area.

Divine Inspiration   150ft   Very Severe   1978
A well positioned route taking the left arête of the face. Start as for Salvationist.
1   150ft   4c.   Follow Salvationist until that route moves back right onto the face, then gain the arête and follow it until level with a horizontal break leading right to the exposed wall of Ultramontane. Finish up this.

Salvationist   150ft   Severe   1958
A good climb which follows the easiest line up the face. Not technically difficult but with an air of seriousness not often found at its grade. Start on the track beneath the centre of the buttress.
1   70ft   Climb a slanting fault to the left edge of the buttress on rather loose rock. Step round right into a shallow corner and follow this to a ledge in the middle of the face above an oak tree, nut belays.
2   80ft   Climb steeply up to the foot of a grassy groove 30 feet up on the right. Climb the groove easily to a large ledge below the final overhang. Move right to avoid this and finish up the top block.

Ultramontane   130ft   Hard Very Severe   1959   ★ ★
A striking line taking the central crackline which goes through the bulges at 40 feet. Start as for Salvationist.
1   130ft   5a.   Climb onto the slanting fault and gain a shallow groove which leads to a pillar on the left. Move up and follow the crack through the overhang to the belay of Salvationist. Climb directly up the face above until beneath the crowning overhang. Traverse strenuously left for 8 feet, then step back right onto the nose and climb the summit block to the top.

Thought Process   140ft   Hard Very Severe   1979
Start 10 feet right of Ultramontane.
1   50ft   5a.   Climb direct to bulging rock (peg runner removed), and trend slightly right and up to a niche. Traverse back left and climb through the bulge to gain the belay of Salvationist.
2   90ft   5a.   Step left and climb directly up the thin wall to the large ledge, finish as for Ultramontane.

Plymouth Limestone

There exist three developed cliffs inside the city boundaries of Plymouth. Radford and Hexton Quarries lie close to Hooe Lake whilst Richmond Walk lies at the Stonehouse end of Union Street. Though not major cliffs they provide a number of worthwhile climbs and offer amusement being ideal for an evening's entertainment.

Radford Quarry   GR 531 505

Park cars at the end of the lake by the dam/bridge and scramble through the hedge to reach the slab. The slab is pretty much featureless, but the following routes offer the best climbing:

Left Edge   100ft   Very Difficult
Follow the slab about 15 feet from the left edge to a nut belay in a short groove just below the top.

Mac's Route   100ft   Very Severe, 4b
In the centre of the slab is the remains of a bolt. Climb directly to this then move left and climb directly to the top.

Strictly Private   115ft   Hard Very Severe, 5a
Climb to the bolt, move right for 10 feet to undercuts, then climb direct to the top.

The Long Slide   100ft   Hard Very Severe, 5c
Climb the slab direct about 10 feet right of the obvious crack.

The Lonely Hold   100ft   Hard Very Severe, 5a
Follow the slab right of the crack to the overlap, then traverse left and finish as for the previous route.

HEXTON QUARRY
This is the quarry at the top of the hill just south of Hooe Lake. A number of short, technical climbs are given by the smooth slab at the back of the quarry, opposite the houses. The best and easiest entry is to abseil from the fence posts above the slab.

Suburbia   65ft   Very Severe, 4c
Climb the slab just left of the right-hand bounding corner.

Ringworld Engineer   65ft   Very Severe, 4c
This climbs the shallow depresssion on the right-hand side of the slab.

Hot Fun   70ft   Hard Very Severe, 4c
Climb directly up the middle of the slab to a thin overlap. Follow this for 10 feet, then step left and climb direct to the top. A fine pitch.

Slippin' and A Sliding   65ft   Hard Very Severe, 5c
Follow Hot Fun to the overlap but move left, then climb to a thin crack. Move back right to climb the blank section to better holds and the top.

Charlie Don't Surf   65ft   Very Severe, 4c
Climb directly to the top via the obvious pocket.

Depression   60ft   Hard Very Severe, 5a
Climb the shallow depression on the left-hand side of the slab to the top.

Richmond Walk   GR 459 544

This cliff lies on private property and permission will have to be gained to climb here. Many climbs were done here in the Sixties and subsequent development has led to the crag being plastered in routes, only the most independent being described here. The cliff is conveniently split into two with the demarcation line being the obvious arête. Left of this the wall is split by a long overhang and left again there is a groove, this gives the line of the first route.

Traffic Jam   Very Severe, 4b
Take a line up the wall just left of the groove and then finish diagonally left.

Traffic Lights   Very Severe, 5a
Climbs the blunt arête right of the groove.

At the far right end of the smooth wall is a groove:

Mayflower   Hard Very Severe, 5b
The groove is followed past some loose rock, finish to the left.

Drake's Circus   E1, 5b
The rounded arête is climbed to the overlap, then move right and climb through a gap in the ivy to the top.

Brec to the Vag   E1, 5b
Climb up to a crack in the roof then over this to a peg, and finish direct.

Brewery Arête   Very Severe, 5a
The arête above the fence is followed to the top.

Cash Investment   Hard Very Severe, 5b
Climb the wall midway between the arête and the overhanging groove.

Diamond Lil   Very Severe, 5a
Follow the groove and exit to the right, then follow a ramp back left to the top.

Night Club   E2, 5c
Climb the wall right of the last route direct.

Right of this route the wall becomes a little mossy and damp; climbs have been recorded here but their quality is questionable.

Chudleigh Rocks   GR 864 788

This excellent crag is very popular with both local climbers and visitors, being only 9 miles from Exeter and adjacent to the A38 dual carriageway, one of the principle routes into Cornwall. It is composed of very sound Devonion Limestone and gives high quality routes in all grades, few of which are serious, thanks to the highly weathered and pocketed rock which almost invariably affords good protection.

There is a regular bus service to Chudleigh from Exeter, but the quickest approach is by car: from the A38 take the exit on the Plymouth side of the village (signposted Chudleigh Knighton), turn left at the top of the slip road (back towards Chudleigh) and then take the second turn on the right, which leads down past the Police Station to parking spaces where the lane widens near a quarry entrance (Palace Quarry). Here a footpath leads off to the right beside a wall. Follow the main path through the woods (which contours the slope) for about 200 yards until it dips sharply to give access to the South Face.

Climbers for the North Face should turn right at the narrow neck of land just before the track dips - a steep muddy path then leads down to the Eastern section of the North Face.

SOUTH FACE

This extensive and fairly complex face provides the best climbing, being very open, quick drying, and having many striking natural lines. Some routes, such as Sarcophagus, Oesophagus and Lute, are climbable in almost any weather conditions, being sheltered from above by overhanging rock. Virtually all necessary pegs are in place and a rack of small to medium nuts is usually all that is required. Routes are described from *right* to *left* as one approaches the cliff.

The first rock encountered is an isolated bluff to the left of the path. This gives several short pitches perfect for novices and one more substantial climb, **Jim's Folly** (30ft Severe), on the side facing the valley.

The South Face proper begins at a cave entrance (Pixies' Hole) where the path from the road makes a steep descent. Just beyond the cave the large corner of Sarcophagus is an obvious feature, and some 60 yards further west, after a more broken section of cliff, is another large cave entrance known as Cow Cave. Above and to the right of this is a ladder of tree roots giving a convenient way down from the cliff top. The highest and most continuous part of the South Face lies to the left (West) of Cow Cave.

Farewell to Arms   95ft   E2   1979
A contrived line up the steep rock above the first cave entrance (Pixies' Hole). Start at a thin overhanging crack 6 feet right of the wide, deep crack taken by Chudleigh Overhang.

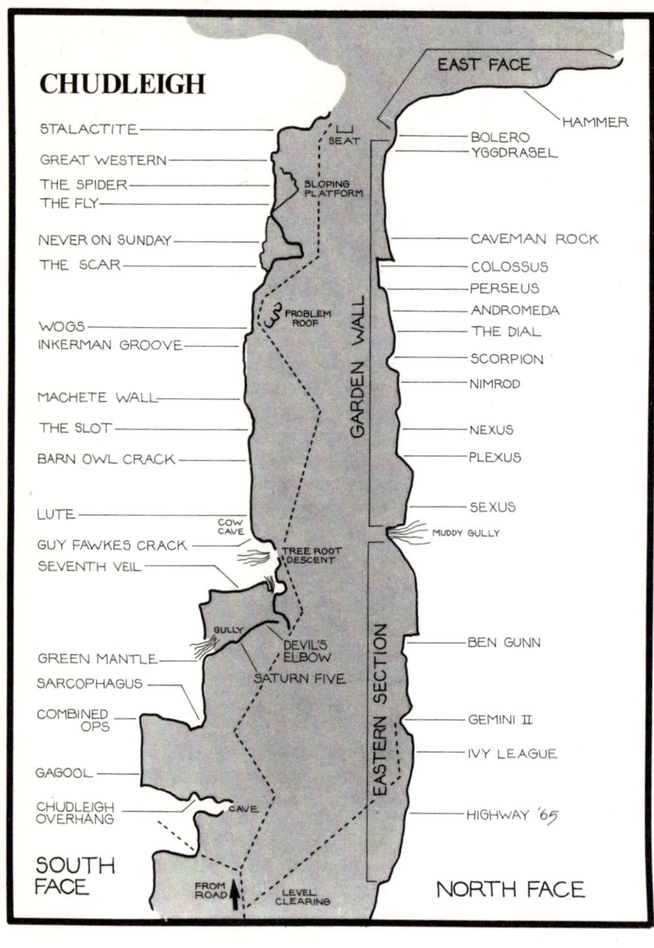
CHUDLEIGH
EAST FACE
HAMMER
STALACTITE
SEAT
BOLERO
YGGDRASEL
GREAT WESTERN
THE SPIDER
THE FLY
SLOPING PLATFORM
NEVER ON SUNDAY
CAVEMAN ROCK
THE SCAR
COLOSSUS
PERSEUS
PROBLEM ROOF
ANDROMEDA
THE DIAL
WOGS
INKERMAN GROOVE
GARDEN WALL
SCORPION
NIMROD
MACHETE WALL
THE SLOT
NEXUS
BARN OWL CRACK
PLEXUS
LUTE
COW CAVE
SEXUS
GUY FAWKES CRACK
TREE ROOT DESCENT
MUDDY GULLY
SEVENTH VEIL
GULLY
EASTERN SECTION
BEN GUNN
DEVIL'S ELBOW
GREEN MANTLE
SARCOPHAGUS
SATURN FIVE
COMBINED OPS
GEMINI II
IVY LEAGUE
GAGOOL
CHUDLEIGH OVERHANG
CAVE
HIGHWAY '65
SOUTH FACE
FROM ROAD
LEVEL CLEARING
NORTH FACE

1 40ft 5c.   Climb the crack, then traverse left on large flat holds (in situ peg) to join Chudleigh Overhang at its crux. Belay in a small cave a few feet higher.
2 25ft 5b.   Traverse right to a cave entrance and pull over the bulge into a short groove. Belay at the base of a large flake.
3 30ft 4c.   Climb the crack and step right onto the top of the flake. Climb straight up the wall above (dubious flake), finishing just right of a large block.

Chudleigh Overhang   80ft   Very Severe   1960   ★
A rather brutal climb of character which goes over the roof on the left wall of the first cave entrance. Start at the wide corner crack leading to the roof.
1 40ft 4c.   Climb the crack and when under the overhang step right to a large foothold. Climb the overhanging crack with difficulty, and traverse left to a stance and peg belays.
2 40ft Step up and traverse right along a line of ledges, passing under a pinnacle, to a short crack leading to a ledge. Go up the short steep wall to the top.

Phoenix on Fire   40ft   E3   1984
Problematic. Start just left of Chudleigh Overhang.
1 40ft 6a/b.   Climb straight up to the overhang, peg runner. Climb past this with difficulty to the stance of Chudleigh Overhang.

Dripdry   90ft   E4   1963/*1982*   ★
Strenuous, dynamic climbing. Start at a thin, polished crack 8ft left of Chudleigh Overhang.
1 40ft 6a/b.   Climb the crack to the overhang (poor thread). Climb past this and continue up the steep wall above (second thread) to the large stance.
2 50ft 5a.   Climb the bulging wall above to the foot of an overhanging white face. Use two aid pegs, then make a strenuous move to reach easier ground. A better alternative is to take Gagool Variation pitch 2.

Gagool Variation   90ft   E1   1965   ★
An excellent route taking the right-hand edge of the steep, smooth-looking face left of the first cave entrance. Start just left of the arête, at a slight groove.
1 50ft 5a/b.   Climb straight up for 15 feet, then move right onto the arête and follow it to a large ledge and belays.
2 40ft 4c.   Move up left onto a large block, then step right into a groove and climb it to reach easier rock on the left.

Direct Start   5c
Climb directly up the right-hand side of the arête – bold.

Gagool Direct   90ft   E2   1979   ★
A good fingery pitch up the centre of the smooth-looking face.
1 50ft 5c.   Climb directly up the wall using small pockets to reach a thin crack. Climb this, then move right to belay.
2 40ft 4c.   As for Gagool Variation.

Gagool Original (E1, 5b 1965) follows the Variation for 15 feet, then traverses to the thin, central crack of the Direct.

Sly Boots McCall   50ft   E4, 6b   1984   ★★
Excellent climbing up the blank-looking face just right of Combined Ops. Two peg runners.

Combined Ops   100ft   E2   1962   ★★
Takes the left edge of the smooth-looking face; a fine sustained pitch.
1 60ft 5b.   Reach the edge by an upward traverse from the right. Follow it for 20 feet to a whitish scoop, then step right and make a hard move to the obvious underholds. After a steep move, easier ground leads to a stance and peg belays.
2 40ft 4a.   Take a diagonal line to the right over blocks till below a double bulge. Make an exposed pull over this using a hidden hold and continue more easily to the top.

Combat   110ft   E3   1971   ★
A steep and difficult route starting just left of the arête of Combined Ops.
1 70ft 5c.   Climb to a projecting flake, which is hand-traversed rightwards to join Combined Ops. Move up into the scoop, then break left up a crack into a niche. Pull out of this with difficulty and continue straight up steeply to a stance.
2 40ft 4a.   Pitch 2 of Combined Ops.

Tendonitis   E4, 6a   1984   ★
A direct variation to Combat. From the flake, climb straight up the wall into the niche. One protection peg.

Oesophagus   100ft   Hard Very Severe   1962   ★
A very strenuous route taking the overhanging crack in the wall right of Sarcophagus. Usually climbable in the wet and invariably so by joining the original exit of Sarcophagus after 50 feet. Start below the crack.
1 85ft 5a.   Steep climbing gains the crack, which is followed to a niche at 50 feet. Step right and climb a pair of cracks to good holds leading to the stance of Combined Ops.
2 15ft   Take the easy break above to the top.

Before The Storm   80ft   E4   1984   ★
A strenuous and committing pitch. Start between Sarcophagus and
Oesophagus.
1 80ft 5c.   Climb directly to the crack of Oesophagus, then move
up and slightly right to a large handhold in the middle of the wall
(microwire runners). Move right into the niche of Combat and finish
up this.

Sarcophagus   110ft   Very Severe   1960   ★ ★
A classic route taking the large obvious corner. Low in the grade and
always dry.
1 30ft 4a.   Climb cracks in the corner to a cave stance.
2 50ft 4a/b.   Climb the chimney to the large overhang. Traverse 10
foot left along a smooth, exposed slab, then go up a short corner to
a ledge.
3 30ft   The broken corner above the stance.

Original Exit
2a 50ft 4a.   Climb the chimney to the large overhang. Step right
and climb a shallow chimney. Exit left by traversing along a wide
horizontal fault to the stance.

Concerto   110ft   E2   1966/*1979*
Strenuous and exposed climbing through the roofs left of Sarcophagus pitch 2. Start as for Sarcophagus.
1 80ft 5c.   Climb for 15 feet, then move out on the left wall and up
to a block. Traverse left for a few feet, then climb direct to a detached
block above the first overhang. Pull past another overhang and
continue to the second stance of Sarcophagus.
2 30ft   As for Sarcophagus.

White Edge   120ft   Hard Very Severe   1966
Start 20 feet left of the start of Sarcophagus, just left of a tree stump.
1 35ft 5b.   Climb a short difficult rib to a ledge. Move out onto
a rib on the right and make a hard move to reach a good jug high up
to the right (peg runner). Pull over into balance, and climb a slab
direct to a small stance. Peg belay.
2 65ft 5a.   Traverse left below the overhangs to the edge of the
slab, peg runner. Move up with difficulty to easy rock leading to a
stance on Green Mantle.
3 20ft 5a.   Climb the overhanging rock directly above the stance.

Green Mantle   110ft   Difficult   1964
A good beginner's route; a bit earthy and vegetated. Some 50 feet
west of Sarcophagus is a small cave entrance with an earthy gully
above it. Start just right of the cave entrance.

1   80ft   Climb for 15 feet using a crack. Traverse right and up a staircase to a vegetated ledge, and continue to another ledge above.
2   30ft   Climb the groove on the left, awkward at first, to the top.

Direct Start   30ft   Hard Severe
1a   30ft   4b.   Climb a short corner to a large ledge right of the cave entrance. From its right-hand side climb the steep slab above to join Green Mantle half-way up the staircase. Two peg runners.

Tar Baby   90ft   Severe   1966
Fairly popular. The prominent crack and corner rising directly from the start of Green Mantle.
1   90ft   Climb Green Mantle to the traverse line, then step up and make an awkward mantelshelf into the groove. Climb to a ledge and continue up the broken corner to the top.

Brer Fox   60ft   Severe   1961
A slight route. Start at the third tree up the earthy gully above the cave at the start of Green Mantle.
1   60ft   Traverse up right on a line of flakes and move around to a steepish wall. Climb this to a tree, then scramble to the top.

Brer Rabbit   60ft   Hard Severe   1961
Climb the groove above the start of Brer Fox, starting as for that climb.
1   60ft   4a.   Climb for 8 feet, then move left to a small ledge beneath the groove. Climb the groove, then go up the staircase straight-forwardly.

The next small buttress is Space Buttress, a remarkable bit of rock which offers a concentration of very steep and enjoyable pitches.

Saturn Five   40ft   E2   1979   ★
Strenuous climbing on good holds. At the top of the earthy gully is a larger cave entrance — start to the right of this, directly beneath an irregular, overhanging crack.
1   40ft   5b.   Pull over the bulge, then follow the crack steeply, past two pegs, moving left onto suspect rock to finish.

Major Tom   50ft   E2   1984   ★
Climbs the overhanging wall left of Saturn Five.
1   50ft   6a.   Follow some good holds, trending right, then climb straight up, lurching for better holds over the lip. Two in situ peg runners.

Ground Control   50ft   E1   1985
A surprisingly independent line up the wall 12 feet left of Major Tom.

1 50ft 5b.   Start up Major Tom, then trend left into the gully. Move right beneath the roof (peg runner) then go straight up on jugs to the top.

Space Odyssey   75ft   E3   1985
A 'cosmic' girdle of the Space Buttress roofs.
1 75ft 5c.   Climb Ground Control to the sharp jugs just above the roof. Follow the break until it joins Major Tom, which is descended for a few feet. Hard moves right gain Saturn Five (peg runner). 10 feet right again, take the roof at its widest point to finish (or escape rightwards).

Squirrel   70ft   Hard Severe   1961
Start just above the higher cave entrance and below an overhang.
1 70ft 4a.   Step up then traverse right, rising steadily for 15 feet. Move up to and over an overhang, then climb easily on the right to the top.

Devil's Elbow   50ft   Very Severe
Start as for Squirrel.
1 50ft 4b.   Climb for 10 feet then traverse left to a big ledge and up to a tree. Traverse right across the blank-looking wall to a small tree. Continue to the top.

Further along from the cave at the start of Green Mantle is a short wall that faces west. On its south side is a large overhang taken by the next climb:

Pigs Might Fly   35ft   E3   1983   ★★
1 35ft 5c.   Climb up to and over the roof using the obvious crack. A way through the roof just left of this has also been found.

Christmas Corner   50ft   Very Severe
Start just right of the lowest point of the wall.
1 50ft 4b.   Climb the groove to an overhang. Skirt this by a semi-circle to the left and continue easily to the top.

Salome   50ft   Very Difficult   ★
A good climb starting on easy slabs at the lowest part of the wall.
1 50ft   Climb the obvious ramp to a small ledge. Climb the final steep section using a crack to the right.

Seventh Veil   40ft   Very Severe
An interesting pitch. Start at a tree stump left of Salome.
1 40ft 4c.   Climb up right to a small ledge. Move left and climb steep smooth rock to the top.

Variation   Hard Very Severe   5b
Climb direct from the tree stump to the top. It is also possible to take an independent line just to the left — slightly harder.

The arête to the left of the Seventh Veil wall gives an interesting problem, **Hot Ice** (25ft, 6a), then the next landmark is Cow Cave.

Guy Fawkes Crack   40ft   Very Severe   4c   1960
The short wide crack to the right of Cow Cave gives an interesting problem, to the right of which an obvious line gives another good little pitch – **T.N.T.** (30ft, 5a).

Smoke Gets in Your Eyes   60ft   E2   1964/*1971*   ★★
A varied and difficult pitch taking the disjointed grooves between Cow Cave and Guy Fawkes Crack.
1   60ft   6a.   Climb the first slabby groove to the overhang, then traverse left and gain a small ledge (protection peg). Move up the groove with difficulty, then exit right by a hard move to reach better holds leading to the top.

An important variation, **Smokey Joe** (E3, 6a), breaks right above the first groove onto the arête and then climbs the wall above to join the normal finish.

Charlie Chaplin Walks on Air   80ft   E3   1980
Left of Smoke Gets in Your Eyes is a fault going over the mouth of Cow Cave. Very strenuous and acrobatic,
1   80ft   6a/b.   Climb up and lurch across the roof to gain a slab, which is followed to join Lute. The huge horizontal roof above has been climbed artificially – **Leo** (A2, 1965)

Lute   80ft   Hard Very Severe   1960   ★
A fine intimidating line which is virtually always dry. Climbs the chimney above Cow Cave. Start on the left wall of the cave entrance, below the narrow chimney.
1   80ft   5a.   Climb up to enter the chimney, which is quitted out left after a few feet. Continue up the open chimney above to the overhang, thread runner. Pull round with difficulty into an overhanging groove leading to the top.

Twang   65ft   E1   1968
An eliminate line giving good, serious climbing between Lute and Spearhead. Start at the rib 10 feet left of the start of Lute.
1   35ft   5b.   Move up to the large ledge 10 feet right of Spearhead, then climb the wall with difficulty to a scoop handhold and peg runner. Move up to stand in the scoop (hard), then climb on better holds and move up left to the stance of Reek.

2   30ft   5a.   On the right is a short corner. Make a move up this, then swing right and climb the rib on widely spaced incuts: strenuous and exposed. Tree belay.

Spearhead   65ft   Hard Severe   1961   ★
Worthwhile despite having very little independence. Start as for Reek.
1   35ft   4b.   Follow Reek to the prominent nose, then move up and right across the wall and climb through the 'spearhead' to the stance of Reek.
2   30ft   As for Reek.

Reek   60ft   Severe   1961   ★★
Technically interesting and deservedly popular. Start beneath the short wall to the left of Cow Cave.
1   35ft   4b.   Climb onto the ledge. Move up left to stand on the bulge, then climb a groove left of the prominent nose to a stance.
2   25ft   Climb the easy slab above the stance for a few feet, then step right and go up a short wall to the top.

Leek   60ft   Hard Severe
Start at the small corner left of the first wall of Reek.
1   40ft   4b.   Climb the corner and traverse left to a terrace. Climb on small holds to enter the groove between Reek and Barn Owl. Follow this to the stance.
2   20ft   The slab above the stance.

Ashtree Buttress   50ft   Very Difficult
From the top of Reek and Barn Owl Crack a buttress can be seen with a tree growing from it. Climb up and pass the tree on the right. Steep pleasant climbing to the top.

Barn Owl Crack   65ft   Hard Very Difficult   1960   ★
This is the obvious break left of Cow Cave. A route of character.
1   65ft   Climb to the terrace below the crack. Climb the crack to the top, the narrow middle section being the most difficult. The crux can be avoided by breaking right to the stance of Reek from the small ledge at 20 feet. Regain the crack 15 feet higher.

Barn Owl Variant   60ft   Very Severe   1967
Start from the terrace below Barn Owl Crack.
1   60ft   4b.   Climb 6 feet up the crack to a small ledge. Step left and climb the left wall by a series of pockets. Take the obvious line on to the arête and climb a tower easily on its left-hand side to the top.

The Slot   55ft   Hard Very Severe   1960   ★
A fine, strenuous pitch. Belay beneath the obvious corner above the left end of the terrace below Barn Owl Crack.

1 55ft 5a. Make steep moves to enter the corner, which is followed for 20 foot to an overhang. Exit to the right with difficulty and climb a steep wall directly to the top.

Panga   60ft   E2   1966/*1979*   ★★
A strenuous and technically difficult pitch. Start on the slab some 10 feet left of the start of Slot.
1 60ft 6a.   Climb the obvious flake (peg runner), then step up left with difficulty to a small foothold. Make a series of hard moves bearing slightly right (peg runner) into a groove leading to easier ground.

Machete Wall   100ft   E1   1961   ★★
An excellent route taking a central line up the wall between Inkerman Groove and The Slot. Start 20 feet to the right of Wogs and just left of a recess.
1 100ft 5b.   Climb easily for 15 feet, then mantelshelf onto a small ledge and continue bearing slightly right to a peg runner high up in a niche. Climb steeply to a second peg and pass it with a hard move. Climb up and left to a good foothold, then move up across the slab on the right to a large pointed block. Standing on this, step left into a groove, which is followed for 10 feet. Step right and climb to a large vegetated ledge. Climb the short steep wall to a tree belay.

South Face (E5, 6b 1983) is a very difficult eliminate near Machete, starting up the overhung niche to its right, then moving left from the second peg runner and up to join Penny Lane.

Penny Lane   125ft   E3   1968   ★★
A fine, intricate and very technical route. Start as for Wogs.
1 25ft   Climb directly to the right-hand end of the first stance of Wogs.
2 100ft 6a/b.   Traverse right and up a short groove, then step right around the rib. Climb the steep wall to a protection peg, then traverse right on very small holds and up to the steep slab beside the perched block of Machete Wall. Move delicately left beneath the overhang, then follow the thin crack above, hard, to better holds on the finish of Inkerman Groove.

Inkerman Groove   110ft   Very Severe   1960   ★★★
One of the best climbs at Chudleigh, taking the long groove to the left of Machete Wall. Start as for Wogs.
1 110ft 4c.   Follow Wogs to a point half-way up its second pitch, from which it is possible to traverse right to the bottom of the long groove. Climb the groove for 30 feet to a small ledge. Traverse right and up to a larger ledge, from which a short steep wall leads to the top.

Inkerman Direct   75ft   Hard Very Severe   *1971*
Useful if one has done Inkerman Groove a number of times, but harder. Start from the first stance of Wogs.
1a   75ft   5a.   Move up right to a peg on Penny Lane. Move left and up a few feet, then pull over the small overhang to enter the groove of the normal route. Climb directly up the groove to reach broken rock and finish easily on the left.

Black Death   100ft   E4   1966/*1982*   ★★★
One of the best and hardest pitches on the cliff, taking the narrow, vertical wall between Inkerman Groove and Wogs.
1   100ft   6a.   Follow Inkerman Groove to a point half-way along its traverse. Climb straight up the wall for 20 feet, then follow a shallow scoop slightly leftwards to its end. Peg runner. Climb the overhanging wall above, bearing right over a bulge, after which easier ground leads to the top.

Wogs   120ft   Very Difficult   1923   ★★
The classic route of its standard with great character. It goes up the obvious fault left of the smooth walls of Inkerman and Machete.
1   30ft   Climb to a ledge by means of a steepish wall. There are many ways of doing this.
2   55ft   Step up above the stance, then traverse left along a narrow ledge. Follow the long crack to a stance on top of the pillar.
3   35ft   Climb to a recess, then step left and go up easier rock to a tree. Or the delicate slab above and to the left of the stance may be climbed — harder.

Variation Finish   Very Difficult
3a   45ft   From above the recess and delicate slab, climb to a projecting ledge on the right then up and over the wall to the top. Worthwhile.

Central Pillar   110ft   Hard Very Severe   1965
A good route, though at present very vegetated. The top pitch is particularly fine and may be climbed independently. The route goes up the face of the pillar between Wogs and Sisyphus. Start at a wide disjointed crack 20 feet left of the start of Wogs.
1   70ft   5a.   Awkward climbing for 10 feet, then step left and go easily up to an overhang split by a crack. Climb the crack to better ledges. Peg runner. Climb the centre of the face of the pillar, by a thin crack-line, to the second stance of Wogs. This is steep and tiring (crux).
2   40ft   4b.   Scramble up above the stance to the large chockstone in the corner above. Traverse up right, using large handholds, then climb up to the overhang. Move right and up a short groove to large ledges. A short wall leads to the top.

Sisyphus   120ft   Very Severe   1961
A less pleasant companion to Wogs, taking the left-hand side of the pillar. Commonly overgrown. Start at a rib 10 feet left of Wogs.
1   70ft   Climb to the obvious traverse line and move left along this for some 15 feet. Break through left of the overhang and continue up right to a stance and chockstone belay, level with the narrow ledge on Wog's second pitch.
2   50ft   Climb the crack above to the second stance of Wogs — awkward. Climb the short delicate slab, then scramble to the top.

Tantalus   115ft   E1   1966/*1979*
An interesting route up the wall between Sisyphus and Never on Sunday. Start as for Central Pillar.
1   50ft   5a/b.   To the left of Central Pillar is an overhanging crack. Climb this, finishing out left. Move up and belay at a horizontal break below an obvious fault.
2   65ft   5a.   Climb the fault for 8 feet to a ledge. Move delicately left and up to a peg. Move left across the wall to good footholds, then go up to gain the bottom of a broken groove. Climb the groove and bear left to the top of Never on Sunday. Or, better, climb directly to the bottom groove on small pockets.

Scar   110ft   Hard Severe   1960   ★
A good climb following a great natural weakness. To the left of Wogs the ground falls 10 feet. Start at the bottom of this dip, to the right of two caves 10 feet up in the rock.
1   60ft   Climb vertically to a small tree stump. Step left then go up a slab to a large terrace beneath a corner with a tree stump in it.
2   50ft   4a.   Climb to the tree stump on gritty rock. Climb the wall above, which overhangs slightly, to a tree belay. Scramble up a path to the top.

Direct Finish   Hard Severe
3   30ft   Standing on the top of the tree, climb to good holds above a smooth scoop then step left and climb the easy wall to the top. Much harder for a short person.

Never on Sunday   120ft   Hard Severe   1961   ★★
A delightful second pitch. Start beneath the two caves 10 foot up in the rock.
1   60ft   Climb to the caves and awkwardly move out of the right-hand one onto slabs. Go up these to the terrace below the tree stump of Scar.
2   60ft   4b.   Just right of the line of Scar, climb a gritty corner for 10 feet then traverse right, rising slightly, to a small ledge around the arête

Variations
2a It is possible to climb a groove directly to the point at which one steps round to the small ledge — Very Severe, 4c.
2b The small ledge has been gained directly by climbing the face beneath it — Hard Very Severe, 5a.

Leap Year Finish   45ft   Hard Very Severe   *1964*   ★
A good finish to Never on Sunday in a very exposed position.
3   45ft   5a.   From the tree at the top of Scar traverse left across the wall, using the tree branch for the first few moves. A hard move brings one to good holds. Peg runner. Climb up and over a bulge, then up steep rock to the top.

To the left of the fault of Scar is a steep buttress about 130 feet high. This is the Western Tower which provides some of the most exhilarating climbing in the area. Its base has recently been cleared of trees and it is now very open and quick-drying.

The Fly   150ft   Hard Very Severe   1962   ★
A good route, exposed and with an air of seriousness. Start 20 feet to the left of the two caves, beneath a ledge at 8 feet.
1   55ft   4b.   Climb to the ledge. Climb the crack on the right to another ledge. Continue up the groove above to the terrace. Peg Belay.
2   60ft   5a.   Walk a few feet right, then move up onto the steep wall. Go diagonally left to beneath the right-hand side of the perched block in the centre of the face. Climb up onto the block, peg runner. Traverse horizontally left from the block for 10 feet, then pull up to a small stance just left of the arête. Block and spike belays.
3   35ft   Climb the rib to a groove leading to the top.

The Spy   130ft   E3   1968   ★
At two thirds height the Western Tower is split by a diagonal fault. This climb follows its upper part, from the perched block. The first pitch may be vegetated. Start 10 feet to the right of The Fly, at a zig-zag crack.
1   50ft   5b.   Climb the crack to a ledge. Move right and climb the wall with difficulty, past a peg runner, to another ledge. Make a difficult move up the corner to reach a small bush and using this climb the slab on the left to the stance of The Fly.
2   80ft   5c.   Move up left to the vegetated ledge. Climb straight up and around the right-hand side of 'the block' and continue up for 10 feet (a few feet right of the line of The Spider) to a good hold and runner. Traverse right beneath the bulge (strenuous) to an enormous jug. Climb the groove above to join the Leap Year Finish. Make a long stride right onto the lip of an overhang, then climb the wall easily to the top.

The Spider   130ft   E1   1964   ★★★
One of the best climbs on the cliff; the final wall is delectable.
Protection is excellent on the crux but rather lacking on the first pitch.
Start as for The Fly.
1   45ft   5a.   Climb to the ledge at 8 feet. Step left then go up a steep
wall to a ledge. From the left end of the ledge (good Friend placement
in horizontal crack on the left) make a difficult move to gain a large
foothold on the slab above. Continue to the second stance of Great
Western. Peg belays.
2   85ft   5b.   Climb rightwards to the vegetated ledge. Move up and
round the left-hand side of the perched block to the small stance
above it. Peg runner. Climb straight up to break through the bulge
and gain small holds on the steep slab above. Go diagonally right to
good finishing holds up and to the right of a small tree, exposed.
Continue straight up to the top, as for the Leap Year Finish.

Great Western   140ft   Very Severe   1961   ★★★
A superb climb, though rather polished and very tricky if wet. Near
the western end of the cliff is a shallow corner just before the face
becomes very fluted. Start here, a few feet to the left of The Fly.
1   40ft   4b.   Climb the corner to the second of two ledges, peg
runner. Traverse left using good high handholds and mantelshelf on
to a ledge.
2   20ft   4b.   A narrow slab leads up to the right. Climb this thinly to
a large ledge. Peg belays.
3   30ft   5a.   Climb the wall ahead until beneath the overhang, peg
runner. Move up into the groove on the left, hard, then climb the
groove to a large stance. Peg belay.
4   50ft   Climb the rib above to the top.

Titan/Pig's Ear   160ft   Hard Very Severe/A1 or E4   1965/*1984*
Start 20 feet left of Great Western.
1   65ft   4c.   Climb on flutings for about 15 feet, then make a difficult
move to a traverse line leading right to the first stance of Great
Western. Climb straight up behind the stance to an overhang. Move
left to clear this, then go up to a stance beneath a large roof. Peg
belay.
2   45ft   A1 or 6b.   Follow a good crack-line across the roof, either
free or using the in situ pegs for aid, to gain the third stance of Great
Western.
3   50ft   Go over a small overhang above the stance to reach an area
of shattered rock between the final pitches of Stalactite and Great
Western. Climb this then scramble to the top.

Stalactite   170ft   Very Severe   1962   ★
A rather rambling route, though with good climbing initially. Start
about 30 feet to the left of Great Western.

1 55ft 4b. Climb for 10 feet on stalactite formations then move right to a ledge. Cross to the right-hand side of this, then go up to another ledge above. Traverse right to reach a deep groove. Climb this to a terrace.

2 25ft 4a. Above is a large overhang. Climb a crack on its left to gain a slab above. Traverse right above the overhang and round to a stance, shared with Great Western.

3 90ft Go up the rib to the left to a small tree. Traverse left onto a slab and climb this to the top.

West End   110ft   Hard Severe   1967
A disconnected and rather vegetated route taking the slabby groove left of Stalactite and the vegetated rock above.

GIRDLE TRAVERSES

South Face Girdle   290ft   Hard Very Severe   1962
A poor route as a whole, but with reasonable climbing in the first and last sections.

1 + 2   55ft   4b.   As for Stalactite.

3   40ft   Traverse right beneath the overhang and down to the second stance of Great Western. Go up right to a vegetated ledge and descend from its right end to the large terrace of Scar.

4   80ft   Cross the terrace to a short, narrow slab. Go up this then traverse right along the obvious line for 25 feet to a scoop. Peg belay.

5   50ft   4b.   Cross the wall of the first pitch of Wogs to a short rib. Make a mantelshelf move (as for Machete Wall) to gain a slab. Traverse right along this to the terrace below Barn Owl Crack.

6   25ft   5a.   Climb a few moves of Leek and step right to join Reek. Move right beneath the nose and cross the steep wall into Lute.

7   40ft   5a.   Either finish up Lute, or abseil off.

The Equation   305ft   E3   1970/*1978*   ★★
A higher traverse of the South Face, from right to left. A difficult and arduous route having a lot of very fine, independent climbing. Start as for Smoke Gets In Your Eyes.

1 70ft   5a.   Climb the slabby groove to the overhang. Hand-traverse left along the horizontal crack, until easier climbing joins Lute. Move left across the smooth wall to a good foothold, then go up through the 'spearhead' to the stance of Reek.

2 70ft   5b.   Move left and down Barn Owl Crack for a few feet. Traverse left and move around the nose of the buttress with difficulty into Slot. Continue left beneath a bulge, using a horizontal crack at first, to gain the groove of Panga. Go up easily for 10 feet to belay in a short corner.

3 70ft   6a.   Move down and left past a block onto a slab. Traverse to the left end of the roof and continue horizontally left to a good underhold

underhold. Pull up left with difficulty into Inkerman Groove. Descend for 10 feet or so, then traverse left across the blank-looking wall to the crack of Wogs, which is followed to its second stance.
4 50ft Traverse across vegetated rock to the tree of Never On Sunday, then go up to the tree at the top of Scar.
5 45ft 5a. The Leap Year Finish.

Eastern Girdle   195ft   Hard Very Severe   1962
This is a traverse of the Sarcophagus section of the cliff. Start as for White Edge.
1 60ft 5b. Follow White Edge for 30 feet up to the slab. Traverse right to the cave stance of Sarcophagus.
2 50ft 5a. Move right to the crack of Oesophagus and climb this to the scoop. Exit right then go up bearing right to the stance of Combined Ops.
3 45ft Move down right and along the obvious traverse line to the stance of Chudleigh Overhang.
4 40ft Pitch 2 of Chudleigh Overhang.

NORTH FACE
The North Face is rather sombre and featureless compared to the South Face, but it nevertheless provides many fine routes on solid rock. The cliff forms the boundary wall of the garden of Rock House, which is privately owned by the Boulton Family. The owners thoroughly approve of climbing, but do request that climbers call at the house to sign a visitors book, so that they know who is on their property.

The foot of the cliff must be approached from the same path used for the South Face, and not by walking through the garden of Rock House. The North Face divides naturally into two separate sections: the 90-foot high Garden Wall immediately behind Rock House, and to the east, beyond a broad, muddy gully, the lower and less attractive Eastern Section. Apart from the far right-hand end, which is composed of calcite, the whole face has been quarried, leaving fewer natural features than on the South Face. The rock is sound however and well supplied with small incut holds.

Climbs are described from left to right as one approaches the face from the narrow neck of land mentioned earlier. On walking westward along the foot of the crag, rock appears first as a mossy and overgrown wall 40 feet high, which has given three poor routes. It is terminated on the right by a muddy chimney, and the first routes are described in relation to this. Beyond the chimney the cliff rises to a height of 60 feet and becomes steeper and cleaner. This comprises the Eastern Section.

Highway '65   55ft   Hard Severe   1965
An interesting pitch on steep rock. Start 25 feet left of the muddy chimney, beneath a perched block half-way up the face.
1 55ft 4b.   Climb to beneath the block, then traverse right for a few feet, peg runner. Move up and step back left, onto the top of the block, peg runner, then climb up to the top on good holds.

Route '66   55ft   Hard Very Difficult   1966
Start 15 feet left of the muddy chimney, below a crack.
1 55ft   Climb up to the corner at the foot of the crack. Move up right then trend back left to a large ledge. Climb the crack on the right and finish over rocks, keeping left of Ivy League.

Ivy League   50ft   Difficult   1965
This climb has a certain character and its low grade makes it useful for beginners. Left of the muddy chimney is the rock staircase forming the climb.
1 50ft   Climb the wall just left of the chimney then step left onto a ledge. Now climb diagonally left to mantelshelf onto a larger ledge, shot hole thread runner. Then go straight up past the tree to the top.

Ancient Mariner   60ft   Hard Severe   1967
Start as for Ivy League.
1 60ft 4b.   Follow Ivy League for 15 feet, then move up right and climb a delicate slab to good holds. Continue up and take the final overhang direct on big jugs.

Gemini II   60ft   Severe   1965
A pleasant, open climb. Start on the right edge of the muddy chimney.
1 60ft   Climb the left edge of the wall, only diverting to the right to avoid two small overhangs at 30 feet and 50 feet.

Gemini I   60ft   Severe   1965
Start some 6 feet right of Gemini II, beneath a small tree root.
1 60ft   Climb for 10 feet then make a rising traverse to the left along a flake with good fingerholds. Go straight up and mantelshelf onto a large ledge. Step right into an open groove, then go up to the right on steep rock, peg runner. Break through the overhangs with difficulty to finish just right of Gemini II.

Tropic of Capricorn   60ft   Very Severe   1963
A clean pleasant pitch with poor protection. Start below some obvious drill marks on the left-hand side of the wall.
1 60ft 4b.   Climb up slightly right on sloping holds. At 15 feet an old wedge runner is reached, followed by a difficult right step and mantelshelf. Continue up steep rock using downward-sloping holds to the top.

Tropic of Cancer   60ft   Very Severe   1963
Start some 15 feet right of Capricorn.
1   60ft   4c.   Climb a slight groove to a ledge at 12 feet. Continue up until beneath a bulge. Climb this direct using poor handholds, then go either left or right to the top

Ben Gunn   60ft   Severe   1963   ★
This climb takes the open groove on the right-hand side of the face. Clean and worthwhile.
1   60ft   Climb a short groove to a ledge. Move up right to a large projecting block, then step left and climb the groove to the top.

The Notch   60ft   Hard Severe   1963
Start near a tree-covered mound close to the cliff, beneath an obvious leftward-slanting corner.
1   60ft   4b.   Climb slabby rock to a small ledge and reach a larger ledge above by a delicate move. Climb the corner, peg runner, then traverse left with difficulty to clear the overhang. Peg runner. Continue steeply to the top.

Two Stroke Banana   70ft   Hard Very Severe   1967
A steep route which is difficult to protect. Start left of and lower than Little Subtleties.
1   70ft   5a.   Climb a shallow groove which leans right and exit right onto a ledge. Step up to a small crack and make a long stride left. Climb the steep wall above, step left, then go up rightwards more easily to the top.

Little Subtleties   60ft   Hard Very Difficult   1965
Hidden at present by a mantle of vegetation. Start left of the foot of Muddy Gully.
1   25ft   Climb the slab until it steepens and traverse left to a ledge. Climb to another ledge, stance and peg belay.
2   35ft   Climb the overhang above by an obvious break. Step left and climb to the top. A line has been climbed just to the left of this pitch, Severe in standard.

Muddy Gully forms the demarcation line between the two sections. It gives an easy way down, which can be tricky in wet weather. The cave exit of the passage through from the South Face can be seen 15 feet from the top of this gully. The ground falls away to the right of the gully and the North Face rises to its maximum height of 90 feet.

GARDEN WALL
All the climbs on this wall are steep and of a consistently high standard. The rock is sound and there is less tendency to the downward-sloping holds that characterizes the Eastern Section.

Unfortunately, it does seem to be possible to climb almost anywhere on the Garden and Grey Walls without exceeding Hard Very Severe standard. However, several routes, such as Nimrod, follow aesthetic and fairly inescapable lines.

Sexus   90ft   Hard Severe   1964   ★
Somewhat neglected and overgrown, but a very pleasant route up the extreme left edge of the face. Start to the right of a small tree which is about 15 feet up.
1   75ft   4a/b.   Climb the steep wall to the right of the tree to a peg runner, and continue up a shallow groove on the left past the tree, to a small overhang. Skirt this by stepping left, peg runner, then go back right again to climb a steep rib on excellent holds. Stance and peg belays under the overhang.
2   15ft   4a   Traverse right from the stance, then pull strenuously over the overhang, to finish by a blackthorn tree.

Garden Wall Eliminate   90ft   Very Severe   1966
A direct line between Plexus and Sexus. Start just right of Sexus.
1   40ft   4c.   Climb the rib left of Plexus to a ledge. Trend left then back right to the stance of Plexus.
2   50ft   4c.   Move left and take the bulge direct, strenuous. Continue straight up to another bulge, which is taken to reach the upper shared section of Sexus and Plexus.

Plexus   100ft   Very Severe   1964   ★★
A fine inescapable line. Right of Sexus are two prominent cracks about 15 feet apart. Start below the left-hand crack.
1   50ft   4a.   Climb the crack for 15 feet then up vertically on the wall to the right of the crack, two peg runners. Peg belay on the sloping ledge below the overhanging wall.
2   50ft   4a/b.   Climb the short crack above, then traverse left beneath a large block to a small ledge, peg runner. Climb straight up to a bulge and peg runner 15 feet from the top. After a steep move, ledges lead easily to the top.

Prometheus   100ft   Hard Very Severe   1965   ★
A steep and exposed route. Start as for Nexus.
1   50ft   Climb the crack of Nexus for 10 feet, then step left onto the slabs. Climb a shallow groove to the stance of Plexus.
2   50ft   4c.   Traverse right for 10 feet then climb steeply to the line of incut handholds leading left. Follow these to a small ledge, peg runner. Climb delicately until a large handhold can be reached above the overhang. Pull up and over, step right and climb the exposed buttress to the top.

Nemesis   90ft   Hard Very Severe   1966
An artificial line, having exposed and very steep climbing. Start as for Nexus.
1   90ft   5a.   Climb Nexus for 25 feet to the jammed flakes. Step left then move up to the bay beneath a large block. Climb the left-hand side of the block and onto a ledge and loose spike. Step up, peg runner, and climb the shallow groove, which leads to an obvious square break in the overhang, hard. Reach high to a peg (probably not in place) above the overhang and use this to pull over. Move left to a small ledge then up the exposed final wall.

Nexus   95ft   Severe   1964   ★★★
Probably the finest route in the Severe grade at Chudleigh; interesting throughout and exposed on the crux. Start below the obvious line of cracks about 40 feet from the left-hand edge of the face.
1   65ft   Follow the crack-line to a very large block on the left. Traverse up on this, then go horizontally right to a small stance and peg belay in the corner.
2   30ft   4a.   Traverse back left and climb the steep wall to a small ledge. Step up left with difficulty to reach good holds leading to the top.

Thornifixion   100ft   Hard Very Severe   1964
An interesting climb, though rather scrappy. Some 20 feet right of the start of Nexus a steep slab runs up for a few feet to the left. Start below this.
1   50ft   5a.   Reach a large ledge at 6 feet, then climb the very delicate slab to good holds. Continue more easily to a good stance and peg belay just below a curious hole in the rock.
2   50ft   4a.   Climb directly over the overhang and continue past the stance of Nexus to the start of a ramp running up to the right, peg runner. Follow this for about 20 feet, pull awkwardly over the overhang and climb easily to the top.

Variation **The Rosy Exit**   4b   *1966*
From the peg at the start of the ramp climb the obvious line above to an overhang split by a crack. Climb this with difficulty and continue leftwards to the top.

Diana   90ft   Very Severe   1966
An eliminate line, very close indeed to older routes. Start just right of Nexus.
1   90ft   4c.   Follow a thin layback edge to the 'hole' on Thornifixion. Move right and up into a slabby groove, peg runner. Go up to a small overhang, which is climbed on its right-hand side, delicate and exposed, to the second 'hole' of Thornifixion. Climb the overhang, a short slab and a final bulge to the top.

Right of Thornifixion there is a wide expanse of wall terminating in the striking cleft of Colossus. This is the Grey Wall. A line of ledges cross the wall about 20 feet up and the first pitches are usually mere formalities, though they serve to add to the exposure. The obvious break right of the centre of the wall is The Dial, whose first pitch is used by some of the other climbs.

Nimrod   90ft   Hard Very Severe   1965   ★★
An excellent climb, sustained and delicate. Start as for Thornifixion.
1   20ft   5a.   Climb the slab of Thornifixion, then traverse right to a ledge and peg belay.
2   70ft   5a.   Move up left to the base of a thin curving crack, which is followed by a prominent peg. Mantelshelf onto the ledge at the foot of a ramp which runs up to the right. Climb the ramp with the aid of a high bore hole on the right to a peg on the lip of an overhang. Move right and continue up steep but easy rock to the top.

Grey Wall Eliminate   90ft   Hard Very Severe   1966
A vague line between Nimrod and Scorpion. Start at a weakness left of the start of The Dial.
1   20ft   4b.   Move up to a ledge from the left-hand side. Step into an open depression and up to the large ledge. Peg belay.
2   70ft   4c.   From the left-hand edge of the ledge move up delicately on slabs, trending slightly left. Move back right and up to a depression, drill mark. Take the bulge above the depression, to emerge at the top of the ramp of Nimrod. Continue straight up and over the final tottery overhang.

Scorpion   90ft   Hard Very Severe   1965
Not too difficult technically, but an intimidating lead which is not well protected. Start as for The Dial.
1   20ft   Follow ledges up to the left to the stance of Nimrod.
2   70ft   4c.   Follow a vague line directly above the stance to a small overhang. Move right and up to a ledge, peg runner. Climb the steep wall on incut holds to a long drill mark, poor peg runner. Reach holds above the bulge and pull over to a ledge with a small sapling. Take the slab to a small final overhang and the top.

Orion   95ft   Hard Very Severe   1965
Despite a rather artificial line it provides interesting climbing. Start as for The Dial.
1   25ft   Climb up the broken corners to the stance of The Dial.
2   70ft   5a.   Climb leftwards to a small ledge, shared with Scorpion, then go diagonally right to ledges. The Dial is just on the right. Move up, then back left under a bulge on sloping footholds and finger incuts. Make a difficult pull over the bulge and finish straight up past a thorn bush.

The Dial   90ft   Severe   1964
This is the obvious weakness up the right flank of Grey Wall, slanting rightwards. Start below this line.
1   25ft   Climb to the highest of a variety of ledges. Peg belay.
2   65ft   4a.   Climb to the large projecting ledge on the right. Move up slightly left on sloping holds for a few feet, then angle gently right on better holds to a steep finish. Two peg runners. This pitch becomes much harder when wet.

Crescendo (Hard Severe) climbs the shallow groove directly above the stance of Dial and continues straight up keeping left of The Dial, with the crux at the final wall.

Cygnus   90ft   Very Severe   1965   ★
A fine pitch giving a good introduction to the more difficult Grey Wall climbs. Start as for The Dial.
1   20ft   Follow the ledges as for The Dial but take a stance a little lower and further right. Peg belay.
2   70ft   4c.   Climb to the projecting ledge, peg runner. Make a long step right and climb an open groove then a short wall, which leads to a sloping ledge and peg runner below a steeper wall. Go up bearing left to easier rock, which is climbed on good but widely spaced holds to finish just right of The Dial.

Andromeda   105ft   Hard Very Severe   1965   ★★
An excellent route which takes a rightward-slanting line up the right-hand part of the Grey Wall. Start 20 feet right of the ledges of The Dial.
1   25ft   4b.   Climb up and make a difficult pull over a bulge in the wall, then move left to a stance as for Cygnus.
2   70ft   4c.   From the right-hand end of the stance climb to a small ledge with a hidden drill hole (slot-in peg runner). Move up and continue bearing slightly right to a peg just left of an overhang. This is normally used as a handhold to traverse right beneath the overhang to the foot of an open groove, peg runner. Climb steeply, on widely spaced holds at first, to a tree belay.
3   10ft   The rock rib on the left.

Andromeda Direct   Hard Very Severe, 5a   1965
From the peg before the traverse right beneath the overhang, climb straight up then rightwards in the general line, passing a bulge with difficulty.

Perseus   90ft   Hard Very Severe   1966   ★
A fine route with probably greater technical interest than any other North Face climb. Takes the wall left of Colossus. Start 10 feet left of Colossus.

1   90ft   5b.   Climb an open corner then traverse left for some 6 feet and climb the smooth wall to a drill hole, peg runner. Move right for a few feet then up to a bay (with a shothole in its floor for a peg runner). Bridge up to a bulge, peg runner, then make a difficult move left to a large foothold. Go diagonally left to a small overhang, peg runner, then up the groove of Andromeda to the top.

Direct Finish
Improves the line but misses the crux move. From the peg runner above the bay make a difficult mantelshelf onto a sloping ledge on the right. Continue slightly leftwards through a break in the overhangs, peg runner, to the top. It is also possible to climb straight up from the initial corner into the bay, via a very difficult mantelshelf.

Colossus   90ft   Very Severe   1964   ★
An imposing line which provides some bold climbing up the great cleft which is the most striking feature of the face. Start in the cave at the foot of the cleft.
1   90ft   4b.   Climb up the left-hand corner of the fissure and continue by a chimneying process until just above a peg runner near the top of the cleft. Make an exposed swing round the overhanging right wall using a prominent flat handhold and continue up the rib to another peg runner. Step back left over the top of the cleft to a large ledge and the top.

Alternative Finish   4c
Climb the slab above the swing-out right, instead of going left again.

The Track   235ft   Hard Very Severe   1965   ★
A high level girdle traverse of the Garden Wall. An excellent route, sustained and on perfect rock. Start at the foot of Colossus.
1   80ft   4b.   Climb Colossus to a tree belay near the top.
2   45ft   5a/b.   Descend the final open groove of Andromeda to the peg runner beneath the overhang. Traverse left with difficulty to join Cygnus at its peg runner, then go up steeply and left to a stance on The Dial.
3   50ft   5a.   Climb The Dial for a couple of moves, then move out left on a delicate slab to the sapling above the crux of Scorpion. Continue left on good footholds to the top of the ramp of Nimrod. Descend this, then make a delicate traverse left to the stance of Nexus.
4   45ft   4c.   Traverse horizontally left for 15 feet to join Prometheus. Follow that route up and across the traverse and continue to the top stance of Sexus.
5   15ft   4a.   Follow Sexus over the overhang to the top.

Variation   Hard Very Severe
More sustained and avoids any deviation in line.
2a 100ft 5a/b.   From the pegs on Andromeda traverse horizontally into The Dial, then make a long step left to reach a peg on Scorpion. Go left again to a drill strike (peg runner) and make a very awkward move left to the foot of the ramp of Nimrod. Continue by the normal route.

Right of Colossus and under the ivy is **Caveman Rock** (80ft, Hard Severe).

Hansel   90ft   Severe   1966   ★
Enjoyable in its grade and taking the narrow slabby wall at the western end of the Garden Wall, just right of the vegetated area of Caveman Rock. Start at a prominent bulge at ground level, 12 feet left of the corner formed by the fluted face to the right.
1 40ft   Climb, using sloping footholds, to a block set in a short steep wall at 25 feet. Step left onto the block (crux), then climb easy slabs to a ledge by a tree.
2 50ft   Climb the steep groove above the ledge, then go up easy slabs to a small overhang, which is surmounted, and the top is reached.

Gretel   85ft   Hard Severe   1966
Start to the right of Hansel and just left of the corner.
1 35ft   Climb easily for 10 feet to the base of a steep narrow slab. Climb the left side of the slab, on very sloping friction holds, to the large ledge above it. Stance and thread belay.
2 50ft 4a.   Climb leftwards to a ledge below a bulging wall 6 feet right of the groove of Hansel. Climb on small holds to reach a good double-handed jug above the overhang and pull up on this (crux). Climb easy slabs above, bearing right to the top.

Yggdrasel   80ft   Hard Very Severe   1967
A good delicate route following the corner formed by the slabby wall and the fluted face. Start at the foot of the corner.
1 80ft 5a.   Climb the corner to the overhang. Turn this on the right, then take the slab on the left to a sloping ledge, peg runner. Step right and gain the smooth groove with difficulty. Follow the slab to a tree belay.

Right of Yggdrasel is the East Face. It is mainly composed of calcite flutings and has a very different character from the North Face. The calcite is not always reliable as it holds together some indifferent base material, however, one or two routes are worthwhile.

East Gully Wall   70ft   Very Severe   1966
A poor route. Start beneath a tree growing out of a grass ramp.
1   70ft   Climb to the tree. Continue up for 10 feet, then traverse 10 feet left. Follow a natural line to finish near a tree which is just left of a large block.

Bolero   70ft   Hard Very Severe   1966   ★
A fine route, steep and strenuous, taking a line straight up from the start of East Gully Wall.
1   70ft   4c.   Climb to the tree. Continue up to a ledge in the middle of the face, then move left for a few feet. Move up and hand-traverse right on good holds until a steep move gains the top.

Alpha One   70ft   E2   1984
Start as for Bolero.
1   70ft   5b.   Climb to the tree, move right onto obvious blocks then go leftwards to the ledge in the middle of the face. Climb diagonally right to finish left of a large block.

Seguidilla   70ft   Very Severe   1968
The initial wall can be avoided by climbing Bolero to the tree then moving 10 feet up the grass ramp. This makes the climb about Hard Severe. Start 10 feet right of Bolero.
1   70ft   5a.   Climb the steep wall with difficulty and make a desperate exit onto the grass ramp. Climb a clean shallow groove and move up left to a huge jug. Go easily up to the large flakes, then climb the wall direct, passing a small sapling on the left, to a mantelshelf gaining the top. Tree belay back right.

Sickle   60ft   Hard Severe   1965
Not particularly worthwhile but the second pitch is in a good position. Start beneath a crack and beside a large metal spike which projects from the rock.
1   30ft   Climb the crack for a few feet then take the wall to the right of this to a ledge. The smooth groove above is climbed to a larger ledge.
2   30ft   Move out left of the large overhang, then climb the wall with caution.

Hammer   50ft   Very Severe   1965
Start 15 feet right of the start of Sickle, beneath organ pipe flutings.
1   35ft   4b.   Climb steeply to the left on rounded holds to a ledge.
2   15ft   The wall to the right of the tree.

Rock House Corner   70ft   Hard Very Difficult   1965
This is the arête which overlooks Rock House. It gives a pleasant pitch with little protection.

PALACE QUARRY   GR 867 787

This is the large quarry seen from the road to Chudleigh Rocks. Details of climbs may change, as quarrying still takes place from time to time. The climbs described are similar in character to those on Chudleigh North Face. The quarry lies on private ground but no access problem exists at present.

On entering the quarry, Tremor Buttress is the obvious clean buttress nearest the gate. Right of Tremor Buttress is a large amphitheatre with a prominent cave, the Grim Grotto, towards its left edge. Descent from all routes is via a path through the woods which leads down left of Tremor Buttress.

Tremor   70ft   Severe   1967
Takes the rib and slab on the left edge of the buttress nearest the gate.
1   70ft   4a.   Climb the rib until level with a small semi-circular overhang then step left onto a steep slab, peg runner. Move up delicately then swing right on good handholds to a large foothold on the arête. Continue to a ledge. Thread belay on the large ledge above. Scramble to the top.

Olympia   70ft   Very Severe   1976
Start on yellowish rock 20 feet right of Tremor.
1   70ft   4b.   Climb to the water-stained niche in the centre of the face. Move right for a few feet, then go up a groove to join the arête, which is followed to the top.

Quiver   60ft   Severe   4a   1969
Takes the front face of the buttress on its right-hand side, two peg runners; scrambling to the top as for Tremor.

The Wild Bunch   110ft   Very Severe   1976
A loose climb which will improve with use. Start on the grass terrace to the right of the Grim Grotto.
1   70ft   4c.   Climb the shattered buttress, then trend rightwards below a series of short cracks to a vague niche with a thread drillhole belay.
2   40ft   4c.   Move left and make a difficult move over a final bulge to finish out to the left on the arête of Tremor.

To the right of the Grim Grotto is the main face, which is broken and vegetated towards its right-hand side. All the climbs on the face start from a two-foot grass terrace (the line of the previous floor of the quarry) 20 feet above the ground, which is approached from the left.

The Bat   120ft   Hard Very Severe   1976
A good route with a sinister air. Start below a finger-crack in the left-hand end of the boat hull-shaped overhang.
1   60ft   4c.   Climb straight up, past an old protection peg, to the finger-crack in the overhang. Climb the overhang with two pegs for aid until a move right leads to easier ground, and a thread and peg belay.
2   60ft   5a.   Climb the slight groove above the stance; then trend leftwards up to the obvious overhang, which is taken with one aid peg at its widest part to gain a steep slab. Delectable climbing on good holds leads to the tree at the top.

Zen   140ft   Hard Very Severe   1969   ★
A good sustained route which partly takes the obvious diagonal fault high on the face towards the right-hand side. Start from the narrow terrace below the right-hand end of a black overhanging wall about 50 feet up.
1   40ft   4b.   Climb to a spike then traverse right and move awkwardly on to a ledge, peg runner. Continue up and left to another ledge and belay.
2   100ft   5a.   Climb a short orange slab on the left, then step right to a ledge. Go straight up to the diagonal crack and traverse left just below this for about 30 feet to a good ledge and thread runner. Difficult climbing then gains a tree near the top (protection peg just right of a short corner).

Routes have been recorded to the right of Zen but these have been so changed by quarrying operations that the face is essentially virgin. It may give worthwhile climbing eventually.

Astral Traveller   300ft   Hard Very Severe   1976
A left-to-right girdle of Palace Quarry. Start left of Tremor.
1   40ft   4b.   Climb a few feet then traverse out to the arête of Tremor and belay.
2   50ft   4c.   Move down and across to the water-stained niche of Olympia. Move right and up a groove to belay on the arête.
3   70ft   4b.   Cross Quiver to a prominent ledge. Move right to a reverse mantle and continue along ledges to the Grim Grotto.
4   40ft   4c.   The slab on the right is followed to a horizontal traverse and a tricky move down to the niche of Wild Bunch.
5   100ft   4c/5a.   Climb a short groove then follow a sloping ramp, crossing The Bat, to join Zen. Either follow this route to the top or head for broken ground further right.

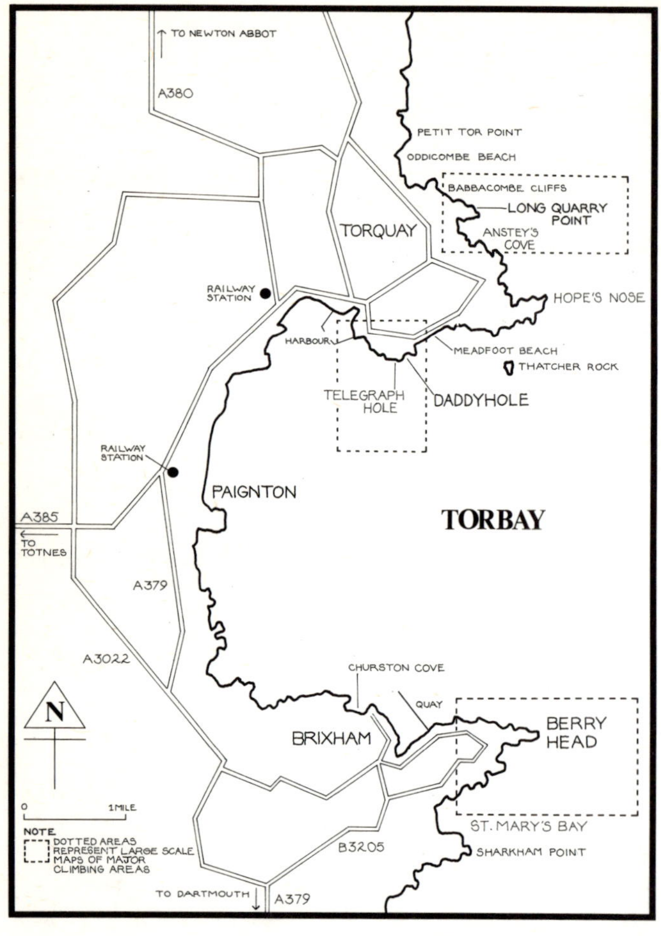

TO NEWTON ABBOT
A380
PETIT TOR POINT
ODDICOMBE BEACH
BABBACOMBE CLIFFS
LONG QUARRY POINT
ANSTEY'S COVE
TORQUAY
RAILWAY STATION
HOPE'S NOSE
HARBOUR
MEADFOOT BEACH
THATCHER ROCK
TELEGRAPH HOLE
DADDYHOLE
RAILWAY STATION
PAIGNTON
TORBAY
A385
TO TOTNES
A379
A3022
CHURSTON COVE
QUAY
BERRY HEAD
N
BRIXHAM
ST. MARY'S BAY
SHARKHAM POINT
0   1 MILE
NOTE
DOTTED AREAS REPRESENT LARGE SCALE MAPS OF MAJOR CLIMBING AREAS
B3205
TO DARTMOUTH   A379

Torbay

Torbay is the major climbing area of South Devon and offers every type of route from the short, safe and sunny to some of the most difficult and dramatic climbing on British sea-cliffs. The rock is a reef limestone and varies greatly from crag to crag, no two cliffs having the same character or appearance. In general the rock demands respect, and only a few cliffs are suitable for the inexperienced.

The two large headlands which enclose Torbay are Hope's Nose to the north and Berry Head to the south. The crags are grouped around these and divide conveniently into three separate areas; the Berry Head/Brixham, Daddyhole, and Long Quarry Areas. They are covered in this order and the routes are described from left to right (south to north) around the coast.

Torbay is well known for its Mediterranean climate and many cliffs give warm, sheltered climbing even in the depths of winter. In wet weather there is no need to be inactive, as some crags are little affected by rain (unless wind-driven). These include the Great Cave area of the Old Redoubt, the Sanctuary Wall, parts of Anstey's Cove, and of course the aid routes and most of the sea-level traverses (if the sea is not too rough).

The sea traversing in Torbay is perhaps the best yet discovered in Britain. There are long, inescapable sections on continuous cliffs and the rock at sea level is often sculpted into superb holds, giving strenuous, high quality climbing. The traverses can give excellent soloing in summer (using the sea as a safety net, buoyancy aid optional) as they enable a huge amount of climbing to be done in a day. In winter they are best tackled with an old rope and a few slings, and should be avoided in high seas.

In situ pegs on sea-cliffs should never be trusted completely, but some are very useful and should be left in place. A few of the peg runners and belays mentioned in the text may not be necessary nowadays, and a nut-pick is very useful for cleaning out cracks to take small wires.

Many of the cliffs have prominent 'No Climbing' signs above them. These are intended to deter tourists and to indemnify the authorities should an accident occur. The only cliff with an official restriction is The Old Redoubt, which is an important Auk colony. In summer, climbing should not take place where holiday makers could be put at risk from falling rock (e.g. parts of Anstey's Cove).

Being a prime holiday area, there is a great variety of accommodation available in Torbay, which is especially cheap and plentiful off-season. For details contact Tourist Information in Torquay. Campsites are widespread and are marked on OS Sheet 202, but some of these are for couples and families only and again the Tourist Office can inform.

In view of the number of recent accidents, it is perhaps worth re-emphasising the seriousness of the Torbay cliffs. The rock here cannot be treated like gritstone or Dartmoor granite, and protection is often far from bombproof. There is a strong case for wearing crash helmets, particularly when seconding, and on several cliffs it is important to consider the difficulties of escape if retreat has been cut off by the rising tide or high seas. In this situation a relatively small problem can result in an 'epic' or a rescue. The Torbay authorities have, in fact, threatened to ban climbing if accidents continue.

Recently, large-scale rock falls in the Long Quarry and Daddyhole areas (where a whole crag containing seven routes disappeared in 1984) gave an insight into the nature of the rock and are potent reminders of the transcience of all things, particularly sea-cliff climbs.

The Berry Head Area

Berry Head is the great limestone headland enclosing Torbay to the south. On its north side is the popular resort town and fishing port of Brixham, from which the Head is well signposted and reached in a few minutes by car. Except for the outlying areas of Sharkham Point and Churston, all the cliffs are approached from the car-park on top of the headland, none being more than ten minutes walk away. A stone's throw from the car-park is the Old Redoubt, perhaps the most important single cliff in Devon. It is however also of great importance as an Auk Colony, and a seasonal restriction on climbing exists from mid-March until July 15th. The climbs affected are marked with an (R). No other cliffs in Torbay have such a restriction so there is plenty of climbing available in this period.

SHARKHAM POINT   GR 936 546 OS Sheet 202
This is the large headland one and a half miles south-west of Berry Head, beyond St Mary's Bay. Its sea cliffs are outside the limestone region but offer worthwhile climbing. On the south side of the tip of the point is an area of curious slabby green rock which is the steep landward side of a narrow zawn. This is known as the Green Cliff. Descend via a track that leads down the right-hand side (looking out) and on to the promontory that forms the seaward side of the zawn. Traverse easily down the landward side of this to the boulder-strewn bed of the zawn. The cliff is dominated by two diagonal seams of iron ore running from left to right.

Rusty Road   100ft   Severe   1979
A pleasant route following the left-hand seam and weaving through the overlaps above. Start at low tide, just left of the seam.

1   100ft   4a.   A delicate start allows the seam on the right to be gained with the feet and followed for 40 feet until beneath an obvious groove. Pull directly over the overlap into the groove and take a zigzag line through the overlaps above until slabs on the right lead to the top.

Traversty   150ft   Severe   1979
A girdle of the Green Cliff from left to right following the obvious fault line at half-height and therefore independent of the tides. Start at a commodious ledge on the descent route, directly above the cave at the back of the zawn.
1   100ft   4a.   Traverse horizontally to a groove, and descend this with care to the obvious break beneath the overhang. Traverse delicately along this line until a large niche is reached, step up and continue traversing until it is possible to step down to a second smaller niche and belay.
2   50ft   4a.   Step right and pull steeply through the break above. Continue diagonally right to the top.

There are several pinnacles around the tip of the point, the biggest of which can be reached and climbed at low tide. On top of the headland is an extensive refuse dump. About 200 yards inland from this is a small limestone crag split by a prominent crack.

Happy Camper's Crack   40ft   Very Severe   1968
Very steep and well protected.
1   40ft   4c.   Climb through vegetation to a little cave. Step right then up left into the crack, which is followed to the top.

THE CRADLE ROCK CRAGS
There is a boulder-filled zawn immediately west of Cradle Rock. Approach from Cradle Rock at low to half-tide or by abseil from an iron stake on the promontory opposite the west-facing wall.

Infidel   70ft   E1   1984   ★
A fine little route taking the west-facing wall of the zawn. Start beneath the middle of the wall.
1   70ft   5b.   Climb straight up the wall keeping just right of a shallow ragged crack, hidden peg on the right, and pull into a niche. Step down left and traverse along the obvious crack line to the arête. Move up right and scramble to the top on steep grass.
Stake belay.

DURL HEAD   GR 940 557
About 10 minutes walk southwards from Berry Head car-park, this minor headland is distinguished by a flat, rocky causeway running out to the 40-foot high monolith of Cradle Rock. On the north side of the head is a steep cliff consisting of two faces at right angles. The

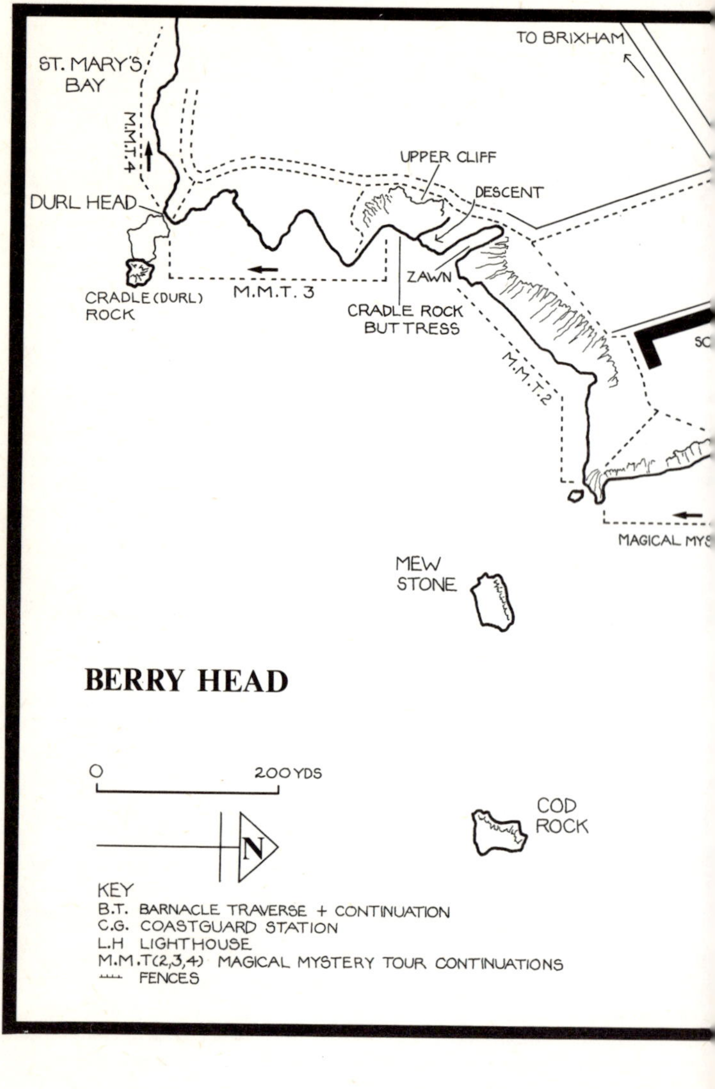

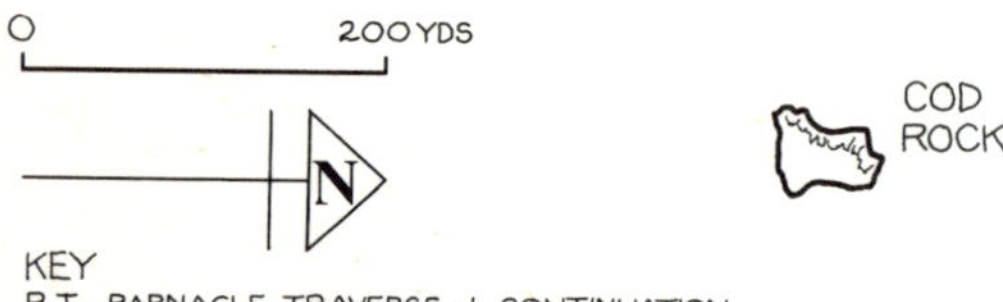
TO BRIXHAM
ST. MARY'S BAY
M.M.T.4
DURL HEAD
CRADLE (DURL) ROCK
M.M.T. 3
UPPER CLIFF
DESCENT
ZAWN
CRADLE ROCK BUTTRESS
M.M.T.2
SO
MAGICAL MYS
MEW STONE
BERRY HEAD
0
200 YDS
N
COD ROCK
KEY
B.T. BARNACLE TRAVERSE + CONTINUATION
C.G. COASTGUARD STATION
L.H LIGHTHOUSE
M.M.T.(2,3,4) MAGICAL MYSTERY TOUR CONTINUATIONS
FENCES

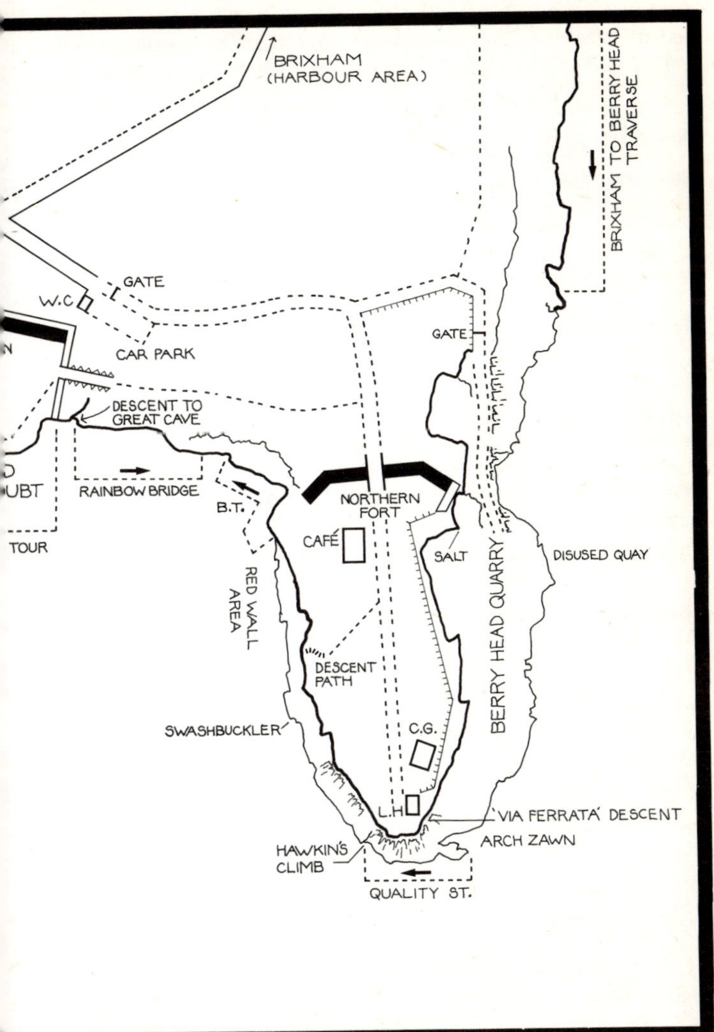

BRIXHAM
(HARBOUR AREA)
BRIXHAM TO BERRY HEAD TRAVERSE
GATE
W.C
GATE
CAR PARK
DESCENT TO GREAT CAVE
RAINBOW BRIDGE
B.T.
NORTHERN FORT
CAFÉ
SALT
DISUSED QUAY
TOUR
RED WALL AREA
BERRY HEAD QUARRY
DESCENT PATH
SWASHBUCKLER
C.G.
L.H.
'VIA FERRATA' DESCENT
ARCH ZAWN
HAWKIN'S CLIMB
QUALITY ST.

left-hand face has a sharply undercut base and the right-hand face is remarkable for its large overhangs. Approach by abseiling to the platform beneath the undercut face, or at high tide climbs on the right-hand face can be approached by scrambling down a grassy hollow on the north side of the cliff to sea level, then traversing into ledges beside the zawn/cave where the faces meet.

Man Bites Dog   80ft   E2   1973   ★
The impressive overhanging crack running up the left wall of the cave at the base of the undercut face.
1 80ft 5b.   Climb the crack very strenuously for 35 feet until the angle relents and the wider crack is followed to the top.

Berry Red Wall   140ft   Very Severe   1970
A leftward traverse across the undercut face. Start on a small ledge on the right wall of the cave/zawn at the junction of the two faces.
1 60ft Climb the greasy cleft and either squeeze through the constriction or pull around the outside to ledges above the first overhang. Move right to a thread belay.
2 80ft 4a/b.   Move back left and step across the cave mouth onto the red wall. Continue leftwards until level with the belay ledge and round a small corner, then go up for 10 feet to a good runner. Traverse horizontally left, then move up and mantelshelf onto a large ledge. Climb the corner above easily to the cliff top.

Fowler's Dolly Mixture   110ft   Hard Severe   1970
A climb with character and good situations. Start as for Berry Red Wall.
1 60ft As for Berry Red Wall.
2 50ft Climb straight up from the belay then step right onto an undercut nose. Move left onto a good ledge beneath a corner and climb the right wall, working out to the arête, followed by easy but exposed climbing to the top.

Lady of Shame   105ft   E1   1978   ★
The first pitch gives spectacular and well protected climbing over a huge roof. Start just right of Berry Red Wall on ledges beneath the obvious roof crack.
1 30ft 5b.   Climb the roof crack very strenuously to a large thread belay on the slab above.
2 75ft 5a.   Move left, step across the cave and traverse left for 10 feet to a vertical crack. Follow this until a step left leads to friable ledges. Move out left to finish.

CRADLE ROCK BUTTRESS   GR 940 558
An interesting crag to the south of the Old Redoubt, reached in a few minutes from the Berry Head car-park. Take the main coastal path along the front wall of the fort and past the top of a repulsive zawn.

until about 100 yards past a stone stile a path leads down leftwards to a platform 30 feet above sea level. The Main Cliff is now to the left (facing seawards) and is approached by a short abseil to boulders exposed at most states of the tide. Above the platform is the smaller Upper Cliff, dominated by the sharp arête of Cut-throat. An alternative approach (giving access to The Pinch and Ganges at high tide and in any sea conditions) is to climb over the wall about 10 yards before the stone stile, then to descend the grass slope to a belt of easy-angled slabs leading down right to the foot of the buttress.

UPPER CLIFF

Solstice   80ft   Very Severe   1980
Climbs the obvious groove to the left of Cut-throat on the Upper Cliff. Belay beneath the overlap.
1   80ft   4c.   Surmount the overlap then climb the crack above, bearing left away from the red chimney. Climb the overhang on good holds and the short wall to finish.

Cut-throat   60ft   Hard Very Severe   1970   ★
The knife-edge arête in the centre of the crag overlooking the platform. A steep and interesting pitch, but the rock requires care.
1   60ft   5a.   Climb a groove in the arête for 20 feet to a small ledge. Move up to a finger pocket, then hinge right round the arête and climb steeply to a large spike. Stand on this then use the arête to reach the top.

Tough Luck   50ft   E1   1983
Start to the right of and higher than Cut-throat, beneath the obvious wide crack.
1   50ft   5a.   Climb a subsidiary crack to a small thread, then move left into the main crack and follow this to exit through the steep corner.

Good Fortune   40ft   Hard Very Severe   1983   ★
Steep and enjoyable climbing up the cracks to the right of Tough Luck.
1   40ft   5a.   Follow the cracks with increasing interest to a projecting block with a good hold on top. A few more steep moves gain the top.

MAIN CLIFF
On the left side of the main crag are two obvious corners, the left-hand being taken by Sidewinder (via the left wall) and the right by Zeta. A deep cave in the centre of the cliff can be crossed at any state of the tide (but not in high seas) by large boulders at the mouth. The

short wall to the left of Sidewinder gives a couple of short, steep pitches at Hard Very Severe.

Sidewinder   200ft   Hard Very Severe   1982
A steep pitch on interesting rock formations. It takes a diagonal line across the left wall of the big blind corner near the left side of the cliff. Start beneath the left wall at a finger-width crack.
1   60ft   5a/b.   Follow the crack until it is possible to step up a shallow niche to rest. Climb diagonally out of this to regain the crack, which leads steeply to the arête. Follow this to a sloping ledge and peg belays.
2   140ft   As for Zeta to the top.

Zeta   230ft   Hard Very Severe   1968
Takes the conspicuous slanting corner above and to the left of the deep cave. Scramble up shaly slabs to nut belays at the bottom of this.
1   90ft   5a/b.   Climb the corner, moving left at 10 feet, to a ledge at 40 feet. Climb the overhanging corner above with difficulty, then move up left to a small stance on the nose.
2   140ft   Descend and traverse a slab beneath an overhang to a long easy slab, which is climbed to finish.

Finn   100ft   Hard Very Severe   1969
A good steep pitch. Start as for Zeta.
1   100ft   5a.   Follow the ramp up to the right for 10 feet, then step up onto the wall. Climb diagonally left for 30 feet, then take the obvious slanting crack and continue diagonally right until about 15 feet from the top. Traverse 10 feet left then a few moves gain the top. Belays well back in an outcrop.

The Pinch   130ft   E4   1969/*1983*   ★★★
An outstanding climb whose second pitch takes the leaning headwall of the main cliff. Start beneath the first corner to the right of the cave.
1   60ft   4b.   Climb the corner to the roof. Traverse left and up to a stance on a block.
2   70ft   6a.   Climb straight up for 35 feet to an obvious round hole in the face. Continue up to an enormous jug, then move slightly left and climb the gently overhanging wall to the top.

Ganges   100ft   Hard Severe   1968
The larger but less attractive corner to the right of The Pinch.
1   100ft   4a.   Climb the corner, exiting right at the top.

THE OLD REDOUBT   GR 943 564
This towering crag plunges straight into the sea from below the first fortress on the right as one leaves the car-park. It is the pre-eminent cliff of Torbay and several of its climbs are as fine and challenging as

any on British sea-cliffs. There is however a seasonal restriction to protect nesting seabirds, and no climbing should take place on the cliff from March 15th to July 15th. Climbers ignoring this restriction could face a £1000 fine. It applies also to the descent to the cave platform.

The crag is approached by descending the grass slope to the left (facing the sea) of the fort and the first broken crags, bearing right lower down to a ramp which ends at a wall dropping sheer into the sea. This is traversed on good holds to a large sloping platform at the mouth of a huge sea cave, the Great Cave, which bites deep into the base of the cliff. Looking from here the most obvious line is the vertical crack system of Moonraker, formed at the junction of the hanging face above the Great Cave with the main mass of crag to its left.

Running along the base of the cliff is the traverse of Magical Mystery Tour, the first 300 feet of which gives access to most of the climbs. This is only possible for about 2 hours either side of low water, and for a much shorter period during neap tides. Normally a low line is taken and the climbing is about Severe standard, but by taking the highest possible line, at a strenuous Very Severe, the period of access or escape is extendable by an hour or so. If the tide is too high or the sea too rough for the traverse, the first stance of Moonraker (which is also a launching-off point for many other climbs) can be reached by a 130-foot abseil.

Needless to say, because of the difficulty of retreat all routes on the Old Redoubt are serious undertakings.

Magical Mystery Tour   1100ft   Hard Very Severe   (R)   1967
The classic sea-level traverse of the Old Redoubt, linking the cave platform with the rocky promontory 300 yards to the south. In anything but calm seas a serious and commiting expedition with some strenuous climbing, no upward escape routes after the first real difficulties, and a zawn swim to finish. Start an hour or so before low tide.
Traverse out of the Great Cave, past the peg cluster at the start of Moonraker, and continue easily at high tide level until beside an overhanging nose. Pass beneath this strenuously at dead low water (4c) or take a traverse line 20 feet above sea level (5a, strenuous) and descend to belay. Beyond is an overhanging buttress. Climb the gully beside it, then traverse on a line about 30 feet above the sea (5a, strenuous) descending gradually to a stance. Continue past a cave, the Green Grotto, to the entrance of a much larger cave, the Blue Grotto, which goes right through the headland. This is crossed by a swim and tyrolean, then easy climbing up to the left gains the top of the promontory.

Magical Mystery Tour II   (Blue Grotto to Cradle Rock Buttress)
1000ft   Hard Very Severe, or E2 with the Blue Grotto pitch   1968
Either start at the southern entrance of the Blue Grotto or if linking up with the first section of MMT start at the northern entrance of the cave at the belays for the Tyrolean. This gives a difficult and fascinating pitch through the cave, as follows:
Traverse to a bulging section, move up then follow a slightly descending line of holds leftwards to easier rock. Continue to a cave and make a rising traverse into this until it is possible to bridge across to a line of holds leading steeply leftwards to ledges. Continue and break through an awkward undercut chimney to slabby rock at the southern entrance of the Blue Grotto (5b, sustained and strenuous). Traverse the slabby cliffs near sea level to the entrance of a large zawn. Make a descending traverse into this (4b), then go out on the opposite wall to a ledge about 20 foot above the water. Move left and down, then steep traversing gains a stance (5a). Climb to the top of a buttress adjacent to the Cradle Rock Buttress descent rake.

Magical Mystery Tour III   (Cradle Rock Buttress to Durl Head)
900ft   Hard Severe   1968
Pitches of 4b, with low tide essential for an initial boulder hop to the point just south of Cradle Rock Buttress (or this has been overcome with a little wading and some desperate climbing).

Magical Mystery Tour IV   (Durl Head to St. Mary's Bay) 2000ft plus boulder-hopping   E2   1969
A good demanding section. Traverse fairly easily to the first obstacle — the impressive cleft of Dove Cavern. Traverse into this on small holds (5b) and out again with similar difficulty. Continue to another difficult pitch above a cave (5b) to a boulder-filled bay. To leave the bay traverse a series of slabby grooves at a relatively high level (5b/c) to reach ledges around the corner. The next obstacle is a steep shale wall, which gives a long and sustained pitch (5b/c), then easier climbing leads to another strenuous pitch (5a) before the beach is gained.

Note The whole of Magical Mystery Tour, from the cave platform beneath the Old Redoubt to St. Mary's Bay, has been climbed 'dry solo' in 2 hrs 20 mins, timing the low tide for Cradle Rock Buttress.

Bismark   120ft   E2   (R)   1980
Climbs the steep white wall towards the end of Magical Mystery Tour — well viewed from the promontory where MMT finishes. The route starts from a stance 10 feet above the sea at the extreme right-hand side of the wall. Reach this by abseil or, more adventurously, by traversing in along MMT.

1   120ft   5b.   Climb up leftwards to reach steeper rock after 25 feet. Trend right up the steep wall to gain a rightwards-leading traverse line beneath overhangs. Follow this for 25 feet until it is possible to gain a small ledge and a short loose wall leading to the top.

Moving Target   130ft   Very Severe   (R)   1973   ★
A good steep route on a remote part of the Old Redoubt. Approach by following MMT for about 500 feet to belay just before the overhanging nose.
1   60ft   4c.   Climb the very steep wall direct, or circumvent it by a long traverse from the right (also steep) to reach a small stance and thread belays.
2   70ft   4c.   Move slightly left and follow a discontinuous groove on surprisingly good rock to the top.

The Long Goodbye   220ft   E1   (R)   1981
An exposed route traversing rightwards from Moving Target. Start as for Moving Target.
1   60ft   4c.   As for Moving Target.
2   80ft   5a.   Follow the groove of Moving Target until it becomes discontinuous after a roof, then traverse right along the obvious line to a small ledge. Peg belay.
3   80ft   5a.   Continue in the same line to a large detached flake then climb up to a peg. Climb the awkward corner above to a ledge then up the vegetated wall above to the grass slopes. Belay on a bluff of rock well back.

Lost Arrow   130ft   Hard Severe   (R)   1968
A reasonable escape route before the main difficulties of Magical Mystery Tour. Start in the small zawn beside the overhanging nose, as for Moving Target.
1   40ft   Climb the wall to the obvious horizontal break leading right onto the first shale band. Peg belays.
2   45ft   Follow the bands up to the left to a corner. Move around left, and climb the brown wall for a few feet to a small stance and peg belays.
3   45ft   Climb the wall above, trending right into a recess, then out left onto the grass. Easily to the top.

Anti-Matter   230ft   Very Severe   (R)   1980
Good climbing and situations. Start as for King Crab, at a curving groove 30 feet left of False Alarms.
1   40ft   4c.   Climb the groove and exit left onto the steep wall, which is climbed to a bird-whitened ledge.
2   90ft   4c.   Traverse left until a short groove breaks through the overlap. Climb this, stepping left to a good stance. Peg belay.
3   100ft   4a.   Move back right and up the obvious groove to the top.

Uncul-Patter   120ft   E1   (R)   1980
A direct variation to Anti-Matter, starting as for that route.
1   40ft   4c.   As for Anti-Matter.
2   80ft   5a.   Pull over the roof above the belay and continue up a crack. Move left then climb straight up the wall above to the top — scant protection and a loose finish.

King Crab   105ft   Hard Very Severe   (R)   1970
Takes a line through the overhangs right of Lost Arrow. Approximately 150 feet left of the initial corner of Goddess of Gloom is an enormous roof 80 feet above sea level. Below its left side, belay 20 feet above the sea in a bay beneath a smaller and much lower overhang, just beyond an arête.
1   80ft   5a.   Climb to the right-hand end of the first overhang and up past it for 15 feet on a stratified wall. Move right and pull strenuously onto a bird-whitened ledge, then move up left and climb the layback crack splitting the final roof. Exposed stance and peg belays on the left.
2   25ft   4a.   Climb the short wall above to the grass slope.

False Alarms   180ft   E3   (R)   1980   ★
A strenuous and spectacular line through the roofs right of King Crab. Some 130 feet left of Goddess of Gloom is a shallow-angled ledge below an enormous roof, 20 feet or so right of King Crab. Belay here at low tide and move down.
1   130ft   5c.   Move right to an overhung crack and climb to ledges. Trend left to a vague groove and follow this to the bottom left-hand corner of the first roof. Layback up to undercut holds leading right to a short groove, which is climbed to gain a line of improving holds leading horizontally right across the lip of the roof to the arête. Continue right for a few feet to a poor stance below a short crack. Nut and peg belays (not in place).
2   50ft   5a.   Climb the crack to a ledge on the right and make an awkward move to gain a shallow groove. Follow this, exiting left to a steep grass finish.

Melinda   180ft   Hard Very Severe   (R)   1970
Takes the third major crack-line to the left of Moonraker, character-ised by its single cave. Start beneath the rounded overhanging rib 40 feet left of the corner of Goddess of Gloom.
1   50ft   4c.   Climb the wall for 15 feet, pull up left then swing right and up into balance on the wall above. Climb straight up for 20 feet to nut belays in a short crack.
2   70ft   5a.   Climb to a peg runner (on Pikadon), then traverse 15 feet left to a thin curving crack at the left end of the bulge. Move diagonally right to another crack, which is followed to a ledge. Good stance and peg belays on the right.

3 60ft 4c.   Move back left and climb the deep groove to the cave. Step up right and follow a groove to some grassy ledges. Belay before scrambing up steep grass to the top.

Pikadon   200ft   Hard Very Severe   (R)   1967   ★
An interesting climb taking the second crack-line, with two caves, to the left of Moonraker. Start as for Goddess of Gloom.
1 60ft 4c.   Climb bearing left up the steep wall left of the corner to an overhang. Break right towards the corner on an ascending ledge, then traverse delcately left and move up to a stance and peg belays under another large roof.
2 70ft 4c.   Traverse 10 feet left and move over bulges to a small ledge, peg runner. Climb the short steep wall on the right, then step right to gain a shallow groove and follow this to a good stance and peg belays.
3 70ft 5a/b.   Step right and climb past the first cave to a good thread in the overhang above the second cave. Climb the smooth corner above with difficulty to a stance on the left. Scramble to the top.

Goddess of Gloom   230ft   Hard Very Severe   (R)   1968   ★★
This takes the thinner crack line to the left of Moonraker and has excellent climbing on the first and last pitches. Start beneath the prominent slanting corner 25 feet beyond the peg cluster of Moonraker.
1 70ft 5a.   Climb easily to an overhang, then move steeply right and up into the corner. Climb this to its capping roof, then break right and move up to a small stance on the first shaly band.
2 60ft 4b.   Climb the crack above until it becomes too vegetated, then climb bearing right up the slab to the second stance of Moonraker. (A harder variant, 5a, is to climb straight up the wall left of the vegetated crack.)
3 100ft 5a.   From the left side of the stance, move up steeply into the groove and follow it to a cave. Break right to a small ledge, then make some difficult moves up to a thin crack on the left and climb steeply to better holds in the final grassy groove.

Torbay

The Quaker   240ft   E3   (R)   1972   ★
A wandering line which provides steep and exciting climbing in sensational positions. Start as for Moonraker.
1 80ft 5b.   Starting 5 feet left of the belay, climb straight up the gently overhanging wall for 20 feet, then bear left to a line of weakness leading to easier rock. Continue to a stance and peg belay on the shale band.

2 60ft 4c.   A vague crack splits the wall above. Follow it to a deep hole, then bear right to join Moonraker above the crack of pitch 2. Swing right and belay in the chimney of The Hood.
3 100ft 6a.   Move out right and climb a white scoop to a faint break in the long roof. Pull over this then move up left to a line of flat holds leading rightwards to a ledge. Climb the short groove to a steep blank wall, high peg runner. Make some very hard moves to a line of holds leading rightwards to a narrow ledge. Step up right, then go straight up on excellent holds.

Moonraker   250ft   Hard Very Severe   (R)   1967   ★★★
The classic route of the Old Redoubt giving steep and exposed climbing on a magnificent inescapable line. It follows the central crack system in the highest part of the cliff. Approach along the first 250 feet or so of Magical Mystery Tour to a restricted stance with a cluster of peg belays just above high water mark, a short way to the left of the lower part of the crack system.
1 90ft 4c/5a.   Make a rising traverse to the right to reach the discontinuous crack and climb this steeply to a large chockstone in a corner. Climb diagonally left for 25 feet to ledges at the foot of another crack.
2 60ft 4c.   Climb the steep corner crack above to a small cave at 40 feet. Traverse left and move up to belays beneath the leaning groove.
3 100ft 4c.   Climb the groove with increasing exposure, using holds on the right wall to pass the bulges. Above this, move left on ledges to a clean corner crack, which leads directly to the top.

The Hood   230ft   E3   (R)   1969   ★
The impressive wide crack to the right of Moonraker — a tough, strenuous climb. Start at a restricted stance some 20 feet
right of the start of Moonraker, in a short corner beneath a large roof.
1 90ft 5b/c.   Traverse right between two bands of overhangs to a niche (often damp) and break up right onto the wall above. Climb bearing right on excellent holds to some big footholds, then move left to join Moonraker and follow this to the stance.
2 40ft 5b/c.   Move up then climb diagonally right across the steep wall (poor peg runner) to gain the wide crack. Climb strenuously to a stance where it widens to a chimney.
3 100ft 5b.   Climb the chimney, overcoming the bramble bush, then traverse left to an overhang. Pull over this and climb the steep groove above to a junction with Moonraker. Climb the shallower groove right of the Moonraker corner to the top.

Dreadnought   310ft   E3   (R)   1969   ★★★
A magnificent climb, one of the finest in the South West, which traverses above the lip of the Great Cave to a prominent hanging

groove in the wall above. Superb, serious climbing in sensational positions. Start as for Moonraker.
1   90ft   4c/5a.   As for Moonraker.
2   80ft   5c.   Reverse to the chockstone, then step up and right to an old peg. Make a slightly rising rightwards traverse on a band of very steep rock to a corner, which leads to the big overhang. Continue rightwards with increasing difficulty to a good handhold, then a further 10 feet of traversing gains a tiny ledge. Stance in slings.
3   65ft   5b.   Step up from the belay then move left to the hanging groove and climb to its capping roof. Move out left, step up to a deep slot and then climb up left again to a large scooped ledge. Climb the short wall on the right to a deep cave with a huge thread belay through its left side.
4   75ft   5a/b.   Step left out of the cave then climb steeply to a shallow groove on the right leading to a ledge and large thread. The steep wall above is climbed to an overhang, which is taken centrally on well-spaced holds. Good holds lead to the top.

Barbican   320ft   E3   (R)   1967   ★★
Though overshadowed by Dreadnought this remains a powerful climb and well worth doing in addition to Dreadnought. Start as for Moonraker.
1   90ft   4c/5a.   As for Moonraker.
2   80ft   5c.   As for Dreadnought.
3   60ft   5a/b.   Step right and climb steeply to a small cave. Continue up the groove on the left to a much larger cave (from which escape rightwards is possible).
4   90ft   5b.   Above the cave is a rounded grey chimney. Gain this and climb it to a footledge leading left into a shallow corner. Climb to the roof and move right into a wide crack, which gives strenuous climbing to slabbier rock above. Move left and follow a wide crack across the slab to shallow cracks leading to the top.

Caveman   395ft   E5   (R)   1982   ★★★
An awe-inspiring line through the massive overhangs above the Great Cave. Exceptionally arduous, sustained and brilliant climbing. Start as for The Hood.
1   80ft   5b/c.   Break rightwards through the initial overhangs as for The Hood, traverse right into a corner then rightwards again to an old bolt and foothold belay on Curse.
2   30ft   6a.   Move diagonally left up to the roof (peg runner) and trend out rightwards on flakes to gain a niche at the inner end of the prominent red flakes hanging down from the flat roof of the cave. Peg belay.

3   45ft   6a.   Move across the first hanging flake to gain an obvious hand-traverse crack leading out to a peg (used to rest) above a projecting red foothold. Move right for 15 feet along the lip of the overhang to a stance.
4   90ft   6a.   Traverse back left to the rest peg. Continue traversing past an awkward bush to join Dreadnought and follow this to the hanging stance.
5   80ft   5b.   Climb the hanging groove on the left as for Dreadnought, but move right at the capping overhang to gain a small ledge at the foot of a shallow groove. Climb this and move left at the top along a horizontal crack to gain a shallow groove leading to the right-hand end of an oblong roof. Climb the short corner to a small stance.
6   70ft   5b.   Move left and surmount the overhang to gain an awkward crack. Climb this and continue straight to the top via the finish of Barbican.

Curse   90ft   A4   (R)   1971
A demanding aid climb across the roof of the Great Cave. Its upper reaches have been superseded by Caveman but the first and hardest pitch remains a testing excercise in aid climbing suitable for cold winter weather. About half-way into the cave climb to a greasy platform just below the roof. Belay 15 feet from a big blowhole.
1   90ft   Climb the mudrock wall to reach a prominent crack going diagonally across the flat ceiling to the centre of the mouth of the cave. Follow this for 40 feet then just before it forks change to a parallel crack on the left, which leads out of the cave to a small stance and bolt belay (on Caveman). From here it is possibe to climb leftwards (5a) to join Moonraker, or to retreat by other means.

Depth Charge   260ft   E4   (R)   1979   ★★★
An audacious climb taking the black, overhanging groove suspended above the right-hand side of the Great Cave. All pegs are in place and the route is unaffected by tides. Start on the cave platform well to the right of the groove, as for Iron Butterfly.
1   45ft   5b.   Climb the initial bulges then go diagonally left to a restricted stance in a corner.
2   35ft   6a.   Climb around the overhang (peg runner) to gain the black groove and ascend this for 10 feet before moving down left to a stance (common with Caveman).
3   45ft   6a.   Move back right and climb the black groove (peg runner),
exiting left at the top to a stance on a flake. Peg belays.
4   45ft   5a.   Move left to join the third pitch of Barbican and follow this to the big cave.
5   90ft   5b.   As for Barbican, or escape easily rightwards.

Lip Trip   (320ft, E4, 1980 ★★★) is another tremendous route, which takes the first two pitches of Depth Charge then continues as for Caveman, thus giving access to the superb upper reaches of Caveman at a slightly easier standard and with no access problems.

Iron Butterfly   130ft   A3 and Very Severe   (R)   1971   ★★
A fine route taking the conspicuous roof crack above the cave platform.
1   100ft   Climb easily for 10 feet then move up left to a projecting foothold. Use 2 bolts, then peg up to and across the roof. Move right below a block then up a groove with difficulty to gain a series of 3 bolts. Exit right under the triangular roof and move up to a small stance in a reddish scoop.
3   30ft   4c.   Climb to the overhang then move left to a peg. Use this then climb direct to belays. Walk off to the right.

The Yardarm   140ft   E3   (R)   1977   ★★
A strenuous and sensationally exposed pitch on good rock. It basically takes the right arête of the sharply overhanging wall of Iron Butterfly. Care must be taken to avoid rope drag as the main difficulties are at the end of the pitch. Belay above the first move of the easy traverse to the cave platform.
1   140ft   5b.   Pull up into a niche, then make a slightly rising traverse to the left for 30 feet to gain some small ledges beneath a slight rib. Climb direct for 15 feet to a thread, then move left and down into an exposed bay. Climb diagonally left out of this to gain a bottomless groove, which is ascended for a few feet before breaking left again to a small roof. Pull around the right-hand side of this and continue direct to a crack leading to a good belay. Walk off right.

Sloop   100ft   Hard Very Severe   (R)   1970
Now a lesser variation to Yardarm but it enables the situations to be enjoyed at an easier standard. Start as for The Yardarm.
1   100ft   5a.   Follow Yardarm for about 50 feet to the thread, then climb bearing right to a projecting ledge. Continue easily to a grass terrace below Ultimate Trundle.

The Ultimate Trundle   70ft   Very Difficult   (R)   1967
Climbs the shattered pillar seen on the way down to the cave platform. Start in the centre.
1   70ft   Climb bearing right to reach the prominent crack running up the right flank of the pillar to the top.

The Seventh Circle   355ft   E2   (R)   1969
A girdle traverse of the Old Redoubt at the level of the upper shaly band. Descend the grassy slope south of the highest part of the crag

and traverse along grass ledges to meet the edge of the face about 60 feet below the clifftop.
1   60ft   5a.   Traverse out onto the wall to a peg runner and descend a crack to a stance on the right.
2   50ft   Continue easily along the obvious line to the second stance of Moonraker.
3   70ft   5b.   Reverse the traverse of Moonraker and swing into the chimney of The Hood. Break right and descend to an exposed ledge, which is followed rightwards until it peters out, peg runner above. Make steep moves to a large scoop, then climb the wall on the right as for Dreadnought to the cave stance.
4   75ft   5a.   Move right, peg runner, and climb to some flat loose ledges. Go right to join the top pitch of Barbican, which is reversed, along the footledge and down the awkward chimney, to the big cave.
5   100ft   Easily up the belt of slabs on the right.

The High Traverse   140ft   Hard Very Severe   (R)   1969
A slight route but with enjoyable and exposed climbing. Approach as for Seventh Circle but belay about 30 feet higher and further right.
1   60ft   4b.   Move down to the right and follow a horizontal crack to the cave on Goddess of Gloom. Step up right and continue the traverse with more difficulty to belay beneath the final corner of Moonraker.
2   40ft   4b.   Continue horizontally right for 30, feet then move up to a stance and thread belay (on Dreadnought).
3   40ft   5a.   Climb the steep wall above, then go diagonally right to the finish of Barbican.

Rainbow Bridge   810ft   E3   (R)   1973   ★★★
An exceptionally fine and sustained traverse on the extensive low cliff to the north of the Old Redoubt. The climbing is mostly on perfect rock well above high water level, making the route a girdle traverse above the sea rather than a sea-level traverse. Only a strong party will manage the traverse in one push; several escape routes exist for the weary. Start from the cave platform.
1   70ft   Climb easily rightwards along the obvious overhung ledge and belay near its end.
2   70ft   5b.   Descend a crack then follow a line of pockets and scoops 10 foot above high tide mark, passing a small thread, to a stance at the foot of a chimney.
3   45ft   5a.   Traverse across slabs to a protection peg under an overhang. Swing around a rib and continue horizontally, strenuous, before moving down slightly to good holds enabling the sloping ledge to be reached.
4   35ft   5a   Continue traversing at the level of the belay: strenuous.

5 40ft 5a.   Move right, peg runner, then climb down and traverse to better holds leading to a remarkable crystal cave, the Hall of Mirrors.
6 90ft 5b.   Climb rightwards onto the wall and up to a thread runner. Move down to the right to some small ledges (peg runner), then climb the steep wall trending right to a shallow groove. Climb the groove (peg handhold) to reach a peg in a horizontal crack. Using this and 2 more pegs for aid (not in place at time of writing) move across to the top of a bottomless groove. Continue traversing to a stance at the base of a gully. (Note: this pitch has been climbed with 1 aid point used to tension traverse to the base of the bottomless groove, which is then climbed — 5c and bold.)
7 50ft 5b.   Traverse horizontally right on a line of pockets in the steep wall to the obvious stance where the chimney is blocked: strenuous.
8 50ft 5a.   Gain the ledges beneath by descending the chimney. Move right and down then swing along a shelf to a good stance in a corner.
9 80ft 5b.   Step down and traverse horizontally about 10 foot above the tidemark until after some strenuous moves on sloping holds an old threaded sling is reached. Either continue traversing with difficulty at the same level or climb down to better holds below high tide level, to reach a small zawn.
10 70ft 5b.   Cross the zawn and climb direct to the roof. Traverse right to a projecting nose, then move down and right with difficulty and continue steeply to a stance and small flake belay.
11 60ft 4a.   Straightforward climbing, past an obvious easy exit, leads to a belay on the edge of the Terminal Zawn.
12 100ft 5b.   Traverse right on the obvious line, very steep, to a small cave. Climb rightwards to an overhang, then pull up and traverse right to slightly less steep rock. Continue rightwards to a groove, which leads to a good stance. An excellent pitch.
13 50ft 4c.   Climb straight up to a ledge, then move left and pull over an overhang to a short wall which leads to the top.

Variation Finish
Shorter and slightly easier than the normal way.
12a 90ft 5b. Traverse right strenuously to the small cave, then climb to gain the obvious crack splitting the wall of the zawn and follow this to the top.

COD ROCK   GR 946 549
This is the fin-shaped stack approximately a quarter of a mile south of the Old Redoubt. Its north-west face offers a number of 60-foot climbs on steep, weathered limestone. Large numbers of seabirds inhabit the rock, so it should be avoided during the nesting season.

Access is by boat in calm seas, and a mooring peg exists just right of centre of the face. A stern anchor would be useful to help keep off the rocks!

Different Kettle of Fish (60ft, Hard Severe, 4a) lies around the left-hand corner of the north-west face and takes an obvious corner above a blowhole.

Blistez (40ft, Severe) takes the obvious crack on the left side of the face.

Shy Talk, Kittiwake, and **Polloks** (all 60ft, Hard Severe) take the crack-lines left of the mooring peg.

Grope and Hope   (60ft, Very Difficult) belays in the boat and takes the crack immediately right of the mooring peg. The easier rock to the right gives **Kaktus**   (Difficult).

BERRY HEAD — MAIN HEADLAND

This comprises the extensive but relatively low cliffs on the south side of the headland and the huge, shady quarry on the north side. The south-facing climbs are quick-drying and generally on excellent rock, which ensures their popularity even in winter. Routes in the quarry are much bigger and more serious, but still on sound rock and very good value in the summer months.

To reach the cliffs of the south side, follow the road through the fort entrance and past the cafe to a path descending gently to the right. The path ends at a polished glacis, which must be descended with care in wet conditions. The Red Wall Area now lies to the right (facing seawards), while the Coast Guard Cliffs are to the left.

RED WALL AREA   GR 945 565

The Red Wall itself is at the far (west) end of the sea-level terraces. To its left are three obvious corners — Red Monk, Chastity Corner and Abbot's Way respectively. Beyond the terrace a slightly tidal ledge system continues westwards and gives access to the first group of climbs. The following route begins where the ledge system ends, beside a prominent overhang.

Barnacle Traverse   Very Difficult   (at low tide)   1967
From the prominent overhang step down and traverse below the high water mark until it is possible to step up and reach a ledge. Continue the traverse across a steep wall to the foot of a shallow corner flanked on the left by a large sea cave. Climb the corner, moving right at the top.

Barnacle Traverse Continuation   300ft   Hard Very Severe   1968
Extends Barnacle Traverse to the large platform to the west. Good climbing, generally 4c with a 5a overhang to finish.

Relay   90ft   Hard Severe   1979
Start as for Barnacle Traverse. After two ribs are passed there is a low roof below a steep pink slab.
1   65ft   Climb the thin crack with a steep move at 20 feet, then move slightly right to a niche below a corner. Nut belay.
2   25ft   Climb the corner facing right; some loose rock.

Pathos   60ft   Hard Very Severe   1979
Start below the prominent overhang at the beginning of Barnacle Traverse.
1   60ft   5b.   Launch out over the roof and climb the steep wall to a large ledge. Continue up the wall above to the top.

Neanderthal   50ft   Hard Very Difficult   1968
Follows the corner formed by the prominent overhang and the wall to its right.
1   50ft   Climb an open crack for 20 feet, then pull out left under the nose and climb the wall above to the top.

Right of Neanderthal an easier-angled wall leads to a cave at 30 feet, above which is an easy groove. This provides a quick way down for routes in the area. To the right of this break is a long overhang 10 feet up, taken by the next climb:

Hot Lips   60ft   E1   1977
Strenuous and problematic. Start beneath a step in the roof 10 feet from its left end.
1   30ft   5c.   Climb to a good runner under the roof and make a hard move to reach holds on the lip. Pull over onto the slab and climb to a belay beneath an overhanging crack.
2   30ft   5a.   Climb the crack strenuously to the top.

Oggie   60ft   Hard Very Difficult   1968
Right of the long overhang and left of the corner of Abbot's Way is a series of small rough holds leading to a prominent nose at 20 feet. Start here.
1   60ft   Climb up to and behind the nose to a large ledge crossing the wall at half-height. Move right to a small bay then go up easier rock to the top.

Cod   60ft   Hard Very Severe   1981
Start 10 feet right of Oggie, at the arête.

1   60ft   4c.   Climb the arête and the wall above to a good ledge. Make some bold moves up and right to reach good holds, and continue steeply to the top.

Abbot's Way   50ft   Very Severe   1961   ★
A steep route taking the left-hand of the three obvious corners left of the Red Wall.
1   50ft   4c.   Climb the main corner for 30 feet, then follow the crack up the slightly overhung left wall to the top.

Abbot's Wall   50ft   Severe
Start at the centre of the wall to the right of Abbot's Way.
1   50ft   Climb the wall then finish up the main corner right of the thinner final crack of Abbot's Way.

Binky   60ft   Hard Severe   1968   ★
Good climbing up the right edge of the wall to the right of Abbot's Way. Start a few feet from the edge, at a thin crack.
1   60ft   4b.   Climb trending slightly right then straight up on small holds to reach a ledge on the rib overlooking Chastity Corner. Finish easily up the short wall above.

Chastity Corner   50ft   Hard Severe   1967   ★
The central corner — a fine little pitch.
1   50ft   4a.   Make a strenuous move to enter the corner and climb it on good jams and laybacks to a ledge. Block belays well back.

The Red Monk   50ft   Very Severe   1967
The reddish right-hand corner. Its capping overhang has recently collapsed, leaving a poor route.

Blood   50ft   E1   1969   ★
An excellent little pitch up the left side of Red Wall. Start 6 feet right of the Red Monk corner.
1   50ft   5b.   Climb easily for 10 feet, then step right and climb straight up the wall above, past a thread, to the half-way ledge. Step left and move up using pockets to a flat handhold. Mantelshelf onto this and so to the top.

Ruddigore   60ft   Hard Severe   1967
Climbs the shallow groove just left of Red Crack, sharing its finish.

Red Crack   70ft   Hard Severe   1961
The obvious wide crack splitting the centre of Red Wall. A pleasant climb.

1   70ft   4a.   Climb a thinner crack right of the main fissure to an obvious traverse line at 40 feet. Move left to reach a shallow corner, which is climbed to a ledge.

Variation   Very Severe
At the traverse line continue straight up to a quartz hole then surmount an overlap to the slab. Trend up and left to the top.

Ruddy Corner   80ft   Hard Very Difficult   1967
The corner bounding Red Wall on the right. Start 20 feet right of Red Crack.
1   80ft   Climb a short wall and flake to reach the red corner. Climb this on doubtful rock to a ledge. Move up and right on poor rock then easily to the top.

Captain's Corner   115ft   Very Severe   1961
Worth doing for the first pitch. It takes the large, blind corner to the right of Red Wall.
1   65ft   4c.   Climb the corner with increasing interest to a large terrace.
2   50ft   Finish up the loose, broken corner above.

Izitso   100ft   Hard Very Severe   1981   ★
Start 15 feet right of Captain's Corner.
1   60ft   4c/5a.   Climb the centre of the slab to a crack and follow this to a suspect block. Move up left on good holds to a ledge.
2   40ft   4c.   Move up onto the wall on the right and continue rightwards until it is possible to step up to good ledges. Continue to a good edge, then climb more easily to a huge thread belay in the back wall.
3   10ft   Climb up on to the block and make an awkward move to easy ground. No belay.

Evening Buttress   60ft   Very Difficult   1961
To the right of the bay of Captain's Corner is a buttress with a slanting crack on its face.
1   60ft   Climb the centre of the buttress, trending right, then move left over an overlap to a ledge. Either finish here or climb the rock above in another pitch.

Evening Arête   90ft   Very Difficult   1967
The last feature before the crag degenerates towards the easy way down is an arête capped by a prominent nose. A pleasant climb.
1   90ft   Follow the edge easily for 60 feet to the nose, thread runner. Climb the steep wall right of the nose to the top.

THE COAST GUARD CLIFFS   GR 947 565

These are the cliffs to the east (left facing seawards) of the descent path. The climbing is on various steep, clean walls rising straight from the sea and on the somewhat slabbier and more vegetated upper cliffs. To reach the first group of climbs from the foot of the descent, walk along terraces towards the point until after a sea-filled crevasse the way begins to rise to about 60 feet above sea level. Below is Swashbuckler Buttress, characterised by the central, bottomless corner of Swashbuckler.

Sirocco   60ft   Severe   1979

Pleasant climbing up the western side of the buttress. Start at the bottom of a crack just to the right of the left edge of the front face.
1   60ft   Climb the steep crack on good holds and continue delicately in the same line to the top.

Broadside   90ft   Severe   1979

Start to the west of the buttress at the top of a short chimney.
1   40ft   Descend the chimney and traverse right about 15 feet above the water, around a rib, and belay on the far side of the next small bay.
2   50ft   Step back left to a ledge then move delicately up and left around the rib and continue past a block runner to the top.

Squall   60ft   Severe   1979

Takes the blunt arête 15 feet left of the corner of Swashbuckler. Approach via Broadside and start beneath the arête.
1   60ft   Climb the arête, straightforward at first, to a deep hole on the right. Climb steeply up the right-hand side of the arête via thin cracks to a ledge, and continue up through a break to the top.

Swashbuckler   100ft   Severe   1968   ★

The impressive central corner gives a surprisingly easy climb. Start on the east side of the buttress at lowish tide.
1   40ft   Make a descending traverse to the face of the buttress and cross this to belay in a chimney just right of the corner.
2   60ft   Move awkwardly into the corner and climb it on good holds to the top.

Douglas Fairbanks Jnr.   60ft   Hard Very Severe   1983

Climbs the overhung groove immediately right of Swashbuckler. Approach as for Swashbuckler at low tide to belay beneath the line.
1   60ft   4c.   Climb the steepening groove past semi-detached blocks to the roof. Move left to a ledge on the arête and finish out right.

Jimjam   50ft   Severe   1979
Takes twin cracks at the eastern end of Swashbuckler Buttress. Start beneath them at sea level.
1   50ft   Climb using both cracks until it is possible to swing left and layback to the top.

To the east of Swashbuckler Buttress is a similar one offering slightly harder climbing. The routes are approached from the eastern side of the buttress beginning at a ledge 20 feet above the sea.

Hidden Groove   110ft   Hard Severe   1979   ★
An interesting excursion. Start on the ledge.
1   60ft   4a.   Descend an awkward crack to a ledge just above the sea (awash at high tide). Skirt round the rib and go up an adjacent groove for 15 feet, then make a slightly descending traverse across the front of the buttress to the 'hidden groove' at the far end.
2   50ft   4b.   Climb the groove with increasing difficulty to the top.

Cloudburst   90ft   Very Severe   1979
Start on the ledge 20 feet above the sea.
1   50ft   4a.   Descend the crack for a few feet (as for Hidden Groove) until a traverse across the steep left wall can be made to the arête. Step across the groove and make a horizontal traverse to a suspended groove in the middle of the face.
2   40ft   4c.   Climb the groove and step left at the overhang to a ledge. Using the discontinuous zig-zag crack make difficult moves up the steep wall to the top.

Calcite Diamond   50ft   E1   1980   ★
Climbs the arête right of Cloudburst — a hard, bold pitch. Approach via pitch 1 of Cloudburst — descend the crack to the ledge, skirt round the rib, then move up to belay on good nuts. (Less awkward solo.)
1   50ft   5b.   Step left then go straight up the edge to a good high handhold. Move up to stand on the handhold, then make a series of tenuous moves up and across the wall until easier climbing on the arête leads to the top.

Although climbs have been described on the upper cliffs above the Hidden Groove buttress they are scrappy and lineless. A short wall in the bay before the last quarried scoop yields a fine series of 'shorties'. Abseil down a cleft near a chimney to a large thread belay on the right.

Tied Line   50ft   E1, 5b   1983
Traverse left at the level of the belay and make a difficult pull leftwards over an overlap to the base of a good crack, which is followed to the top.

Placebo   35ft   Very Severe, 4c   1983
Traverse up to the left from the belay to reach good discontinuous cracks after 10 feet. Finish up these.

Ray Zazorn   40ft   Very Severe, 5a   1983
This is at the left end of the wall. Descend to the tide line and step out right onto the wall via hard moves to a good hold and a crack leading to the top.

The next worthwhile routes are in the last quarried scoop before the tip of the headland, where the crags are bigger, steeper and more continuous. They are bounded on the right by a blank red wall topped by a glacis, from which the clifftop can be reached by scrambling. Above the glacis is the steep slab taken by Flying Fifteen.

Thursday Rib   80ft   Severe   1961
This is the rib forming the left edge of the quarried scoop.
1   80ft   Climb the right flank of the rib until the rock steepens. Move diagonally left to a scoop in the edge of the rib then continue to a ledge.

Thursday Corner   80ft   Hard Very Difficult
The corner to the right of Thursday Rib, breaking left to the arête when it becomes too vegetated.

Schizophrenia   150ft   Hard Severe   1967
Start at the bottom right-hand corner of the steep grey slab right of Thursday Rib.
1   70ft   Climb the right-hand side of the slab, stepping right to pass a bulge. Peg belay below a steep wall.
2   80ft   Climb the steep wall, then either continue up loose terrain to the top or traverse right to the final corner of Gugu Wack.

Right of Schizophrenia the cliff is gradually shortened by a glacis running up to a smooth terrace. At the left end of the terrace is a vegetated, crystal-filled crack taken by the following climb.

Gugu Wack   130ft   Hard Very Severe   1969
Unless recleaned, this is an awkward route which is difficult to protect. Start beneath the 'crystal cake' fault.
1   70ft   4c.   Climb easily to where the fault steepens then move up with difficulty to the slab above which leads to a large sloping terrace and a peg belay.
2   60ft   Above and slightly left is a solid corner in an area of loose rock. Climb this to the top.

Flying Fifteen   70ft   Hard Very Severe   1968   ★
A fine poorly, protected pitch starting 10 feet right of Gugu Wack, at an overlap in the terrace.
1   70ft   5a.   Climb the wall for 15 feet then move diagonally right to a ledge with a poor peg runner above. Traverse left for 10 feet then climb directly to the sloping terrace and peg belay of Gugu Wack.

Crystal Corner   50ft   Very Difficult   1961
A slight route taking the corner formed by the blank red wall with the main mass. Low tide start.

Blind Pew   45ft   E4   1983
Climb the red wall right of Crystal Corner, employing a peg runner at 12 feet and a skyhook on the bulge.
1   45ft   6a.   After a boulder problem start, hard moves lead to the bulge. Climb past this (crux) and up the wall above.

Hawkin's Climb   120ft   Hard Severe   1961   ★★
An excellent climb taking the steep open slab on the buttress right of the smooth red wall. Start at low tide, as for Crystal Corner.
1   50ft   Traverse right below high water mark, past Crystal Corner, until it is possible to move up and right to a small ledge on the far side of the buttress.
2   50ft   4a.   Climb to a thin crack running diagonally up the slab. Follow this to reach a stance and belay behind a large flake.
3   20ft   Traverse right for 15 feet then climb easily to the top.

The low seacliff on the tip of Berry Head provides a very enjoyable traverse, Quality Street. It may be climbed in either direction but is best from right to left as it takes in Hawkin's Climb. The approach, which can also be used for climbs in Berry Head Quarry and Arch Zawn, is by the 'via ferrata' handrail which descends the quarry face from just in front of the lighthouse. Clamber down this and continue towards the sea over the top of a natural arch to reach some terraces. Quality Street starts beside the chimney formed by the south side of the arch.

Quality Street   230ft   Hard Severe   1968   ★★
Possible at any state of the tide but not during high seas.
1   40ft   Cross the chimney about 5 feet above high water mark and traverse left to a large ledge. Move on up to a cave and belay.
2   40ft   4a.   Traverse horizontally for 15 feet, then climb diagonally left acros a gritty wall to a small ledge. Thread belay.
3   60ft   Continue more or less horizontally left to a thread belay at the far end of a long ledge.

4 70ft 4a.   Traverse for 20 feet to the foot of a light-coloured slab and climb this via a thin diagonal crack (as for Hawkin's Climb) to a stance at a big flake.
5 20ft   Move right and up a crack to a large terrace. Scramble back to the top of the headland.

Milky Bar Kid   50ft   E1   1983
A fine little route centred on the overhanging white wall above the first pitch of Quality Street. Start from the large ledge at the end of Quality Street's first pitch.
1 50ft 5a/b.   Climb up rightwards into the cave. Move over the roof to its left then go up slightly right to finish through the obvious slanting break.

ARCH ZAWN
On the north side of the natural arch at the start of Quality Street is a square-cut zawn formed by a detached platform. Boulders in the bed of the zawn are uncovered at low tide and may be reached by a descending traverse from the seaward end of the platform. The cliff forming the landward side of the zawn is 80 feet high and gives some interesting routes.

Seaworm   90ft   Hard Severe   1970
A climb of character. Start at the obvious slimy corner towards the left side of the face.
1 50ft   Climb the corner to a bulge at 20 feet and move over this onto a small pedestal. Move right and climb a crack to a large ledge and thread belays.
2 40ft   Climb up on the right to an upper ledge composed of calcite blocks. Follow this leftwards and crawl up a tunnel to the clifftop.

Stag Party   90ft   Severe   1970
Start at a crack 20 feet right of the initial corner of Seaworm.
1 60ft   Step right into the crack and climb to the overhang. Move right and up the widening crack to ledges and a thread belay in a cave.
2 30ft   Step left onto the pillar and climb steeply to a cave. Take the final overhang direct.

Rastus   95ft   Hard Very Severe   1971   ★
A steep and interesting route. At low tide, start at a crack 10 feet right of Stag Party. At higher tides, traverse in from Seaworm.
1 70ft 4c.   Climb for 10 feet then move right and swing into the cave. Climb the slab on the right, then pull up left into the crack and follow it to ledges.
2 25ft 4c.   On the left is a short overhanging corner above a recess. Climb this to the top.

All Because   45ft   E1, 5b   1983
Climbs the seaward arête of the wall via a thin finger crack, reached by a leftwards traverse from the ledge around the corner from the zawn.

Sunkiss   30ft   E1, 5b   1983
The short but impressive arête to the right of All Because.

The obvious black corner on the opposite side of the zawn from Rastus, All Because etc., is taken by **Man In Black** (E1, 5b, 1983). The next buttress to the west of Sunkiss gives **Crunchie** (60ft, Hard Severe, 1983), which follows an open corner.

BERRY HEAD QUARRY   GR 944 567
This is the very large, shady quarry on the north side of the headland. It has been disused for several years but any future developments may affect climbing. The best routes are on the oldest and most seaward face, directly beneath the Coastguard station, where the rock is most solid and presents a series of fine lines. The crag cannot be recommended in winter, when the rock stays damp due to a covering of lichen, but in summer it offers big, often serious routes in a pleasant, secluded environment and is particularly useful in the nesting season when the Old Redoubt is out of Bounds.
    One approach is by the 'via ferrata' handrail in front of the lighthouse, but the usual way is to walk in by the old quarry road, which begins at a gate in the fence about 200 yards inland from the entrance of the main fort.

Malteaser   100ft   Hard Very Severe   1983
Climbs the vague crack system in the wall above the handrail descent.
1   100ft   4c/5a.   Follow the cracks until a short traverse right at 85 feet enables the obvious wide crack in the red headwall to be climbed to the top.

The most prominent feature of the seaward cliff is a slender buttress on the left-hand side. This is bounded on the left by the open groove of Beggar's Banquet and on the right by the deeper corner of Boo-bah Plost.

Arncliffe   150ft   Very Severe   1970
About 50 feet left of Beggar's Banquet are some small caves. Care with rock needed. Start 10 feet left of these, at a niche with a honeycombed roof.
1   50ft   4b.   Climb the back of the niche and pull straight over the roof to a small ledge. Continue to a small stance and peg belays.

2   50ft   4c.   Move diagonally left then back right to the foot of the groove above the stance. Enter this, peg runner, and climb it to a cave. Thread on the left.
3   50ft   4a.   Pull straight out of the cave on huge holds, then a move right gives easier climbing to the top.

Graunching Gilbert   150ft   Hard Very Severe   1970
Start 25 feet left of Beggars Banquet. Peg runners used.
1   90ft   4c.   Climb bearing slightly right to a small overhang with undercuts on its lip. Move right under this and up to a V-groove, which is climbed on small holds. Above is a niche with a shothole in its back wall for a peg belay.
2   60ft   Finish easily over ledges to the top.

Beggar's Banquet   140ft   E2   1970   ★
An exposed and serious route taking the long, open groove left of the slender buttress.
1   30ft   4a.   Climb to a small hole then step left and up to a small stance. Peg belays.
2   60ft   5a.   Climb to a shothole thread then step left and move up into a short corner, which is quitted out left after a few feet. Continue past a hollow block to a stance.
3   50ft   5b.   Climb diagonally right to exposed ledges, peg runner, then move up and left with difficulty to more ledges. Climb directly to the top on steep rock.

Boo-bah Plost   160ft   Hard Very Severe   1970
The original route of the quarry — a fine line which would improve with traffic. It takes the groove bounding the slender buttress on the right and starts at the shallow groove forming the base of the line.
1   60ft   4b.   Climb the groove then step right and up to a ledge. Climb past the recesses then move right to a larger sloping ledge. Peg belays.
2   100ft   5a.   Climb the calcite groove for 30 feet then move right into the main groove, peg runner. Follow this for 20 feet then move right and climb steeply to ledges. Gain a ledge about 20 feet from the top, then step left and climb the final corner (peg runner).

Paranoid   160ft   E1   1970   ★★
An excellent sustained route taking a sinuous crack in the light-coloured wall 30 feet right of Boo-bah Plost. Slings needed for thread runners. Start below the cave which is 20 feet up the cliff.
1   25ft   4c.   Climb straight up to the cave. Belay on threads.
2   75ft   5b.   Move right then back left above the cave. Climb the crack above until it peters out, then follow the thin, leftward-slanting crack to a good hold and continue to a poor thread. Move up right with difficulty to gain a small stance below a V-groove.

3 60ft 5b.   Climb the groove to the roof and move rightwards on poor holds to a small ledge (peg runner above). Step left into an open groove and climb steeply on good holds to the top.

Home Brew   170ft   Hard Very Severe   1970
Mainly follows the right-hand of two parallel cracks in the centre of the face. Peg runners used. Start 10 feet left of a vegetated cave, below the line of the left-hand crack.
1 50ft 4b.   Climb for some 25 feet then traverse right to gain some ledges and the cave.
2 60ft 4c.   Move right out of the cave then climb directly to a small stance below an overhang. Peg belay.
3 60ft 4b.   Climb the overhang on the right then traverse left on ledges to a larger ledge. Climb the wall behind, bearing right, to the top.

Direct Start 4b
Start directly beneath the cave stance, under a large fin of rock. Gain the fin from the left and step up to a horizontal crack. Move over a bulge and up to the cave.

Burning Bridges   150ft   E3   1983   ★★
A route of quality taking the large, blank-looking corner in the centre of the face. Start beneath the corner.
1 150ft 5c.   Climb the wall fairly directly to the blank corner and follow it to the top. Tree belay.

Sunset Boulevard   150ft   E4   1983   ★★
Takes the impressive wall left of Burning Bridges. An excellent, well protected and strenuous route.
1 150ft 5c/6a.   Climb the crystal wall then trend right into the corner (hand-slotted peg in borehole). Move up to a runner placement, make a rising traverse left until the crack system is reached and follow this (crux) to a large ledge. From its left end climb easier ground up and left until the top can be reached via a rightward-slanting crack/scar. Extra rope needed to belay unless the pitch is split.

Desparête   150ft   E3   1984   ★
A fine route up the obvious right arête of the Burning Bridges corner.
1 150ft 5c.   Climb directly up the wall beneath the arête (threads). Move up the right-hand side of the edge, then cross the overhanging red wall diagonally left to hinge round the arête on a hidden pocket (situ thread) and go up to a ledge. Follow the line to the top with magnificent exposure.

Dust Devil   170ft   E1   1970
Start at the apex of a very large mound of earth, left of the much smaller mound at the start of Yellow Rurties, and below the big blank corner of Burning Bridges. Peg runners used.
1   70ft   4c.   Climb the broken buttress to a stance and thread belay at the foot of the blank corner.
2   50ft   5a.   Traverse horizontally right to the edge of the buttress and move up for a few feet before breaking right over a delicate slab. Climb the corner to another good stance and peg belays.
3   50ft   5b.   Climb the steep wall on the left and make difficult moves over a bulge into a short chimney. Finish to the left on the obvious line.

Yellow Rurties   170ft   Hard Very Severe   1970   ★★
A fine route, sustained and on good rock. The first pitch is sparsely protected. It works rightwards to the obvious clean-cut corner high on the right-hand end of the face. Start at a small grassy mound to the right of a much larger mound that abuts the cliff.
1   110ft   4c.   Climb straight up for 25 feet to a borehole (slot in protection peg). Move up into the groove on the right and climb to a large thread. Continue for 15 feet to a peg runner in a borehole (also giving backrope if required) then gain some ledges above. Traverse right until 5 feet beyond a large flat foothold (peg runner), then climb up on the right to a stance above.
2   60ft   5a.   Traverse left and climb the wide crack, exiting right to ledges. Move up to a good hold then rightwards to the final corner and climb to the top.

Dirt Eater   150ft   E4   1983   ★
A good clean route taking the steep walls and exposed buttress to the right of Yellow Rurties. Start 30 feet right of Yellow Rurties.
1   150ft   6a.   Climb the obvious finger crack splitting the reddish wall, moving right then back left (peg runner) to gain the ledge. From its left end climb to join Yellow Rurties, which is followed to its stance. Move right and climb the square white groove above. Traverse 10 feet right to a thread runner. Climb the wall above to a ledge, then traverse back left to the arête and finish up cracks.

Opus Dei   510ft   E2   1971   ★
A good sustained girdle crossing the face at two thirds height. The climbing is reasonable apart from one hard section. Start as for Graunching Gilbert.
1   40ft   4b.   Ascend rightwards to a small stance on the arête below a shallow corner. Peg belay.
2   70ft   4c.   Move into the corner then traverse the obvious line, peg runner, to meet Beggar's Banquet just below the stance. Move up to this.

3   50ft   4c.   Climb for 10 feet then step right to a small ledge, which is followed till it ends, peg runner. Step down, traverse the very exposed face and move round into Boo-bah Plost. Climb the right-hand crack to a stance on a block on the right.
4   90ft   5b.   Traverse right, descending slightly, to join Paranoid in the groove below the roof. Make hard moves right to a small ledge, peg runner above, then continue horizontally right to a crack (peg runner) and step across a sandy band to a comfortable bay. Peg belays.
5   110ft   4c.   Traverse to the groove of Home Brew and continue awkwardly to a small ledge beside an impressive wall. From the peg on the right, abseil and pendulum to a small stance (on Dust Devil) below the great smooth corner.
6   50ft   5a.   As for Dust Devil — step up onto the rib and climb rightwards, peg runner, to a corner. Stance and peg belays 10 feet higher.
7   100ft   5a.   Move up above the belay and gain the rib on the right. Traverse under a roof and descend a short slab to the final corner of Yellow Rurties. Climb 10 feet then cross onto the exposed buttress. A horizontal crack leads to a vertical crack and thence to the terminal grass slopes.

To the right of the main, seaward face is a huge quarried bay, whose left edge provides **Foos Won't Moos** (180ft, Severe) and whose right edge gives **Salt** (200ft, Hard Severe, 1970), both of which are esoteric gems left to rediscovery. Another climb, **Winterlude** (Very Severe) takes the calcite wall 20 feet left of the start of Salt. A cave system in the seaward side of the isolated pinnacle opposite the western end of the main face gives **Labyrinth** (Severe), an interesting excursion.

In the first quarry reached from the entrance gate is **Semi-Detached** (40ft, Hard Very Severe, 4c, 1984), which takes an obvious flake crack running up a blunt arête above a pile of boulders, midway between two pools and on the left wall of the bay. The red slabs on the right wall of the quarry give:

Caius   80ft   E1   1984
Climbs the red slabs above the pool, just left of centre.
1   80ft   5a/b.   Trend left into a gully; climb this and the slab above to some vegetation. Climb the steeper wall above then scramble up to the road on the left.

FRESHWATER QUARRY   GR 923 567
This large crag just north of Brixham harbour has provided one climb (**Animals Are People**, 110ft, Severe, 1968) taking the big corner on the left side of the main wall. Climbing here is discouraged however, as there is a car-park beneath the cliff.

CHURSTON SEA CLIFFS AND QUARRIES   GR 918 ,571 to 915 572
A minor area but with some charm, lying about half a mile along the
coast from Freshwater Quarry. Take the coast road from Brixham
harbour, turn right into the Freshwater Quarry car-park and follow the
coastal path to the twin beaches of Churston Cove. (Good low tide
bouldering at the start of the path.) Cross the cove and climb the far
slope, from which the small sea cliffs can be seen along the coast.
   The cliff behind the boulder-beach is 60 feet high and abounds in
cracks and corners, many of which are somewhat grotty.

Gremlin   50ft   Very Severe   1975
Approaching the cliff from the left, the first major feature is a big
corner. Start beneath this.
1   50ft   4b.   Climb the steepening corner and exit direct by some
tricky moves.

Merlin Rocket   60ft   Hard Very Severe   1967
A strenuous crack climb with good protection. About half-way along
the boulder-beach is a large, pointed triangular block. Scramble up
past this and the tree above then rightwards to a calcite corner.
1   60ft   5a.   Climb the corner to the niche. Step up right and climb
the overhanging crack to a large spike in a second niche. Follow the
crack and pull out over a hawthorn at the top. Tree belay well back.

Hornet   60ft   Very Severe   1975
The corner right of Merlin Rocket. Start just left of it.
1   60ft   4c.   Use the obvious flake to move into the corner and
climb it steeply on good holds to a loose finish. There is no option but
to abseil from bushes back down the line.

The seawashed walls are shorter but sounder and begin at a large
block. Except at low tide one has to climb through the narrow cleft
behind the block to get to the first bay, which contains Enterprise.
Beyond this is a tangle of blocks, cracks and chimneys too short to
record, and a wide crack at the right-hand end of the bay gives easy
access to the top of the cliff.

Enterprise   50ft   Severe   1967
A good little climb taking the clean, slightly curving crack-line in the
first bay. The last few feet are the most trying.

The quarries lie beyond the sea cliffs and are reached by a path down
through the woods at the very top of the point. The first quarry seems
quite extensive but on close inspection only a few of the lines appear
worthwhile.

Bloodhound   100ft   E2   1969
Takes the main challenge of the quarry, a large buttress, starting up a crack-line right of the central rib. Scramble up from the right to a stance on a large ledge.
1 50ft 4c. Climb the crack strenuously then move left along a narrow ledge into the half-way cave.
2 50ft 5b. Move left along the ledge for 10 feet till beneath a steep slab, peg runner. Stand on two flat holds above, then make a series of hard moves bearing slightly right to the start of a thin vertical crack (peg runner). Another move, then better holds lead to the top.

Further along the coast towards Paignton are two more quarries, reached by a pleasant path from the first. The second quarry is fairly large but loose and featureless, having no routes at present. The third is also loose except for a large isolated block in the centre with a dark slab facing seaward. This gives **Slipshod** (50ft, Very Severe, 4b, 1969), which climbs the left rib for 20 feet and then goes diagonally right to the top.

The Daddyhole Area

This section includes all the climbing between Torquay harbour and Meadfoot Beach, although the major cliffs are situated around and below the car-park on Daddyhole Plain. To reach this from Torquay harbour take the Babbacombe road for 100 yards and turn right at some traffic lights. From here the way is amply signposted. If travelling on foot from Torquay, follow Rock End Walk from the harbour eastwards along the coast, reaching the Plain in about 10 minutes.
   The first route, a sea level traverse, starts from the little cove (Beacon Cove) beside the large building just east of Torquay harbour.

Five Star Traverse   1000ft   Very Severe
Traverses the low cliff under the Imperial Hotel. Pleasant and not sustained, an enjoyable solo. Start at lowish tide. Easy climbing on slabs for some 300 feet leads to a small zawn. Traverse this (4c) to a second zawn, which gives a problem of similar difficulty. Continue past the private beach of Peaked Tor Cove and continue awkwardly (4b) to a smooth-looking wall behind Saddle Rock. Fine climbing across this wall (5a) leads to the rocky base of Dyers Quarry. The traverse can be continued on the low walls beneath the quarry almost as far as London Bridge, but this is harder and rather artificial.

SADDLE POINT   GR 922 628
Opposite Saddle Point Rock is a small crag giving a cluster of interesting climbs. The most obvious feature is a wide, rather grotty

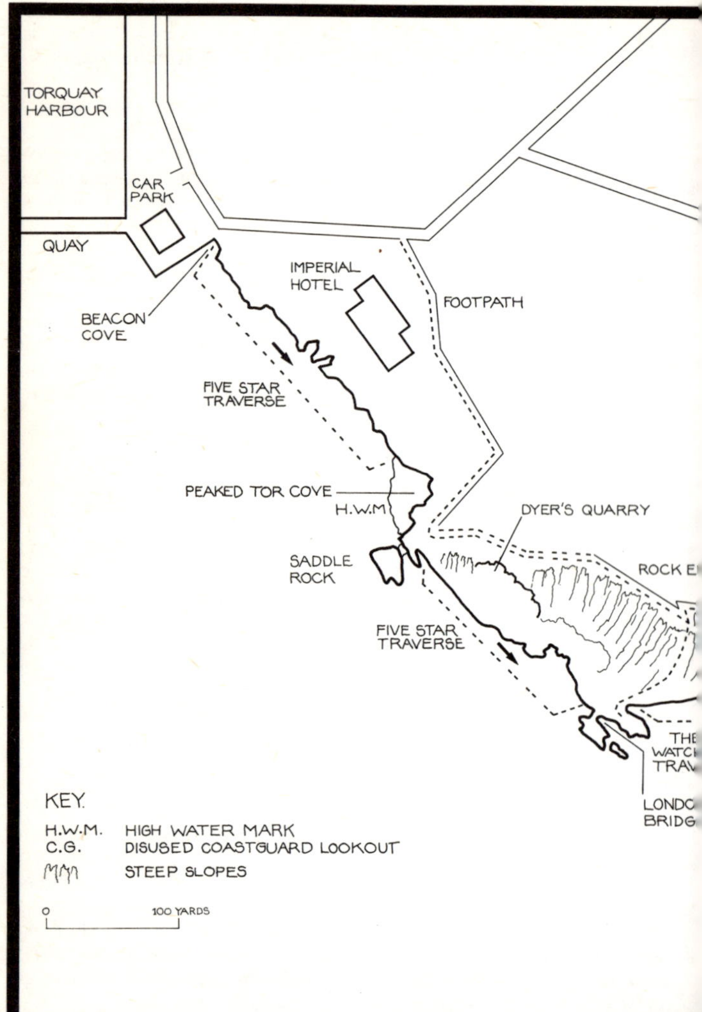
TORQUAY HARBOUR
CAR PARK
QUAY
BEACON COVE
IMPERIAL HOTEL
FOOTPATH
FIVE STAR TRAVERSE
PEAKED TOR COVE
H.W.M
DYER'S QUARRY
ROCK E
SADDLE ROCK
FIVE STAR TRAVERSE
THE WATCH TRAV
LONDO BRIDG
KEY.
H.W.M.   HIGH WATER MARK
C.G.   DISUSED COASTGUARD LOOKOUT
         STEEP SLOPES
O   100 YARDS

DADDYHOLE AREA

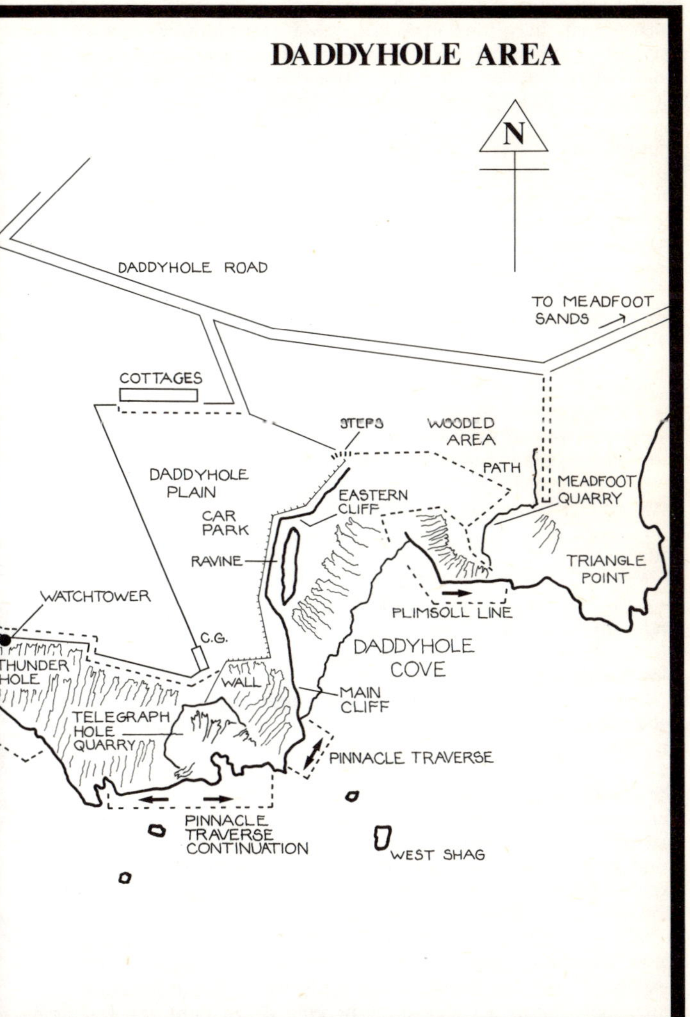

corner-crack defined on the left by the arête of Date with the Devil and on the right by the narrow slab of Mass Murderer. Climbs are best approached by fixing an abseil rope, which can also be used as a belay below loose finishes. Alternatively, traverse in either from Peaked Tor Cove to the west or Dyers Quarry to the east.

Blue Monday   70ft   E2   1984
Follows cracks up the left side of the slab to the left of Date with the Devil. Start on the ledge beneath the slab.
1   70ft   5b.   Climb the crack-line until a difficult rightward-rising traverse gains the fine continuation jamming crack above. Loose finish.

The Devil's Alternative   65ft   E2/3   1984
Takes the slab left of Date with the Devil. Start on the ledge beneath the slab.
1   65ft   5c.   Climb trending rightwards to some good ledges. Tackle the bulge above by stepping slightly left and move up to an in situ peg. Climb the wall above between a thin crack and a vague flake, to a ramp-line on the right leading to the top.

Date with the Devil   60ft   E1   1984   ★
The striking arête which bounds the wide corner crack. Start beneath the corner.
1   60ft   5b.   Start in the corner then swing up and left over the roof to gain the arête. Follow this, past a protection peg, to a loose finish (belay on abseil rope advised).

Mass Murderer   60ft   E2   1980
1   60ft   6a.   Climb the narrow, featureless slab to the right of the wide crack. Three bolt runners in place, to be clipped at leader's discretion.

The Watchtower   600ft   E2   1969   ★★
This is a traverse of the cove to the east of the natural rock arch known as London Bridge, which is about 500 yards from the car-park on Daddyhole Plain. The climbing is always good and occasionally excellent, although the last few pitches are escapable. It is possible at all states of the tide unless a high sea is running.
From the car-park on the Plain follow Rock End Walk westwards for some 300 yards, past the watchtower itself, until just after some descending zigzags in the path. Inconspicuously climb through the fence then follow a vague track bearing down right and scramble down a scoop to the sea, just east of London Bridge.
Roughly 250 feet of climbing (moves of 4b) leads to a thread belay at the mouth of a deep zawn known a Thunder Hole. Climb the highest of the flake cracks leading up into the zawn until it ends at a

flat-topped spike. Fix a sling, pendulum across the zawn to holds on the opposite wall and climb to a peg. (Note: the zawn was originally crossed by swimming and this is still an option). The tape can now be flicked off to avoid rope drag and the second man pendulums from lower down using a tight rope from the peg, then either prussiks or swarms up the rope for a few feet. Traverse horizontally right for 25 feet then move up to an overhang (good thread runner high up). Continue rightwards with difficulty (peg runner) to good holds on the edge of the wall, then descend to belay (5b, a superb pitch). Move right and climb a groove for 10 feet before bearing right across the slabby wall to a break leading easily rightwards to a tree belay near the top of the cliff (5a). Step around the corner and descend a groove to sea level. Traverse on good holds to smoother rock then climb steeply to ledges (4a). Continue traversing to a long ledge with a thread belay at its right-hand end (4a). Step up to a good foothold then climb directly on small holds (5c) to easier ground, serious. Continue straight up to belay in the bushes, then a forested scramble regains Rock End Walk.

Jeckyll and Hyde   80ft   Hard Very Severe   1968
About 15 feet before the thread belay on the edge of Thunder Hole (see The Watchtower) is a line of a crack and projecting flakes. A useful escape.
1 80ft 4c. Follow the crack-line to a chockstone. Step right and follow a shallow groove, taking care with the rock at the finish. Tree belay. Scramble to the top of the cliff.

TELEGRAPH HOLE (PARSON'S HOLE)   GR 925 627
A sunny and secluded little cliff situated in a small cwm above the sea. It offers some excellent slab climbing and many other climbs of character. From Daddyhole Plain follow the clifftop path to Torquay (Rock End Walk) until about 30 yards after the first arch (near the coastguard look-out), then break left down a faint track which arrives at a stone wall above the cliff. Follow this until a retaining wall is reached, then climb the wall and descend an easy rib to the flat base of the quarry. The main part of the cliff consists of impressively smooth slabs bounded on the left by the corner of Nardly Stoad's Climb and on the right by the stepped corner of Discuss the Thoughts of Chairman Mao. Right of the latter is a less attractive face notable for its many downward-sloping ledges and a central niche with a tree in it (the stance of Mighty Atom).

The Mad Hatter   50ft   Difficult
Starts about 10 feet right of the easy way down and follows the rib all the way. Traverse right to avoid the stone wall.

Mock Turtle   50ft   Moderate
The shallow grassy groove on the right.

The White Queen   75ft   Severe   1969
The second pitch gives a pleasant and delicate piece of slab work.
1   30ft   As for Nardly Stoad's Climb.
2   45ft   A small rib just left of the corner is climbed until a short traverse left can be made. Climb the slab, finishing to the left.

Nardly Stoad's Climb   70ft   Severe   1967
Start 10 feet left of the lower tree and just left of a small corner.
1   30ft   Steep rocks lead to a stance below the corner.
2   40ft   Bridge up the corner above to a small ledge. Continue up steeper rock, finishing by a small tree.

The Slithy Tove   70ft   Hard Very Difficult   1967
Just right of Nardly Stoad's Climb is a small corner.
1   70ft   Climb the corner and rib above, which leads to within 10 feet of the top. Step left and finish up Nardly Stoad's Climb.

Bird Scarer   90ft   E2   1983   ★
A line near the left edge of the main slab, giving bold and interesting climbing. Start a few feet right of the tree.
1   100ft   5c.   Climb to a ledge, then follow a vague groove slightly rightwards (peg runner) to reach the protection peg on Blinding Flash. Climb up to another peg, step left and continue steeply to the top.

Blinding Flash   100ft   E4   1983   ★★
A bold and sustained route up the most continuous part of the main slab. Start 15 feet up the slope from the large tree at the base.
1   100ft   6a.   Climb straight up for 40 feet to a very thin crack running up left towards a protection peg. Make a series of thin moves to the peg, step up then climb the steep slab above, bearing right, to better holds and the top.

Flashdance   90ft   E2   1983   ★★
Excellent climbing up the natural line of weakness on the main slab. Start beneath the right-hand side of the slab, 10 feet up the slope from Blinding Flash.
1   90ft   5c.   Climb to a protection peg at 20 feet and continue to some small wire placements 10 feet higher. Move left to gain a sloping ramp and twin protection pegs, then climb the steep slab above, past a projecting peg, to reach a large handhold above a further peg. Move up to a narrow white ledge and so to the top.

Crinoid   90ft   Hard Very Severe   1967   ★
A fine route taking an elegant line up the right edge of the main slab.
Start as for Flashdance, 25 feet up from the lower tree.
1   90ft   5b.   Climb for 20 feet to the peg runner. Move up and right
onto the rib and climb this (two peg runners) to a thin diagonal fault,
which leads leftwards to a large flat handhold and the top.

The Midas Touch   70ft   Hard Very Severe   1967   ★
This pleasant route follows a shallow scoop right of the rib of Crinoid
and starts 15 feet up from the higher tree.
1   70ft   5a.   Climb bearing left for 30 feet, then go straight up
delicately before moving left and up to the top on small holds.

Total Control   70ft   E1   1983   ★
Start as for The Midas Touch.
1   70ft   5b.   Climb the wall to a large flake and move off this to
reach a ramp leading left. Traverse 10 feet left along this, and pull
rightwards over the bulge to the slabs above. Continue directly up the
slabs to the top.

Liaison with Lenin   70ft   Hard Very Severe   1980   ★
Start as for Discuss the Thoughts of Chairman Mao.
1   70ft   5a.   Move up to gain the ramp, which runs up diagonally
left. Follow this to its end, then climb directly up steeper rock to
finish.

Buzby   280ft   E2   1981   ★★
A rising traverse of the main slabs of Telegraph Hole, providing fine
sustained climbing. Start at the left side of the cliff, by the descent
route.
1   130ft   4b/c.   Climb the short rib and follow a rising traverse line
at two thirds height, to reach a sloping ledge on the main slab beyond
the groove of Nardly Stoad's Climb.
2   70ft   5c.   Climb rightwards to a good foothold in a crack. Move
right to a projecting peg and make hard moves straight up to a good
hold, peg runner. Move right and belay at a large flake on Midas
Touch.
3   80ft   5c.   Climb down right for 10 feet and make hard moves
across to an obvious ledge level with the belay. Climb a short ramp on
the left, pull up right over the bulge and continue with interest to the
top.

Discuss the Thoughts of Chairman Mao   80ft   Very Severe   1967
Follows the corner formed by the junction of the two main faces.
1   80ft   4b.   Climb the corner to a bulge and bridge over to the
ledge above. Continue up the corner over the next bulge, then break
out right to the top.

Jericho   80ft   Very Severe   1983
Start 10 feet right of Chairman Mao.
1 80ft 4b. Move up and step right onto a projecting ledge. Continue to a massive iron pin then trend left up slabby rock, keeping the steep reddish wall on the right. Move up steeply to stand on a loose-looking block on the right, continue to a peg, then an awkward move gains easier ground.

Swing Low   80ft   Severe   1967
An unsatisfactory route which takes a slanting line on the wall right of Chairman Mao and starts below the tree in the niche.
1 20ft Straight up to a stance just below the tree.
2 60ft Follow the obvious line joining the top part of Chairman Mao. Two peg runners.

The Mighty Atom   85ft   E1   1967   ★
Interesting climbing on solid rock. Start at a series of sloping ledges beneath and some way to the right of the tree, at a shallow black groove.
1 40ft 4a. Climb over the ledges past a large iron spike to belay in the niche.
2 45ft 5b. Behind the tree is a corner with a small overhang part way up. Climb the corner by layback and exit right onto a sloping ledge (strenuous). The stone summit wall is reached more easily and overcome by an exposed traverse left.

Mighty Cheese   130ft   Severe   1967
A rambling route abounding in loose blocks. Start about 30 feet right of the most forward part of the buttress, below a projecting block.
1 80ft Climb to the block (peg runner) and overcome it to the left. Scramble up loose rock to belay by some large unsound blocks.
2 50ft Ignore the corner above and traverse left towards The Mighty Atom. A corner on the right is taken, finishing to the left.

Below the left side of Telegraph Hole is a ramp which can be descended to a small bay containing three routes.

Saline   40ft   Severe, 4a   1983
Climbs a smooth, white-looking corner around to the left side of the bay.

Praline   40ft   Very Severe, 5a   1983
Takes a vague groove to the right of Saline and to the left of the two curving cracks taken by Aquiline. Exit leftwards.

Aquiline   60ft   Hard Very Severe, 5a   1983
Follow two obvious curving cracks to reach some stepped overlaps.
Trend rightwards through these and up the slabby wall above. Belay
in the wall.

The next routes are on the stratified wall below the telegraph pole.

Stratagem   60ft   Very Severe   1978
Start in the obvious niche reached by an abseil down the groove to the
right of the wall (looking out).
1   60ft   4c.   Traverse right out of the niche to a break in the
ovrhang. Go up through this and step right. Climb straight up the wall
above to finish with difficulty.

Megatarts   60ft   Very Severe, 4c   1983
Five feet right of Stratagem is a niche in the overlap. Climb through
this, then go up the groove/corner above.

DADDYHOLE MAIN CLIFF   GR 926 627
The cliff forms the west side of Daddyhole Cove, which is directly
below the car-park on Daddyhole Plain. One of the major crags of
Torbay, it is notable for its generally good rock and striking lines, and
is well viewed from Meadfoot Quarry. To approach, take the path
from the Plain towards Meadfoot Beach for 100 yards then turn right
along tracks through the trees to the spur forming the east side of
Daddyhole Cove, above Meadfoot Quarry. From here a narrow path
leads down to the boulder beach in the cove. Cross the boulders to
the cliff, the foot of which is well above high water level.
    Three obvious corners dominate the cliff. The smooth left-hand one
is taken by Last Exit to Torquay; Triton takes the dark, slanting corner
in the centre, while the more broken corner high on the right gives
the second pitch of The Pearl. Either side of Last Exit are the fine arêtes
of Gargantua and Zuma. There are three ways off from the top of the
cliff: 1) Scramble down the seaward slope and reverse Pinnacle
Traverse, 2) Abseil 130 feet back to the base from a tree midway
between the finishes of Triton and The Pearl, 3) Follow a track up and
leftwards through the thorn bushes to regain Daddyhole Plain.

Pinnacle Traverse   60ft   Very Severe   1967
This skirts around the left corner of the cliff to Telegraph Hole, and is
also useful as part of the descent from the clifftop. Possible at any state
of the tide. Start in the boulder-filled cleft at the left end of the cliff,
at a smooth groove.
1   60ft   4a.   Climb the groove (or, if the tide is right in, move in from
further right) to a traverse line of huge jugs leading around the arête.
Follow this and the obvious line beyond (peg for aid on a steep section
or 4c free) to reach the saddle above the Pinnacle.

Pinnacle Traverse Continuation   500ft
This runs from Pinnacle Traverse to the headland just beyond the finish of The Watchtower. It is possible in either direction and, though discontinuous, it offers some good 5a climbing if the best line is taken.

Caliban   90ft   Hard Very Severe   1969
A line on the extreme left end of the cliff. Start from low to mid tide on a boulder around the corner to the left of Pinnacle Traverse. At high tide the first stance can be reached via Pinnacle Traverse.
1   45ft   4c.   Climb straight up the wall to join Pinnacle Traverse at the peg. Climb leftwards past this and belay in the niche.
2   45ft   4c.   Move up to the overhang and make an awkward, strenuous traverse up to the right to a small ledge. Step left and reach the top from a red groove.

Tobacco Road   80ft   Very Severe   1967   ★
A good route on superb holds — low in the grade. It takes the tobacco-coloured wall leading up to the large overhang near the left edge of the cliff. Start as for Pinnacle Traverse.
1   80ft   4b.   Climb the groove then move left and up the wall until beneath the roof. Traverse delicately left to the edge then climb with care to the top.

Rocketman   100ft   E3   1979
A spectacular and serious route through the overhangs above Tobacco Road. Start as for Tobacco Road.
1   60ft   5c.   Climb to the large overhang of Tobacco Road, then traverse right across a hanging wall to a horizontal spike. Move right along a sloping ledge and belay (pegs).
2   40ft   5b.   Step down and traverse right to join Pantagruel at a protection peg. Reverse a few moves to gain a short groove. Pull over the roof above to the large detached flake before escaping left to easy ground.

Pantagruel   125ft   E4   1967/1977   ★
A fine challenging climb with poor protection in the upper part. Scramble over boulders to a stance below the obvious overhanging corner right of Tobacco Road.
1   100ft   5c.   Climb straight over the initial bulge into the corner and follow this strenuously past a protection peg, making a difficult exit to less steep rock. Peg runner. Traverse right to a small ledge (poor peg) then step up and continue rightwards with difficulty to reach a corner crack. Restricted stance.
2   25ft   4b.   Climb the corner to the top.

Readymix   140ft   Hard Very Severe   1967
A strenuous route on curious rock, taking the obvious curving crack left of the arête of Gargantua. Start as for Pantagruel.
1 80ft 4c. Make a rising traverse right below the big roof then move over a bulge, peg runner, into the corner. Climb steep rock on the right for 15 feet to a restricted stance.
2 60ft 5a. Climb to the bulge and follow the corner crack with difficulty until the angle eases. Step left and finish as for Pantagruel.

Gargantua   140ft   E1   1967   ★★
This excellent route climbs the big arête between Readymix and Last Exit to the niche on Gates of Eden, then weaves through the overhangs above. Start at a bank of shale below the corner of Readymix.
1 30ft 4c. Scramble up the shale for a few feet, then climb rightwards to a flake crack which leads to a small ledge with peg and nut belays.
2 60ft 5a. Climb into the open groove above then move up left, past a protection peg, to a good resting place. Take the bulge above direct and continue up the steep wall until a step right gains the arête, which is followed to the niche.
3 50ft 5a. Traverse right using a line of small holds then step up and move back left above the bulge on much better holds. Move up into an overhanging groove then break left to easier rock and the top.

Gates of Eden   130ft   Hard Severe   1967   ★★★
The classic of Daddyhole — an interesting and exposed climb in impressive surroundings. Beneath the corner of Last Exit is a huge leaning block, the left side of which forms a wide chimney. Start here.
1 60ft   Climb the chimney for a few feet then ascend the wall on the left to a ledge. The flake crack above leads into the corner, which is climbed for 10 feet to peg belays.
2 35ft   Climb the corner until it begins to overhang then traverse left and step up into a niche. Peg belays.
3 35ft   Step down left to the foot of a wide corner crack and climb this to the top.

Last Exit to Torquay   120ft   Hard Very Severe   1967   ★★
A steep and exposed pitch on perfect rock. Start as for Gates of Eden.
1 60ft   As for Gates of Eden.
2 60ft 5a/b. Climb the corner to the first overhanging section and make some difficult bridging moves, peg runner, to better holds above the bulge. Continue to a second overhang, which is passed using holds on the right wall. Easy climbing to the top.

Zuma   140ft   E4   1977   ★★
Climbs the magnificent arête to the right of Last Exit.
1   60ft   As for Gates of Eden.
2   80ft   6a.   Climb for a few feet then step right into a tiny groove (protection peg, on Snakecharmer). Climb the face above to reach good jams beside the obvious projecting block. Climb slabby rock on the right for 10 feet to regain the arête where it becomes smooth and overhanging. Move up the arête then use pocket holds on the left before trending right towards the arête to finish.

East of Eden (Very Severe and A1) aids its way up the thin cracks in the left wall of Triton.

Triton   165ft   Very Severe   1967   ★
The big central corner gives interesting and well-protected climbing on solid rock. Start as for Gates of Eden.
1   90ft   4a.   Follow Gates of Eden to the top of the flake crack then continue up the edge of a large flake on the right until some steep moves lead to ledges in the corner. Belay beneath an overhang.
2   75ft   4c/5a.   Move over the bulge to a ledge. Continue up the corner crack until a difficult move gains better holds on the left wall and the top.

Neptune   150ft   Very Severe   1967
Climbs the slabby right wall of Triton. Start at the narrowing chimney on the opposite side of the block to Gates of Eden.
1   30ft   4a.   Climb the chimney to a stance.
2   120ft   4c.   Climb a crack above to the rib then traverse left into the centre of the wall. Climb the wall until a horizontal crack leads rightwards to the rib, which is followed to a tottery finish.

The Bead   150ft   Very Severe   1967
Takes the right-hand rib of the Triton Corner. Start as for Neptune.
1   30ft   4a.   As for Neptune.
2   120ft   4c.   Climb the crack above to gain the rib at a good ledge. Step right and climb a pink slab to good holds then continue bearing rightwards up various slabs and walls to a loose finish.

Fandangle   180ft   Hard Very Severe   1967   ★
Excellent climbing in the upper part compenstaes for a vegetated, but still pleasant, first pitch. Start by scrambling up the loose shale rake beneath the right-hand part of the crag to belay beneath an overhang with a very prominent flake forming its right-hand side.
1   110ft   4b.   Climb up to and past the overhang using the flake then continue straight up for 30 feet, past a peg runner, to a groove with a layback crack in it. Follow the crack until it peters out then climb the slab to good nut belays at a large flake.

2   70ft   5b.   Double ramps run beneath the overhanging wall on the right. Move along the lower ramp until small incuts enable the higher one to be gained. Peg runner. Use the thin crack above to make a hard move onto the sloping ledge on the right, then continue easily to finish as for The Pearl.

The Pearl   190ft   Hard Severe   1967   ★
A good varied route taking the right-hand of the three great corners. Start as for Fandangle.
1   120ft   4a.   Climb to the peg runner then make a rising traverse to the right, two further pegs runners, to reach a gully, which leads to a good stance.
2   70ft   Climb the corner above, with a diversion to the left at 20 feet to avoid a bulge.

Mukdah's Wall   200ft   E4   1984
Climbs the overhanging white wall right of the final pitch of The Pearl.
1   120ft   4a.   As for The Pearl.
2   80ft   5c.   Climb the red flake and the blunt arête on its right-hand side, before moving back left along ledges. Follow the crack system to within a few moves of the top, where it is best to continue direct rather than take the deceptive, left-hand crack.

Snakecharmer   355ft   E3   1976   ★
A rising traverse of the main cliff, having sustained difficulties and a lot of fine climbing. Start as for Tobacco Road.
1   100ft   5c.   Climb to the first overhangs then move right using a flake crack into a smooth groove, peg runner. Break through this onto slabbier rock then traverse right, rising gently, to join Pantagruel. Peg runner. Continue horizontally rightwards, below the line of Pantagruel, to join Readymix, which is descended for a few feet to its stance.
2   35ft   5a.   Follow the obvious line rightwards, peg runner, to the arête of Gargantua, then traverse easily to a peg belay in Last Exit.
3   80ft   5c.   Climb for 10 feet then step right across a tiny groove to a poor peg runner. Move down rightwards to better holds leading to the arête and climb this for 20 feet to some large blocks, where runners can be fixed to protect the second. Continue horizontally right to a stance and huge thread belay in Triton.
4   70ft   4c.   Move up a little then traverse the slabby wall to the arête5   70ft   5b.   Pitch 2 of Fandangle.

DADDYHOLE UPPER CLIFF   GR 927 628
This is the short cliff directly beneath the car-park on Daddyhole Plain. It suffered a masive rockfall in 1983, when half the routes were

destroyed. The remaining climbs may still prove useful for an evening or for rounding off a day's climbing in the area. Descent is possible via a chimney reached by climbing over the fence at the right edge (facing seawards) of the park tarmac, and also by descending a ramp at the eastern (Meadfoot) end of the cliff. Both descents are messy.

End Crack   45ft   Very Difficult   1969
A pleasant route on the wall right of the descent chimney.
1   45ft   Climb the crack and corner behind the tree to a small ledge. Step right, then back left and climb the slab and groove above.

Imperial Wall   60ft   Hard Very Severe   1977   ★
The fine arête to the right of End Crack. Start at a detached flake just left of the arête.
1   60ft   5a.   Climb the wall direct with difficulty to reach a crack system above and follow this, finishing to the right of a tree.

Romeo and Juliet   70ft   Very Difficult   1968
Climbs the obvious chimney to the right of the large overhang which caps the left side of the crag. A scrappy route.

Ramshackle   65ft   Severe   1969
A worthwhile climb following the zig-zag crack some 20 feet right of Romeo and Juliet.
1   45ft   Climb a narrow slab to some large wedged flakes. Continue up the crack to a ledge and chockstone belay on the left.
2   20ft   Climb the wide crack then finish diagonally right.

Sabre Tooth   60ft   Hard Severe   1969
An interesting route starting beneath the large horizontal fang of rock half-way up the cliff to the right of Ramshackle.
1   60ft   Climb the reddish-brown slab and gain a sitting position on the fang. Step right and take the rightward-slanting line to the top.

Brass Bound Crack   55ft   Hard Very Severe   1969
A good route taking the obvious crack in the right wall of the groove some 30 feet right of Sabre Tooth.
1   55ft   5a.   Climb the groove until the crack can be gained from a subsidiary right-hand branch. Move up to a resting place then go directly up the overhanging groove.

Eubulus Williams   45ft   Very Severe   1969
Starts 15 feet right of Brass Bound Crack and follows a leftwards slanting groove.
1   45ft   4c.   Climb straight up for 15 feet then layback leftwards into the groove, which leads more easily to the top.

PLIMSOLL LINE CLIFF

Between Daddyhole Cove and Meadfoot Quarry is a slabby cliff giving a pleasant and useful traverse, which is possible in either direction and at most states of the tide.

Plimsoll Line   200ft   Hard Very Difficult   ★
Start from the boulder beach in Daddyhole Cove.
Cross the slab, about 10 feet above high water mark, to the arête. Continue mainly at this level, stepping down occasionally, to finish up an obvious diagonal ramp leading to the floor of the quarry. The traverse has also been extended to, and around, Triangle Point to give good summer soloing.

Prime Time   60ft   Very Difficult   1983
Start about one third way along Plimsoll Line at an obvious diagonal crack.
1   60ft   Follow the crack for 40 feet to a small overhang. Take the obvious groove right of this to the top. Tree belay behind.

Back Brain Stimulator   60ft   Very Difficult   1983
Start 15 feet right of Prime Time, just right of a small niche.
1   60ft   Climb the wall and slab trending right to a large flake (possible stance). Climb leftwards to finish up a rightward-sloping slab/groove.

Splash Down   60ft   Hard Severe   1983
Start about two thirds of the way along Plimsoll Line.
1   60ft   Climb directly to an obvious pale scoop and continue up the steep black wall above via a diagonal line from the left.

Vista   60ft   Hard Very Difficult   1981
Some 15 feet to the left (facing seawards) of the finish of Plimsoll Line is a faulted cleft, by large boulders. Scramble down the cleft for 25 feet and belay on good nuts.
1   60ft   Climb easily across a slab to a leftward-slanting crack-line in a steeper slab. Follow this to join Plimsoll Line then move straight up the steep wall on good holds to the ridge.

MEADFOOT QUARRY   GR 928 628

The crag is set in a small cwm behind Triangle Point, the rocky promontory between Daddyhole Cove and Meadfoot Sands. It is a pleasant and popular cliff thanks to easy access, a sunny south-easterly aspect, and the fact that the climbs are not too serious by Torbay standards.
    From the car-park on Daddyhole Plain, follow the path towards Meadfoot Beach for 200 yards then turn right on another path

overlooked by a slabby cliff. This ends at a shoulder above Triangle Point from which a short scramble leads down to the base of the quarry.

On the left side of the face are a couple of easy-angled slabs, bounded on the right by the elegant Diamond Rib. Right of this is the slab of Mayday then the steeper 'coal face', to the right of which and high on the cliff is the large tree reached by Nest Egg and Tree Root. The slabs on the far left can be climbed anywhere at Difficult standard.

Central Slabs   80ft   Very Difficult   1966
Start beneath the inset slab to the left of Diamond Rib.
1 50ft   Climb the slab to an iron spike then move onto a stance on the right.
2 30ft   Move back left and climb the steeper slab, making an exit through prickly bushes.

Diamond Rib   80ft   Hard Severe   1967   ★
A fine delicate pitch. Start beneath the rib.
1 80ft   4b.   Follow the rib with increasing interest until a small block is reached towards the top. Step right then finish direct.

Mayday   90ft   Very Difficult   1967
Start beneath the clean slab to the right of Diamond Rib.
1 70ft   Climb easily up the slab before moving into a shallow groove. Climb the corner above, step right, then move up left to a stance on more broken rock.
2 20ft   Climb bearing left up the final wall.

Third Time Lucky   100ft   Hard Very Severe   1981   ★
Fine climbing up the steep face just right of the Mayday slab. Start right of Mayday and just left of Median.
1 100ft   5a.   Climb directly to the bottom of a shallow groove, which is followed to a poor ledge below a thin edge. Use this to reach the slabs above and thence to a ledge with a quarry spike at its right-hand end. Finish directly over the loose overhang.

Demeter   100ft   E1   1979
Start as for Median.
1 100ft   5b.   Follow Median for 30 feet to the peg runner, then move left and up to a shallow groove. Move up to a sloping ledge, just right of another shallow groove, then climb the steep wall to the obvious overhang. Better holds lead across the groove to an iron spike, above which the right wall leads more easily to the top.

Median   100ft   Hard Very Severe   1970   ★
A good and interesting route. Start at a line of grooves right of the slabs of Mayday.

1 70ft 5a.   Climb the grooves for 25 feet then move right, peg runner, and mantelshelf onto a ledge in the centre of the black wall. Ascend slightly leftwards, making use of a crack, until it is possible to gain a cramped stance.
2 30ft 5a.   Climb the groove to the roof then traverse right (peg runner) to reach easier ground and the top.

Grand Slam   100ft   E2   1980
Start about 15 feet right of Median and belay with a peg on the highest ledge.
1 100ft 5b.   Climb directly up the wall (poorish peg runner in crystalline rock on the right — not in situ) to a narrow ledge. Difficult moves via a brittle crack lead to easier ground. Follow cracks diagonally left to the top.

Revolver   110ft   Hard Very Severe   1976   ★
A good climb starting just left of Rubber Soul, beneath the 'coal face'.
1 80ft 5a/b.   Climb the steep wall until a step right is made to a shallow ramp, which is followed to a good hold on top of a block. Climb with difficulty to gain a prominent peg on the girdle, and continue straight up to make a stance beneath the overhang.
2 30ft 4c.   Step down then make a rising traverse to the right to reach the top.

Rubber Soul   100ft   Hard Very Severe   1967
This climb runs up the right-hand side of the 'coal face' and starts beneath the projecting square block.
1 80ft 5a.   Climb up on to the block and move up to a small ledge, peg runner. Follow the broad rib above, little protection, then move right to belay at the tree.
2 20ft 4a.   Move left and make an exposed traverse above the 'coal face' to finish on good holds.

Nest Egg   100ft   Severe   1967   ★
An enjoyable route on excellent rock. Start directly below the tree.
1 80ft   Climb straight up to a small ledge at 30 feet and continue up the shallow grooves above to the tree.
2 20ft   Climb the groove behind as for Tree Root, but finish out right.

Tree Root   100ft   Very Difficult   1967
Start at the foot of the fault running leftwards up to the tree.
1 80ft   Climb without undue difficulty to the tree.
2 20ft   Climb the groove behind, moving left at the overhang.

Pegs' Progress   75ft   E2   1969   ★
A fine steep route taking the left-hand of the two thin cracks in the gently overhanging wall right of Tree Root. Start just right of Tree Root below the niche on the girdle.
1   30ft   Climb up to belay in the niche.
2   45ft   5c.   Just left of the niche, move up to a good handhold then a strenuous move gains another good hold high left. Climb the crack above then move left to more large holds before climbing steeply rightwards to finish. Alternatively, from the top of the crack finish up the obvious rightward-slanting crack — more strenuous.

Clotted Cream   70ft   E4   1969/*1984*   ★★
Just left of the arête of the cliff is an obvious thin crack in the gently overhanging wall. A fine strenuous pitch.
1   70ft   6a.   Climb a groove on the left until the crack is reached. Follow this to the top.

Hermeda   60ft   Very Severe   1968
An interesting route taking the grooved arête which bounds the cliff on the right.
1   60ft   4b.   Move into the corner from the right and climb to the obvious pointed block. Climb to an overhang, which is turned on the right to a crack leading on to easy slabs.

Malingerer   60ft   Very Difficult
A nicely situated route making the best of the rock right of Hermeda.
1   60ft   From the start of the corner of Hermeda, move up rightwards to a small ledge. Continue directly up the slabs above to the top.

The Meadfoot Girdle   260ft   E2   1969   ★
A rising traverse of the cliff having sustained climbing and a good line. Start as for Diamond Rib.
1   80ft   4b.   Follow Diamond Rib for 60 feet to the small block, then traverse right into Mayday and descend 5 feet to a stance and peg belay.
2   80ft   5a/b.   Move around a rib then climb diagonally right past a peg runner to a small ledge in the 'coal face'. Step up rightwards past a prominent peg and traverse right to join Nest Egg, which is followed to the tree.
3   30ft   4a.   Traverse beneath the impending wall on the obvious line to a niche.
4   70ft   5c.   Above is a diagonal crack, which is hand-traversed to gain the groove of Hermeda. Follow this around the overhang to the easier slabs.

The small pinnacle on the seaward side of the quarry basin gives a pleasant little climb, **Gulliver** (Difficult), on its seaward face. And on Triangle Point itself, the landward corner of the prominent pointed block is taken by **Pig's Ear** (40ft, Severe).

The Long Quarry Area

To reach this area from Torquay harbour, take the Babbacombe road for just over a mile to a sharp right turn signposted to Anstey's Cove. Either park on the roadside just past this and walk up a track (beside the vast new garden centre) leading up onto an open common (Walls Hill Downs) above the cliffs, or take the next right turn to a large car-park at the Babbacombe end of the common. The clifftop above Anstey's Cove and Long Quarry Point is a five-minute walk back eastwards from here. An alternative approach (though expensive and congested in summer) is to park at Anstey's Cove and walk across the beach. This gives good views of the Sanctuary Wall and Anstey's Cove cliffs. The huge blocks on the beach offer some good boulder problems.

Running out to Hope's Nose from Anstey's Cove is the traverse of **Morning Town Ride** (6000ft, Hard Very Severe with pitches of up to 5a) an entertaining excursion if begun at high tide.

ANSTEY'S COVE   GR 935 650

Best reached from Walls Hill Downs via a flight of steps leading down into the cove. The steps descend initially through a bay formed by a vertical wall on the right (looking down) and a bulging buttress on the left (Mitre Buttress). The first routes are on the vertical wall.

Crooked Man   80ft   Hard Severe   1968
Takes the obvious curving line towards the left side of the vertical wall. The rock is rather poor.
1 80ft 4a.   Climb a short wall to gain a ramp, which is followed rightwards to below a steep corner. Climb this and the earthy ramp above to the top.

Small Change   40ft   Hard Very Severe   1975
Rather overgrown with ivy at present but a good steep pitch taking the wall to the left of Little John. Start just left of the deeper cracks of that climb.
1 40ft 5a.   Climb bearing left to an obvious flat hold, then move up into a niche. Step left and climb the face to reach large doubtful holds and the top.

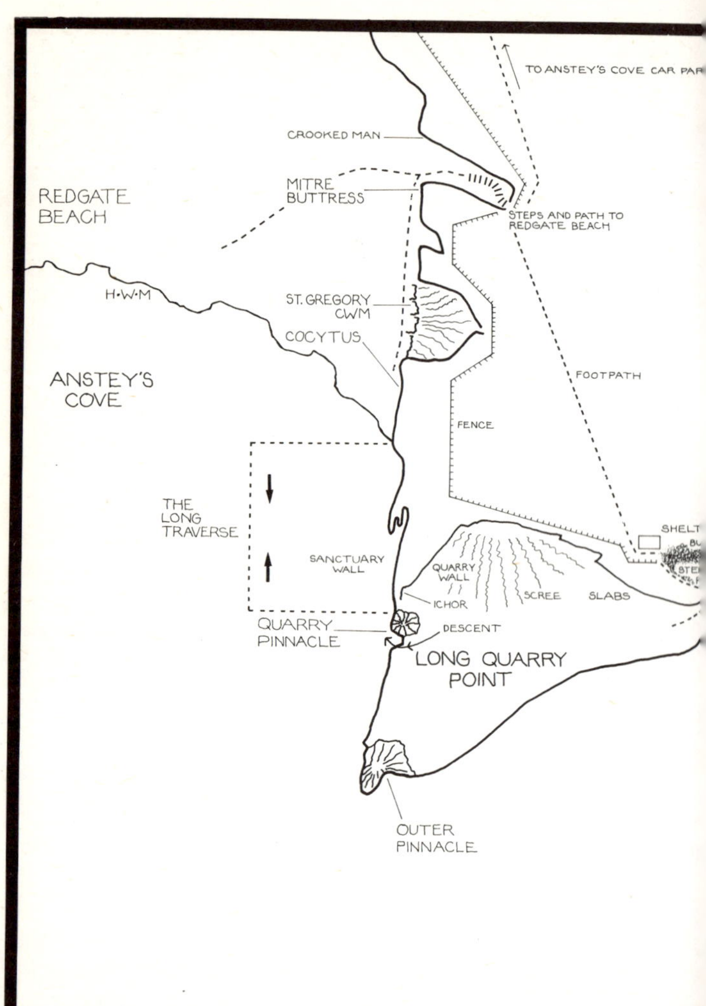
TO ANSTEY'S COVE CAR PAR
CROOKED MAN
REDGATE BEACH
MITRE BUTTRESS
STEPS AND PATH TO REDGATE BEACH
H.W.M
ST. GREGORY CWM
COCYTUS
ANSTEY'S COVE
FOOTPATH
FENCE
THE LONG TRAVERSE
SANCTUARY WALL
SHELT
BU
STE
QUARRY WALL
ICHOR
SCREE
SLABS
QUARRY PINNACLE
DESCENT
LONG QUARRY POINT
OUTER PINNACLE

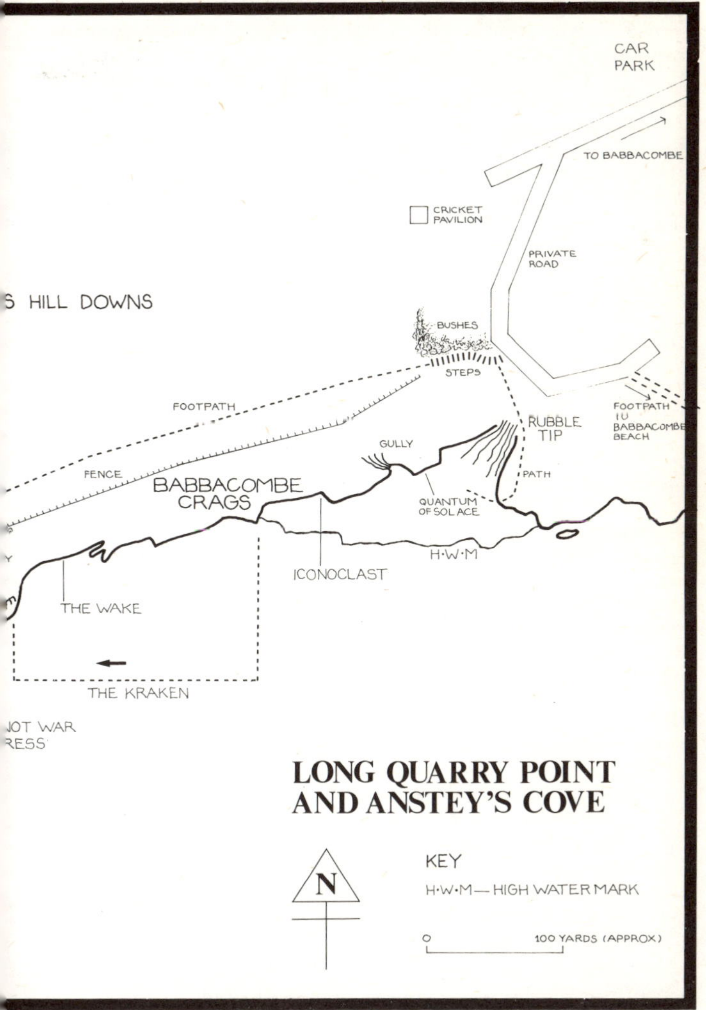
CAR PARK
TO BABBACOMBE
CRICKET PAVILION
PRIVATE ROAD
HILL DOWNS
BUSHES
STEPS
FOOTPATH
RUBBLE TIP
FOOTPATH TO BABBACOMBE BEACH
GULLY
FENCE
BABBACOMBE CRAGS
QUANTUM OF SOLACE
PATH
H·W·M
ICONOCLAST
THE WAKE
THE KRAKEN
NOT WAR PRESS
N
LONG QUARRY POINT AND ANSTEY'S COVE
KEY
H·W·M — HIGH WATER MARK
0   100 YARDS (APPROX)

Little John   35ft   Severe   1969
Start about 20 feet left of the steps, at a zig-zag crack below an obvious V-groove.
1   35ft   Climb the crack to a steep scoop. Step up and right then move left into the niche at the top. Strenuous.

Big Jim   35ft   E1, 5b   1984
Climbs the wall to the left of Tiny Tim.

Tiny Tim   35ft   Very Severe   1969
At the left end of Mitre Buttress is a slanting crack. Start beneath this.
1   35ft   4c.   Climb to the crack proper. Continue with difficulty for 10 feet, then better jams and jugs lead to the top.

Crook Bruce   70ft   E4   1977
A strenuous pitch up the left edge of the great bulging wall forming the left side of Mitre Buttress. Start some 30 feet left of The Mitre's arête at a leftward-slanting groove which disappears into ivy.
1   70ft   5c.   Climb the groove for 15 feet then take the overhanging crack on the right till it ends. Traverse up to the right with difficulty to a small nose then climb directly to the top.

Just One More   80ft   A2 and Hard Severe   1969
Technically difficult and continuously overhanging. Start 10 feet left of the foot of The Mitre's arête.
1   80ft   Go straight up to a wedge in a horizontal crack at 25 feet, then more diagonally left to another just below the bulge. Two more pegs and then a free move gain a small ledge near the top of The Mitre. Step up right then easily to the top.

The Mitre   100ft   E2   1968   ★★★
An excellent pitch, sustained and on good rock. Start 10 feet right of the arête of the bulging buttress.
1   100ft   6a.   Climb to a peg at 10 feet and pass this with difficulty, moving left to gain a large recess on the arête. Pull directly over the bulge above and continue (peg runner) to an uncomfortable niche. Step left to a small spike then swing up on good holds to the start of a sloping ramp (peg runner on the right). Climb diagonally left across the vertical wall to good footholds around the rib. Step up right then climb more easily to the top.

Variation Start
It is possible to climb directly up the lower arête to the recess — inferior but much easier.

Original Finish 4b
A natural line but it avoids the climax of the route. Continue easily up the sloping ramp for 10 feet, then layback onto a second ramp. Break right, then climb easily to the top.

The Cope   90ft   Severe   1968
The right-hand retaining slab of Mitre Buttress. Pleasant at first. Start beneath the slab.
1   90ft   Climb up to the left of the shallow groove and continue up the left edge of the slab until the angle eases. Easily to the top.

Epoc   70ft   Very Severe   1968
Immediately right of The Cope is a square bay. Start 5 feet right of the right-hand corner of it.
1   40ft   4b.   Climb the cracked wall to a small ledge then go diagonally right to a terrace and peg belay.
2   30ft   Move left and pull into a groove, which leads to the top.

Era   75ft   Very Severe   1968   ★
A fine pitch starting 10 feet right of Epoc at a rightward-slanting crack.
1   40ft   4c.   Climb the crack to the top of the pedestal. Continue directly up the wall above to the peg belay on the terrace.
2   35ft   The easy groove on the right.

Right of this the cliff splits into two tiers. The lower tier is continually overhanging and gives a superb route on its left edge as well as good artificial climbing. The upper tier has provided some routes but they are short and loose and do not merit individual description.

Devonshire Cream   70ft   E5   1984   ★★★
A serious, stunning pitch. Start beneath the arête.
1   70ft   6a.   Climb the arête past two peg runners.

Ferocity   60ft   A2   1969
A strenuous and difficult route up the centre of the tier. Start 25 feet from the left-hand arête (arrow).
1   60ft   Peg the wall slighly rightwards until a very long reach enables a peg to be placed below the first of five bolts. Follow these then step right onto grassy slabs. Large thread belay 25 feet back on left. From here one can escape leftwards and up to the top pitch of Era.

Lynch   50ft   A2   1969
Start about 35 feet right of Ferocity, at an arrow.
1   50ft   Go straight up to a shallow groove and follow it to the second of two threads, just below the top. Traverse 10 feet right then move up to a stance. Peg belays. Either go up right to the finish of St. Gregory or leftwards to the top pitch of Era.

Mars   170ft   Hard Severe   1969
Right of Lynch is an overhanging groove with a slabby rib on the right forming the left edge of the St. Gregory slab.
1   60ft   Move right onto the rib and climb it to a smooth brown slab, which is taken direct to a peg stance in a reddish corner.
2   50ft   Step left horizontally then climb the smooth slab direct to a loose corner right of the large overhanging wall. Peg belays.
3   60ft   Swing right from the stance and climb the exposed corner on sound but small holds. The overhang is turned on the left, peg runner, to finish up a shallow groove.

The next feature rightwards is a large quarried basin or cwm with a long white slab on its left-hand side. There are two old drill spikes plainly visible in the centre of the slab.

Saint Gregory the Wonder Worker   180ft   Severe   1967   ★★
A pleasant climb on clean rock taking the centre of the slab and the steeper rib above.
1   110ft   Climb the slab fairly easily to the second of the two spikes. Belay.
2   70ft   Traverse left along the smooth slab for 10 feet, then climb straight up the rib to traverse right round the nose on the obvious line a few feet from the top.

Little Wonder   80ft   Very Difficult   1969
Just right of the back of the St. Gregory cwm is an obvious ramp rising towards the sea.
1   80ft   Climb to the left end of the ramp and traverse seawards. Finish up the steep wall where the ramp becomes narrow and exposed. One protection peg.

Weeble   90ft   Hard Very Severe   1981
Start below the ramp of Little Wonder and belay on the buttress by a prominent black wall.
1   60ft   5a.   Move across onto the black wall and up to a ledge on the right. Climb on widely-spaced holds to the overlap, step up right to a flake, then make awkward moves onto the easier slabs above. Nut belays.
2   30ft   Climb the groove above or escape more easily via the rib on the left.

Moonshot   70ft   E1   1968   ★
A dynamic little route which breaks out of the prominent cave in the smooth wall forming the right-hand side of the quarried cwm. Scramble up to a peg belay below the cave.

1   70ft   5a.   Follow a line of flakes to the cave, step up on the left
then traverse back right across the top of the cave, keeping low, to
good holds at a small bush. Move up and slightly left then go straight
up the slabby face to the top.

St. Jude   160ft   Severe   1969
A poor route. Below and to the right of the start of St. Gregory is a wall
of solid limestone leading into the quarried basin. Start at a shallow
corner — roughly at the centre.
1   80ft   Climb the centre of the wall on clean, crystalline rock. Stance
below the edge of the cwm.
2   80ft   4a.   Move out right and climb the exposed edge of the
cwm,
loose.

Aornis   80ft   Severe   1968
The next feature to the right is a curved groove with a black right wall.
1   40ft   Climb the groove to a large perched flake. Step right then go
up to a ledge. Peg belays on the right.
2   40ft   Move back left 5 feet and follow the line of cracks above to
easy rock. Bear right to peg belays. To finish from here, scramble
diagonally left into the quarried basin or take the top pitch of St. Jude.

To the right is a steep wall terminated by the groove of Cocytus, and
right of this is an amber-coloured wall, set back slightly and shrouded
by a huge slanting roof.

Dumb Blonde   70ft   E3   1983
Climbs the left-hand of two weaknesses in the steep wall between
Aornis and Cocytus.
1   40ft   6a.   A hard, boulder problem start gives way to easier
climbing leading to the belay of Cocytus.
2   30ft   5b.   As for Cocytus.

American Express   70ft   E4   1984   ★★
The right-hand weakness — excellent.
1   40ft   6b.   Climb the wall via the vague groove to the second peg.
Layback the arête to the third peg, finishing left of a bulge.
2   30ft   5b.   As for Cocytus.

Cocytus   70ft   E2   1968   ★★
A superb little route, safe but testing, which takes the strikingly
smooth groove bounding the left side of the amber wall.
1   40ft   6a.   Climb the groove, two peg runners, to a stance on the
left.

2   30ft   5b.   Climb for a few feet, then traverse right across a slab and pull round a bulge into the continuation of the groove. Finish out left by an exposed layback. Peg belays 20 feet back on the left (shared with Aornis).

Blonde Bombshell   80ft   E5   1983   ★★
Excellent climbing with scant protection up the centre of the amber wall. Start 10 feet right of Cocytus, beneath a peg at 15 feet.
1   80ft   6b.   Climb to the peg and continue up the face to a red scoop. Move up on the right then back left to an overhung ledge. Climb the bulging wall above via a layback edge to reach better holds leading to the top. Belays back right.

Groove and Slab   120ft   E1   1976
An interesting climb running up just right of the huge overhang which shrouds the amber wall, some loose rock. Start about 25 feet right of Cocytus and 10 feet left of Acheron.
1   80ft   5b.   Climb to a ledge and ancient peg, then pull up into a groove. Climb the groove then hand-traverse a shelf leading righwards to a small ledge on the arête of Acheron's corner. Climb the slab direct to a horizontal crack, above which is a sharp-edged slanting crack forming the continuation of the line. Climb this and the slab above to the stance.
2   40ft   Step up and right onto a slab, then climb diagonally right to the top.

Acheron   130ft   Hard Very Severe   1968   ★
A fine route taking an impressive slanting corner above and to the right of the overhang which shrouds the reddish wall. Start by scrambling up a short groove to a chockstone belay right of the smooth initial corner.
1   80ft   5a.   Climb the corner to a sloping ledge beneath the overhang. Continue up the smooth, leftward-leaning corner, then move up and left across the slab to a good stance. Peg and low thread belays.
2   50ft   Climb up for 5 feet then traverse 30 feet right. Climb up left of bushes to the grass slope. Iron spike belays.

Lethe   95ft   Very Severe   1968
An exposed, but perhaps inferior variant to Acheron.
1   45ft   4c.   Take pitch 1 of Acheron as far as the overhang, then traverse right to a small stance and peg belay.
2   50ft   4b.   Climb the overhanging groove above. Swing left on reaching the roof then continue up to join Acheron near the top.

Right-hand Finish.
2a 30ft 4b. Step right into the bottom of a corner, which is climbed direct to the top (exposed).

Gut Bucket   40ft   Severe   1968
The chimney right of Acheron. Slightly better than it looks.

The Long Traverse   350ft   Very Difficult   1962   ★
This is a sea-level traverse running out to Long Quarry Point from Anstey's Cove. It is used to approach the Sanctuary Wall routes (from either direction) and is an enjoyable and popular climb in its own right (making a particularly good round trip via The Ridge and The Grey Tower). Start from the boulder beach and traverse on good holds to The Sanctuary, an impressive zawn which is very difficult to cross at high water. Continue beneath the Sanctuary Wall then skirt around the base of Quarry Pinnacle to reach Long Quarry Point. Alternatively, exit just before the pinnacle via a short steep wall (5a, 2 peg runners).

LONG QUARRY POINT   GR 937 651
This large headland encloses Anstey's Cove to the north. It basically consists of a flat, quarried platform about 20 feet above high water level, which is backed by two large cliffs of sharply contrasting character. To the right are large, grey, boiler-plate slabs and to the left a rather featureless wall, Quarry Wall. Seaward from this is the twin-summited Quarry Pinnacle, much diminished by a recent rockfall, while on the tip of the point is another broad pinnacle, Outer Pinnacle, which is easy-angled on three sides but has a steep seaward face. Descent to the point is by a steep path beginning in front of a prominent shelter on Walls Hill Downs (see map).

The first cliff described may be approached from either Anstey's Cove or Long Quarry Point, the former being easier at low tide and the latter easier at high tide.

SANCTUARY WALL
This is the large wall running out to Long Quarry Point from Anstey's Cove (i.e. overlooking the second half of the Long Traverse beyond The Sanctuary). It is acutely overhanging and provides some of the most spectacular and nerve-racking climbing in the area. The main feature of the cliff is a huge central fault which begins as a wide overhanging crack and becomes an open, vegetated corner higher up. The fault itself gives a poor route (**Cinqtus**, Hard Severe and A1), and a much finer one, Sacrosanct, up its right-hand edge. All climbs are approached via the Long Traverse.

Sacrosanct   120ft   Hard Very Severe   1969   ★★
A strenuous and exposed climb taking the crack-line in the right-hand edge of the central fault. Approach via the Long Traverse and belay in

a small corner about 30 feet above high tide level and 15 feet right of the wide crack/fault.
1 40ft 4c. Move up to a peg then make a strenuous leftward traverse to the wide crack. Climb to a large stance a few feet higher.
2 80ft 5a. Traverse right across the slab and climb its right edge to an exposed ledge. Climb the overhanging crack above to reach easier ground and the top. Difficult belay (pegs useful).

Call to Arms   130ft   E4   1980   ★★★
A route of 'grotesque steepness' following a superb line. The first weakness right of Sacrosanct is an open groove which overhangs sharply. Start beneath this.
1 80ft 5c. Climb the groove to reach a small stance in a larger groove coming in from the right (Incubus).
2 50ft 5c. Climb straight up above the stance by exposed bridging, passing the overhang on the right with difficulty. Trend rightwards above to belay on the iron spike.

Incubus Direct   140ft   E3   1970   ★★
A very strenuous pitch taking the sharply overhanging wall below the groove of Incubus. Start about 50 feet back along the Long Traverse from Quarry Pinnacle, at a disjointed crack and small arrow below and right of the groove.
1 70ft 5c. Climb for 15 feet and make a hard move to reach holds on the wall above. Climb bearing left to a peg and continue leftwards very steeply to gain a jutting ledge. Thread runner. Climb the smooth, slanting groove on the left to the stance of Incubus.
2 70ft 5a. As for Incubus.

Incubus   95ft   Hard Very Severe   1968   ★
An impressive and worthwhile route taking the leftward-slanting groove at the right-hand end of Sanctuary Wall. Start from Long Quarry Point, at a notch at the foot of The Ridge.
1 25ft 5a. Step down and traverse left on steep rock to take a stance on the slabby left wall of the groove.
2 70ft 5a. Climb the groove to the overhang. Pull round its left-hand side and move up the corner for a few feet until the sounder wall on the left can be climbed to finish. Peg belay useful.

Madness   250ft   E5   1983   ★★
The obvious soaring traverse line across the Sanctuary Wall. A phenomenal route giving very strenuous and intimidating climbing in positions of utter exposure. Approach via the Long Traverse (either from Anstey's Cove or Long Quarry) to the promontory forming the outer edge of The Sanctuary. Climb the slab above the promontory, moving to the left arête and up to easy ground. Continue scrambling to reach a belay spot near the start of the line.

1   60ft   5c.   Traverse to a groove with a good crack for protection. Continue rightwards along the shelf to a hanging stance at another corner.
2   80ft   5c.   Move around the corner and traverse to where the ledge ends at some suspect incuts. Swing down right and continue at a slightly lower level to a long overhung ledge. Move up from the right end of this to an obvious hold, then swing up and around the rib on the right. Descend until a crack on the right can be reached and climbed to a good stance (on Sacrosanct).
3   110ft   6a.   Move right and up the arête, as for Sacrosanct, to a small ledge (optional stance). Launch out across the traverse line, which becomes very difficult and strenuous, and follow it to join Incubus at its crux bulge. Climb leftwards to the top as for Incubus, or pass the bulge on the right finishing as for Call to Arms.

QUARRY PINNACLE
Since the rockfall this is now virtually two separate pinnacles, divided by a conspicuous corner. The long face of the higher pinnacle gives:

Afterglow   100ft   E1   1983
Start left of Storm Child, below the obvious line.
1   100ft   5a.   Climb trending slightly right until below the groove in the upper part of the face. Traverse left for 10 feet then go up and rightwards to the top.

Storm Child   50ft   Severe   1978
The central corner, a pleasant pitch. Start beneath it.
1   50ft   4b.   Move up left then go rightwards up a crack into the corner, which is followed to the top.

Sea Slip   55ft   Severe   1978
Takes the obvious curving groove in the right-hand pinnacle. Start among boulders at the foot of the pinnacle.
1   55ft   4a.   Climb an overhanging crack for a few feet then step left into the bottom of the groove. Take this and the wall above to the top. Starting the cracked slab further left makes the route Very Difficult.

Crêpes Suzettes   50ft   Very Severe   1978   ★
A pleasant climb up the seaward face of the right-hand pinnacle. Start at an overhanging crack.
1   50ft   4c.   Climb the crack strenuously then move left to a scoop. Climb out of the scoop delicately, following the very thin crack above to the top.

Flambé   45ft   Severe   1978
Start right of Crêpes Suzettes.
1   45ft   4a.   Climb the steep crack on to the slab then follow the thin crack above pleasantly to the top.

OUTER PINNACLE
The pinnacle on the tip of the point has a long seaward face.

Jumping Jack Flash   100ft   Very Severe   1968
Start at the left side of the pinnacle (facing seawards).
1   60ft   Traverse in about 15 feet above sea until a diagonal ascent can be made to a band of overhangs. Step down and across to a cave. Thread belays.
2   40ft   4c.   Climb a crack on the left until it is possible to move into the corner, peg runner. Climb this on layaways to steeper, white rock, where an escape left is made. (The original finish continued over the overhang, giving harder climbing — Hard Very Severe, 5a).

Alternative Start   40ft
Beginning on the other side of the pinnacle, slide down a slot in the rock about 15 feet from the sea. Climb diagonally right into the cave. Interesting.

High and Dry   90ft   E1   1968
A steep and nasty crux on suspect rock. Start as for Jumping Jack Flash.
1   40ft   Take the traverse of Jumping Jack Flash to make a stance on the slab beneath a rounded ramp running up left.
2   50ft   5a/b.   Climb the ramp and move delicately left to a good foothold. Move up left into the corner, peg runner, then step right and up with difficulty using undercuts, finishing with a hard move left to good jugs.

The other pinnacles around the edge of the basin give many short pitches, up to about 30 feet, which are enjoyable by virtue of their proximity to the sea, but not sufficiently important to warrant description.

THE RIDGE

The Ridge   70ft   Very Difficult
This is the rib above Quarry Pinnacle and overlooking Sanctuary Wall. It makes a good continuation for the Long Traverse, especially when combined with Grey Tower.
1   70ft   Move on the rib from the right and follow the crest to an area of bushes above the Sanctuary Wall. From here a thorny path wanders up and leftwards to the clifftop or the base of Grey Tower.

Grey Tower   60ft   Hard Severe   1964
A pleasant and exposed pitch taking the rib formed by the upper edge
of Quarry Wall. Approach via The Ridge and belay (peg in a borehole)
beneath a white rib.
1   60ft   4a.   Climb the white rib to the grey slab, peg runner. Follow
the right-hand edge of the slab to the top.

ICHOR SLAB
Right of The Ridge is a smooth-looking, dark grey slab giving three
short but interesting pitches.

Ikon   60ft   E2   1979   ★
A good pitch on clean solid rock. Start 15 feet left of Ichor,
below a thin crack.
1   60ft   5c.   Climb the crack to the overlap, move over this and
continue until footholds on the right can be reached. Finish direct.

Ichor   70ft   E2   1968   ★
The most obvious weakness on the slab, often rather grassy. Start
approximately in the centre of the slab, at a line of holds.
1   70ft   5b/c.   Climb for about 25 feet to a peg, then make a hard
move up and left to a thin crack, which leads with difficulty to a flat
handhold. Continue to the slanting grassy crack, which is followed,
moving right to a ledge at the top.

The Big 'Y'   70ft   E2   1983   ★
A line to the right of Ichor. Start on the arête.
1   70ft   5c.   Climb the arête until a rising traverse can be made to
clip the peg of Ichor. Move right along the undercut flake (crux, peg
runner). Climb the thin crack to finish.

Between Ichor Slab and the start of Cross Route is a rather lineless
area of slabby rock giving easy grade climbs.

QUARRY WALL
While undoubtedly of an esoteric nature this crag can offer good
sport to those prepared to 'give it a go'. Pegs (especially blades) and
hammer are standard equipment for most routes.

Cross Route   150ft   Severe   1969
A scrappy route. Start 20 feet to the left of The Magus and a few feet
right of a huge flake.
1   40ft   Scramble to a shallow groove and climb it to where it
steepens. Bear right for a few feet then move back left and up the left
wall of the corner to a stance. Peg belays.

2   70ft   Climb onto a calcite ledge then traverse right, making two big steps, to a small sloping ledge. Climb the block and wall above to a slab then traverse to a ledge below a large crack.
3   40ft   Cross the slab by a rising traverse on small footholds to the top.

The Magus   310ft   Hard Very Severe   1969   ★
A long and interesting expedition taking a line which appears to wander but is in fact largely natural. The pegs needed are mainly thin blades. Start at an obvious arrow half-way between the start of the Gilded Turd and the Ichor Slab and about 50 feet below a very big drill strike forming a shallow groove.
1   50ft   4a.   Climb more or less straight up, peg runner in a shothole, to a good stance and peg belays at the foot of the strike.
2   60ft   5a.   Move down right for 15 feet and pull right with difficulty to ledges. Move diagonally right for 20 feet, two peg runners, until a hard move gains a good ledge. Climb steeply up to another ledge containing an iron spike. Belay.
3   60ft   4b.   Go up left and awkwardly onto a larger ledge, peg runner. Traverse left along the slab, peg runner, and step down where it becomes a steeper ramp. Continue across left then move up to peg belays in the obvious slanting corner crack. A delightful pitch.
4   60ft   4c.   Move up to an earthy recess and step right onto a block, peg runner. Go up steeply to a ledge, peg runner, then move right and pull with difficulty onto a large terrace. Peg belay.
5   20ft   4c.   Move to the left end of the terrace and climb steeply on doubtful rock to the bushy slope. Go up 5 feet to a peg belay in a shothole at the foot of the white rib.
6   60ft   4a.   The Grey Tower. Climb the white rib to the grey slab, peg runners. Follow the right edge of the slab to the top. Exposed.

Steppenwolf   260ft   Hard Very Severe   1969   ★
An impressive route taking a direct line up the shallow rib bounding the open groove of Gilded Turd on the left, before being forced out right by the final tower. An arrow marks the start, which is about 30 feet left of the start of Gilgamesh and 50 feet left of The Gilded Turd.
1   80ft   4c.   Climb the rib for about 25 feet then step left to a borehole, peg runner. Continue left for a few feet then up to a small ledge, from where the overhanging left rib can be gained. Climb this, peg runner, until a line of undercuts leads right to another peg runner. Stance and peg belays above.
2   50ft   4c.   Go up Gilgamesh to the rib on the left of the layback crack, peg runner, from where a short traverse left gains a large doubtful flake. Climb over this leftwards then straight up to a cave stance.
3   40ft   4c.   The overhanging rib on the left is gained by an awkward pull and taken until a step right gains a stance and peg belays.

4   50ft   5a.   Move up right to a sloping ledge and climb a short wall to the top of the chimney on the girdle. Move strenuously right to the girdle stance. Thread belay.
5   40ft   5a.   Climb the overhanging crack above to reach a sloping ledge. Continue up a short groove to the top.

Direct Finish   E2   ★
An exciting pitch which greatly improves the route.
3a   70ft   5b.   Move up and right to beneath the final wall. Climb bearing left and make difficult moves to a good hold. Stand on this using a (dubious) peg above as a handhold, then climb directly up the steep wall until the angle eases. Step left to a slab leading pleasantly to the top.

Gilgamesh   280ft   Hard Very Severe   1969
Ascends a not-too-obvious buttress to the left of the Gilded Turd and just to the right of Steppenwolf, starting at an arrow and the letter 'G'. Peg runners used.
1   70ft   4b.   Work up trending left to a series of overlapping slabs. Move back slightly right to an overhung corner. Stance and peg belays above (shared with Steppenwolf).
2   70ft   4b.   Move up easily for a few feet then climb the corner and up to the large cave stance.
3   50ft   4b.   Traverse right for 20 feet, then move up and continue to the right to a corner below a red wall. Thread belays.
4   40ft   4c.   Traverse left across the red wall to a spike then climb strenuously up to the large ledge.
5   50ft   4a.   Take the obvious line out to the left over doubtful blocks to finish on the summit of the Grey Tower.

The Gilded Turd   210ft   Hard Very Severe   1969   ★★
A fine route taking an intricate line on the right-hand side of the quarried wall. Low in its grade but requires a certain 'cool' due to outward sloping holds and sparse protection. The start, marked by an arrow, is about half-way up the scree slopes, beneath a vague triangle of whitish rock.
1   90ft   4c.   Climb to the top of the white triangle, peg runner. Move a few feet right then diagonally left to a glacis, peg runner on left. Climb the steeper wall to good holds then go up left to a short corner, which leads to a good stance and peg belays.
2   70ft   4c.   Move 10 feet left then climb for 25 feet to a horizontal crack (peg runner). Step up awkwardly and climb a vague groove on the right with difficulty (peg runner) to a glacis. Move right then up left to a big stance. Peg belays
3   50ft   4a.   Traverse left to a shattered rib, which gives pleasant and exposed climbing to the top.

The Girdle Turd   320ft   Very Severe   1969
The obvious horizontal fault line at about two thirds height. Start at a crack formed by a large flake, near Cross Route, on the left end of the buttress.
1 80ft 4a.   Climb the crack to a rib, which leads to a small roof; traverse left under the roof until it is possible to pull into an overhang-capped groove. At the top exit left and up to a chockstone belay on the fault.
2 40ft 4b.   Follow the fault line rightwards to the third stance of The Magus.
3 80ft 4b.   Go up The Magus for a few feet, then traverse right on undercuts to a small ledge on the arête. Round this is the cave stance of Gilgamesh. Follow this route for 20 feet to a stance below a chimney.
4 40ft 4c.   Climb the chimney to a chockstone and step right onto a block. A grass ledge above to the right provides a stance and thread belay in the corner above.
5 80ft 4a.   The narrowing gangway on the right leads awkwardly to an iron spike, which is used to gain a ledge on the right. Walk along the ledge until it peters out, then step down and move right to a loose groove leading to the top.

THE SLABS
Despite tenacious vegetation in the cracks, the Slabs provide some excellent climbing, especially on the more open, harder lines. Protection is sometimes sparse and some of the rock is flaky and should be treated with caution. A nut pick is very useful for cleaning out nut runner placements.

Osram   80ft   Very Severe   1967   ★
A good pitch taking the clean-cut, curving corner formed by the junction of Quarry Wall with the slabs. Start beneath the corner.
1 80ft 5a.   Climb awkwardly for 15 feet, then step left to a ledge. Move up into the corner and follow it, large thread at the bulge, until beneath broken rock at the top. Go diagonally right on the slab and up to a grass terrace. Peg belays. To reach the top from here follow an indistinct path leftwards across the loose slope to near the top of the quarried wall. Or as a continuation one can do The Odyssey or pitch 2 of Ulysses.

Ulysses   170ft   E2   1969
A fine first pitch but with poor protection. Start as for Osram.
1 90ft 5b.   Climb Osram for about 30 feet and fix a good runner at the foot of the corner proper. Reverse 10 feet and climb across to a ledge on the right, peg runner. Move up to the obvious rising ramp, which is followed to a good foothold and poor peg runner. Go up to

another poor peg and make difficult moves to gain a line of sloping footholds. Follow these to where the angle eases. Bear left to peg belays.
2 80ft 5b.   Climb the slab above for 20 feet then traverse left to a peg runner. Move delicately up to good holds beneath the conspicuous short corner, peg runner. Exit right from the top of this, peg runner, then go straight up to the top on rather poor rock.

The Odyssey   185ft   Hard Very Severe   1969
A worthwhile continuation to Osram. Start at the peg belay above that climb.
1 110ft 5a.   Climb the steep slab to the obvious traverse line. Follow this rightwards on good holds for about 60 feet, until the cracks peter out, peg runner. Continue thinly right to the smooth niche of Jaywalk, peg belays.
2 75ft 5a.   Move diagonally left for 10 feet to a smooth rounded groove, peg runner. Climb the groove, delicate in places, to finish up easy-angled vegetated slabs.

Jaywalk   120ft   Very Severe   1969
An exposed and serious pitch offering an alternative finish to Grip Type Thynne. Start from the top stance of this route.
1 120ft 4b.   Make an exposed traverse left for 45 feet on vegetated rock at first, and move into a smooth scoop, peg runner. Move up right into a groove then follow the obvious line diagonally left to a white ledge where the slabs are less steep, peg runner. Climb up for 5 feet then diagonally left over grassy rock to the top.

Normal Hero   80ft   E3   1973
An alternative start to Grip Type Thynne, starting about 50 feet left of Ruby in the Dust, at a rightward traverse line across the steep wall.
1 80ft 5c.   Traverse right and slightly up for 30 feet to a thread runner. Traverse rightwards to the obvious block, move up 5 feet then make a 20-foot traverse to good holds beneath a bottomless corner. Climb this to the stance at the end of pitch 1 of Grip Type Thynne.

Ruby in the Dust   180ft   Very Severe   1973   ★
A pleasant route of singular character, following the conspicuous crack-line which rises across the slabs from left to right. Protection is sparse on the first pitch, where technical difficulty is not high, while on the second pitch the harder climbing is very well protected. Start some 40 feet left of he lowest point of the slabs, where the crack begins.
1 100ft 4b.   Follow the crack, sometimes using it for the feet, until it rounds a slight rib to an easier-angled, vegetated area. Narrow grass stance and peg belay.

2 80ft 4c.   Continue rightwards on a gently rising line for 40 feet to the edge of a smoother slab. Peg runner. Make a difficult high right step (peg runner above to protect the second), then continue more easily to the right to finish on the edge of the crag.

Black Ice   210ft   E3   1973   ★★★
An excellent direct route up the steep central mass of the slabs. Difficulties are sustained and the rock is generally clean and solid. Start at the extreme left end of the quarried wall at the base of the slabs.
1 120ft 5c.   Climb steeply to a protection peg then either make hard moves to better holds leading to a white scoop, or move right then climb leftwards to the scoop (easier). Step up to reach the rising traverse of Ruby in the Dust. Move a little right then climb the wall above for a few feet before traversing left (poor peg runner) to better holds. Climb bearing slightly right up a line of thin cracks to gain some ledges on the right with difficulty. Peg belay on the left.
2 90ft 5c.   Move right and climb to a narrow ledge, peg runner, and continue to the obvious horizontal crack which is followed leftwards on to the final steep wall. Move up until a crack can be reached high left, then a few steep moves gain easier ground.

Variation   5c
An alternative start has been made to the left of the one described, following a thin crack which rises diagonally right to the scoop

Grip Type Thynne   300ft   E1   1968   ★
A long and fine route despite a smattering of vegetation. It takes a natural oblique line on the slabs. Start about 20 feet right of the extreme left end of the quarried wall at the base of the slabs.
1 130ft 5b.   Climb to the top of the short wall then follow the slab diagonally left, peg runner, and move with difficulty into a white scoop, peg runner above. Climb up to good holds in the grassy crack, move a little right then climb the wall above for a few feet before traversing left (poor peg runner) to better holds where the angle eases (as for Black Ice). Climb diagonally left to a grassy ledge. Peg and spike belays.
2 30ft 5a.   Step up then traverse right for 10 feet and move delicately up to good holds. Go diagonally left to the large grass band and move right along this to good peg belays just left of the wide curving crack.
3 80ft 4c.   Pull up into the crack. Climb this then up over grass to a clean grey slab. Traverse left across the slab then diagonally left over more vegetation to a large grassy stance.
4 60ft 5a.   Above and to the left of the stance is a ramp leading onto the exposed final wall. Climb the ramp and pull onto the wall. Step right then up on good holds, moving steeply right to the top.

Band of Rusty Gold   280ft   Hard Very Severe   1973
A devious route, not recommended. Start below a red scar near the top of the quarried wall at the base of the slabs.
1   80ft   Take the easiest line to below the red scar. Traverse right and up to the peg belay of Coup de Grâce.
2   30ft   Traverse left along vegetated ledges, past the next slab line, to a peg belay under a steep wall.
3   90ft   4b.   Climb the wall onto the slab, and follow it leftwards to below a white scoop. Climb the wall above to the peg belay and small stance of Safari.
4   30ft   4c.   Traverse right to the high step of Coup de Grâce and the end of pitch 2 of that climb.
5   50ft   5a.   Traverse left for about 30 feet to a difficult move up into an easy groove. Climb this to a peg belay. Scramble to the top.

Coup de Grâce   210ft   Very Severe   1967   ★
The original route of the slabs and still worthwhile, although the main pitch is split by a band of vegetation. Start beneath the highest point of the quarried wall, some 30 feet from its right edge.
1   80ft   Climb the wall to a large grass ledge. Move left to belay on pegs beneath a slab running up to the left.
2   90ft   5a.   Climb up a flake to a peg runner at hand level then make a thin traverse left to good holds. Move easily up the slab, bearing left, until the flake crack thins and curves over, peg runner. Make a high right step onto the smooth slab, move up, peg runner, then traverse 10 feet right to a ledge. Move onto the ledge above, peg belays (escape is possible from here).
3   40ft   4c.   Step back to the lower ledge then move up left to beneath the bulge. Over this and the perched flakes above to move left beneath the final overhang; exposed. Easily up right to the top.

Magic Carpet Ride   160ft   Very Severe   1969
Takes the smooth slab right of Coup de Grâce. Rather grassy but pitch 2 gives sustained and quite serious climbing. Start about 15 feet in from the right-hand end of the quarried wall, at an arrow.
1   75ft   Climb to a thin crack then leftwards up a ramp. Follow a vague groove to grassy rock then a grass stance. Peg belays.
2   85ft   4c.   Go straight up to another grass ledge, peg runner. Step up and delicately left to good holds. Continue left for 10 feet then follow a line of thin cracks and holds, past a prominent peg runner, to the top.

Transference   310ft   E1   1973
A low level traverse of the Slabs, from right to left. Start at the right-hand side of the quarried wall.
1   100ft   Cross the quarried wall at about half-height to a stance and peg belay below and right of a large prominent flake.

2 60ft 5a.   Climb up and left to the flake. Traverse left and belay on joining Ruby in the Dust.
3 80ft 5b.   Climb the wall above for 10 feet then traverse left with difficulty past a protection peg to join Grip Type Thynne, which is followed diagonally left to a stance.
4 70ft 5a.   Move to the left end of the ledge then climb down and step left into a niche. Move up and traverse left into the large corner fault and either climb this or scramble down the grass.

Safari   555ft   Hard Very Severe   1969   ★★
Traverses the whole of the Slabs from right to left. A fine expedition and pleasantly sustained. After pitch 4 it may be preferable to finish up Grip Type Thynne. Start as for Magic Carpet Ride.
1 75ft   As for Magic Carpet Ride.
2 70ft 4c.   Take the traverse of Magic Carpet Ride, but when that route begins to climb vertically continue traversing left for a further 20 feet, peg runner, until steep climbing on good holds leads to the second stance of Coup de Grâce.
3 70ft 4c.   Traverse left for 15 feet, peg runner, then step down and reverse the 'high right step' of Coup de Grâce to a peg runner. Continue more or less horizontally left for 30 feet, two peg runners, then step down and traverse to a large white ledge. Peg belays.
4 60ft 5a.   Left of the ledge is a sharp flake which should be treated with respect. Go along this until it peters out then thin moves lead to better holds on a smooth ramp on pitch 2 of Grip Type Thynne. Go leftwards up the ramp to the grass stance.
5 80ft 4c.   Pitch 3 of Grip Type Thynne to the large grassy stance. Now either finish up pitch 4 of Grip Type Thynne (5a) or:
6 50ft 4a.   Traverse horizontally left as for Jaywalk to take a stance in the smooth scoop. Peg belays.
7 150ft 5a/b.   This pitch combines parts of The Odyssey and Ulysses. Move down left for 5 feet, then thin moves horizontally left gain good holds on the obvious traverse line, peg runner. Follow this for some 60 feet quite easily then delicately again for 20 feet to a peg runner. Climb up with difficulty to the foot of the conspicuous short corner, peg runner. Climb this and exit right, peg runner, then climb straight up to the top taking care with the rock. Iron stake belays near the edge.

BABBACOMBE CRAGS   GR 934 653
This is a jumble of crags between Long Quarry Point and Babbacome Beach. They offer private, secluded climbing even in the height of summer and the routes are interesting and worthwhile, though some show signs of neglect. Approach to the first big grey cliff is made via a traverse which starts about three quarters of the way down the path to Long Quarry Point. Begin by scrambling up a wide crack then a narrow grass ledge leads to a cave, from which the way down is

obvious. Descent can also be made by the gully on the left side of the cliff, the top of which is reached by descending the grass slope about 20 yards north of the white shelter.

Snoopy   150ft   Very Severe   1969
Takes the area of dark grey slab right of the gully. Start at the sycamore tree.
1   70ft   Climb easily for 40 feet, peg runner, then traverse right along the smooth slab to a good stance. Peg belays.
2   40ft   4b.   Traverse back left 15 feet at a higher level and move awkwardly onto a good foothold, peg runner. Move up to a borehole, slot in peg for runner, and continue straight up to a sloping stance at another borehole, peg belays.
3   40ft   4b.   Move up to a groove then up right for 5 feet, peg runner. Traverse left round the bulge and follow the groove (care with rock) until the angle eases. Belay on pegs.

Love Not War   255ft   Hard Very Difficult   1967   ★
This follows the large, grey, vegetated buttress which begins as a rib. An enjoyable route with fine situations and uniquely weathered holds on the upper pitches. Start at the foot of the rib, on a terrace 10 feet above the sea.
1   50ft   Climb the rib (loose and exposed), or the open corner on its left, to a large ledge. Peg belays.
2   25ft   Climb the wall left of the vegetation to a ledge. High thread belays.
3   60ft   Go diagonally left on the obvious line then back right to a narrow stance.
4   120ft (30 feet of rock climbing).   Go diagonally right for 15 feet, overlooking the sea, then up to a terrace. Aim for the ash tree ahead and scramble over shrubs to reach it. Belay.
The way off is left of the white buttress above.

Original Finish   Hard Severe
A less pleasant finish, not in keeping with the rest of the route.
4a   100ft   Climb about 6 feet and exit from the face by traversing left over loose rock. Climb and scramble up through a small ash tree to good thread belays on the left.

The Exile   70ft   E2   1971
Lies on a short wall right of the top of the Love Not War buttress, reached by descending the grass slope about 50 yards north of the white shelter on the Downs. Start beneath the large depression 20 feet up.
1   70ft   5b.   Climb the bulging wall into the depression then move rightwards to another resting place. Continue bearing slightly right to

a good handhold, then climb straight up the wall using small pockets. Tree belay well back.

To the right of the Love Not War buttress is an impressive, overhanging wall taken by The Wake, beyond which lower walls lead to the next group of crags at the reappearance of a backshore. The quickest approach to this area is to use the car-park at the Babbacombe end of Walls Hill Downs, then to walk down the private road until it curves down to the left, at which point one goes straight on through a gate to a flat scrubby area — the top of an old rubble tip. A steep muddy path runs down the seaward side of the tip then swings right to the grassy platform beneath the cliffs. The top of the rubble tip can also be reached in a few minutes by taking the clifftop path from the shelter above Long Quarry Point. A better approach (once located) is by descending the grass slope about 200 yards north of the shelter above Long Quarry Point to the top of a gully identified by a small tree a short way down (not to be confused with a much steeper gully 50 yards to the south). This tree is the belay for Neophron and is so far back from the clifftop that it is worth fixing a loop of rope from it before starting the climb. A vague path continues down the gully, via a short smooth corner, to the flat grass area at the base of the crags.

The Kraken   700ft   E1   1969
A sea-level traverse linking the cliffs near the rubble tip to Long Quarry Point. A difficult and interesting traverse if climbed 'clean', but the crux areas are short and easily overcome by swimming or rope moves. Start at low tide, or just before. Easy climbing from the end of the boulder-beach leads to a smooth corner. Cross the top of this (4b) or 'boulder hop' at very low tide. Continue more easily past inlets, to the base of a larger, overhanging cliff. Step onto an overhanging wall from a high boulder and pull leftwards to better holds leading round an arête onto a slab (5b, strenuous). Continue to a steep wall, which is traversed using small pockets (4c). Go up on good holds then descend leftwards to an overhanging nose, which is passed by hard climbing, (5b) gaining the platform beneath 'Love Not War'. Cross the platform then traverse on excellent rock about 20 feet above the sea to a small ledge above a cave (4b). Step up and follow a crack leading down leftwards to slabby rock (4c). Continue traversing (moves of 4c) to the smooth-looking plateau wall of Long Quarry Point. Traverse the base of this for some 60 feet then climb to level ground.

The Wake   130ft   E2   1976   ★
A remote climb on the imposing cliff half-way along The Kraken traverse. Pitch 2 gives fine climbing in a good position, while the first pitch is fierce and strenuous. Approach by traversing the first 250 feet of The Kraken (two hours either side of low water in a calm sea) to the

impending wall at the start of the real difficulties. An overhanging groove rises above a tall boulder beneath the wall.
1   30ft   5b.   Step off the boulder and climb for 10 feet to a large flat flake. Move up to a rightward-slanting crack and climb this, exiting left to a spacious stance. Nut belays.
2   70ft   5b.   Climb the open groove above the right-hand end of the stance to reach some sloping ledges. Move right and follow the obvious diagonal crack strenuously to a resting position where it ends. Pull round a bulge to good holds in a steep groove leading to another spacious stance. Nut belays.
3   30ft   4c.   The obvious corner behind the stance, then 30 feet of steep scrambling to a tree belay.

The two main outcrops of the Babbacombe Crags are a steep, dark crag at the base of the rubble tip and the bulging, white Neophron cliff about 40 yards to the left. The left side of the latter has recently suffered a large rockfall and starting the following climb may be tricky to say the least.

Fear of Flying   190ft   E3   1976
After a dirty start this gives interesting, steep climbing along the rising traverse line beneath the rim of the cliff. Start near the left end of the Neophron cliff.
1   100ft   5c.   Traverse in from the left along muddy ledges, heading for a shallow groove with a prominent peg and sling at its top. From the peg traverse right with difficulty to another peg then move up to excellent holds above a bulge. Continue rightwards to a big flake, which is traversed with care before descending to a stance. Peg belays.
2   90ft   5c.   Climb diagonally right past a peg runner to reach big holds on sharply bulging rock. Climb slightly left and up to a pocket hold beneath an overhang, then make a long reach right and traverse to a resting place at a large crack. Very strenuous. Continue to a deep slanting slot, then move down and across the wall of Iconoclast. Follow Iconoclast up and across its traverse, then continue traversing to join the final crack of Neophron.

Iconoclast   80ft   E2   1969   ★★
A strenuous and exposed pitch taking the impressive corner which bounds the bulging buttress of Neophron on the left. Start by scrambling up to a short awkward wall which leads to a spike belay (tape) at the foot of the corner.
1   80ft   5b.   Climb to a bulge at 30 feet, which is passed with difficulty. Continue to the top of the corner, then make a difficult rising traverse to the right for 10 feet to a good hold. Climb the short wall above until at the top a step left can be made to a reasonable exit onto the grass.

Neophron   120ft   E3   1969   ★★
An excellent route whose upper part provides steep, sustained climbing. On the bulging white wall is a line of three grooves forming a boomerang shape. Start behind the largest tree in the clump at the foot of the wall.
1   30ft   4a.   Climb a few feet then traverse 10 feet right. Go up the wall, peg runner, to a ledge. Move up right then back left to a stance. Peg belays (may not be in place).
2   90ft   5c.   Make a rising traverse left to beneath an area of unusual crystal rock. Step up right, peg runner (probably not in place), then move up awkwardly to a peg above a shelf of white rock. Steep and difficult climbing rightwards across the wall gains the bottom of the first groove. Climb the wall above and continue up the second groove to a big hold and tiny spike runner at its top. Layback round left into the final groove and follow the crack in its right wall to the top. Tree belay well back (fix beforehand or pull up one rope).

Quantum of Solace   60ft   Severe   1967
A pleasant route on sound rock. At the foot of the rubble tip is a steep grey face with a crack in the centre of it. Start 10 feet right of the crack.
1   60ft   Climb to ledges then move left into the crack, which is followed to the top. Tree belay.

Krapp's Last Fake   90ft   Very Severe   1968   ★
Right of Quantum is another wall set back slightly. Steep and very well protected. Start some 30 feet right of the start of Quantum.
1   50ft   Follow the cleanest line to a stance and peg belays in an earthy bay.
2   40ft   5a.   Move up onto the ledge on the left, peg runner. Make a very awkward move into the corner and follow it to finish by a step left over the rib.

Fake's Last Krapp   120ft   Hard Very Severe and A1   1968
An exposed route taking a shallow groove on the projecting buttress right of Krapp's Last Fake.
1   50ft   As for Krapp's Last Fake.
2   70ft   5a.   Move up into another bay on the right. Use a peg to place another in the irregular crack on the left. In the same crack use another peg and three nuts for aid, then pull into the groove on finger-jams. Move up right to a thread, step back into the groove, peg runner, and climb it to the rib, which leads to easy ground. Peg or tree belay well back.

All That Fall   100ft   Hard Very Severe   1969   ★
The best route on the buttress: direct, exposed, and well protected. Start as for Krapp's Last Fake.

1 50ft 5a.   Climb for 10 feet then rightwards across the slab to the foot of the obvious right-angled groove. A hard move starts the groove, which is followed to a good stance and peg belays.
2 50ft 5a/b.   Pull over the roof strenuously (peg runner) into the open groove. Climb this then straight up the wall above to exit right at the top. Peg belays.

The first reasonable rock southward from Babbacombe beach is a squarish buttress with a cave on the right and a chimney on the left. The chimney gives **Siddaw Bwurda** (80ft, Very Difficult).

PETIT TOR POINT, ODDICOMBE   GR 927 662
Torquay's most northerly limestone outcrop; well seen from Long Quarry Point or the Babbacombe Crags.
   Easy traversing northwards from Oddicombe Beach leads to a quarried basin whose edge forms a narrow cliff about 80 feet high. Its base is seawashed at high tide and can be reached by steep traversing from either direction or by a short abseil at the northern side.

Cunard Line   200ft   Hard Severe   1979
A natural traverse line running from left to right across the cliff. Start at a scoop just above the sea, beside the steep rib that bounds the crag on the left.
1 120ft 4a.   Step up until steep moves can be made around the rib to a ledge on the large slab beyond. Traverse along a discontinuous ledge system to the belay of Deadline, beneath the slabby upper wall.
2 80ft 4b.   Step up to a scoop and traverse right along a ramp. Move up for a few feet then continue rightwards for 40 feet until it is possible to gain the top and a tree belay 20 feet above.

Deadline   110ft   Very Severe   1971
Start some 20 feet left of a low cave, at a faint weakness in the steep initial wall.
1 40ft 4c.   Climb the wall to the large horizontal fault and traverse left along this to a stance beneath the slabby upper wall. Peg belays.
2 70ft 4b.   Move up to the rightward-slanting line and follow this for 15 feet to crystal pockets, peg runner. Go straight up to a ledge (peg runner), then climb for 5 feet and traverse left to a large foothold, peg runner. Move up to the roof then step left and up a short rib to the top.

Minor Crags

Hazard Quarry

GR 755 592

An esoteric crag but with some climbing of interest, it lies roughly 3 miles west of Totnes, just off the B3210. The turn-off is marked Hazard Farm, and permission to climb must be obtained here. A short drive along a twisty Lane leads to a parking spot at a disused limekiln, behind which is the cliff.

The quarry is about 300 yards long and 120 feet high, the central feature being an enormous overhang obove a shattered-looking, black-streaked wall. Left of the overhang is a blunt rib with a tree at 70 feet. The rib is bounded on the left by a slabby and somewhat vegetated wall. Some routes have become overgrown and are not fully described.

The left end of the slabby wall is taken by **Meadow Fly** (120 ft, Very Severe, 4c, 1979), which climbs up and left to an overhang then finishes up an arête on the left.

Green Ranger   115ft   Hard Very Severe   1979
Start roughly in the centre of the slabby wall.
1 50ft 4b.   Climb up to obvious cracks. Step right then climb straight up past a small oak tree on the left before traversing left to a tree belay.
2 65ft 4c.   Continue up behind the tree on small holds to gain a sloping ledge. Move up left to reach a superb thread then climb the groove and edge awkwardly to exit by a large tree. This pitch is sparsely protected

Two routes climb the obvious cracks and caves right of Green Ranger. The left-hand line is taken by **Twilight** (Very Severe, 4c, 1979) and the right-hand crack is **Pastoral** (Very Severe, 4c, 1979).

Dumnonia   120ft   Hard Very Severe   1978
Start at the bottom of the blunt rib left of the overhang, beneath a vague groove.
1 70ft 5a.   Climb past the loose block at 15 feet then move right to good runners in a crack. Move back left then step up to the first shale band. Climb boldly to the tree in the large groove.
2 50ft 4b/c.   Climb the groove and wall until it is possible to move onto the edge. Step onto the slab and follow this to the top.

Samurai   90ft   E2/3   1979
A fine and commiting route which climbs the right-hand of the two overhanging prows, on its left-hand side. Start at good cracks right of an elder tree.
1 90ft 5c.   Climb the deep cracks until it is possible to traverse left on good undercut jams. Step down to a small hold by a shothole, then difficult moves lead to a huge thread on the arête. Surmount this and the slab above to the top.

A number of climbs have been made on the walls right of Samurai, the best being **Haphazard** (Hard Severe, 1979), which climbs the centre of the obvious slabs, finishing left of the overhang.

Galmpton Quarry   GR 876 561

An extensive quarry offering pleasant lower-grade climbing and considerable potential for more routes in the middle grades. The rock is rather featureless so the climbs are somewhat lacking in protection, however the friction is excellent, the limestone sound, and the cliff is a sheltered sun-trap.

All the climbs are on the Main Face, which is bounded on the left by an unclimbed rib and on the right by a vegetated corner.

Port Tack   90ft   Very Severe   1966
Start at the left side of the face, just right of a bramble gully.
1 90ft 4b.   Climb the wall past an oak sapling at 20 feet. Make a gentle traverse right then a long leftward traverse about 10 feet from the top.

The Main Mast   90ft   Severe   1966
This takes a vertical line in the centre of the face.
1 50ft   Climb up to the right on good sloping ledges to a stance.
2 40ft   Climb the wall into a shallow groove, which leads to an earthy exit.

The Final Taxi   110ft   E1   1984
Unprotected but with sound rock and good holds. Start about 10 feet left of a large tree on the right of the Main Face.
1 110ft 4c.   Climb up to the left on clean rock to a small bush at two thirds height – the last runner. Climb the wall above for 25 feet then move right and finish on the edge.

Up The Creek   60ft   Severe   1984
Start as for The Final Taxi.
1   60ft   Follow the obvious dark band directly to the top.

The Ropeway   60ft   Severe   1966
Start behind the large tree, 10 feet right of The Final Taxi.
1   60ft   Climb the open scoop, angling left, to a good belay.

Slipway   60ft   Severe   1966
Start some 20 feet right of The Ropeway.
1   60ft   Climb angling slightly left, parallel to The Ropeway, moving
left at the top to belay as for that climb.

Chipley Quarry   GR 807 722

This lies about 4 miles west of Newton Abbot on the A383 near
Bickington. On the map it is under the letter 'p' in the word Chipley.
The face opposite the quarry entrance reaches a maximum height of
80 feet and the rock is igneous, possibly akin to dolerite.

Isca   60ft   E1   1983
The best climb on the face taking the leftward-slanting crack in the
centre.
1   60ft   5b.   Follow the crack till under the overhang (peg runner).
Step left with difficulty and layback the crack for a few feet until better
holds lead to a large ledge. Tree belay on top.

Ivy Route   45ft   Hard Severe   1983
Start 15 feet right of Isca, at a quartz-lined hole in the rock. Climb a
rib for 15 feet and step right to a large ledge. Finish directly up the
wall.

At the extreme right of the face are **Doing a Dalby** (Very Difficult, 1983),
which takes a prominent crack, and **Dalby** (Very Difficult, 1983) on the
short wall to its right.

Torbryan Quarry   GR 825 665

Famine (60ft, E2, 5b, 1980) is the obvious cleaned line on the right-hand
side of this very isolated quarry.

The Ladram Bay Stacks

GR 096 850

A unique area, which consists of a number of offshore pinnacles, the bases of which are cut off the the sea at high tide. The pinnacles are composed of new red sandstone, giving climbing which is serious but entertaining. Various methods of protection are available but a selection of ice pegs and 'drive-ins' will be found very useful. Most of the pinnacles can be approached on foot at low tide but is maybe necessary to swim or wade back to Ladram Bay if one's timing is wrong. The absence of belays on the summits can pose a problem, particularly when rigging descents. Simultaneous (see-saw) abseils are probably the safest.

Big Picket Rock   140ft   Very Severe   1971   ★★
The classic ascent of the area. Start beneath the south face.
1 60ft   Climb up leftwards on easy ledges then back right to a cave.
2 30ft   Climb above the cave, exiting right onto a steep wall with cut holds. Follow a ledge rightwards to a stance.
3 50ft   Traverse right and then climb a groove to the summit plateau. Descend is by a simultaneous abseil.

Lost World   60ft   Hard Severe   1971
Start at the south side of the seaward nose.
1 30ft   Climb a steep wall, exiting left, past a rusty six-inch nail, to a large shelf.
2 30ft   Climb the corner crack above to easy slopes leading to the summit forest.

Bonetti Tower   80ft   E2   1971
1 40ft   Climb the slab on the seaward face.
2 40ft   Climb the corner above with great care and difficulty (previously aided). Descent by simultaneous abseil.

The Razor   90ft   Hard Severe   1971
1 20ft   Climb the short wall at the seaward arête.
2 40ft   Traverse left by a stomach-crawl and then climb the wall above to big ledges.
3 30ft   Climb the corner behind and the earth arête to the razor sharp summit. Return to the second stance to abseil off.

Tower of Babel   50ft   Severe   1971
Start beneath the seaward face.
1 30ft   Climb the steep wall using a six-inch nail for aid, then step left onto a large terrace.
2 Climb the corner above to the flat summit.

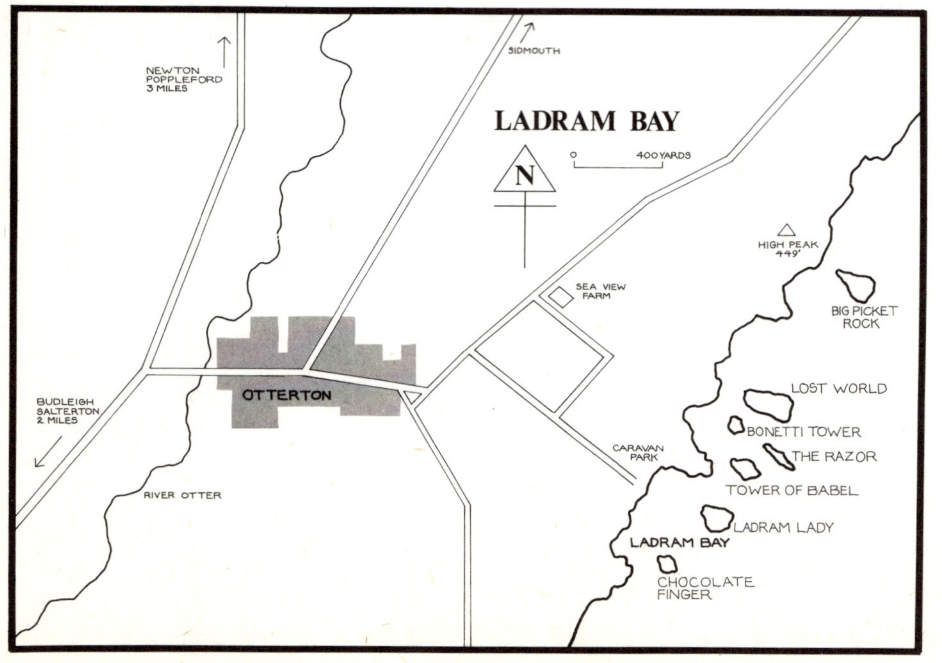
SIDMOUTH
NEWTON POPPLEFORD 3 MILES
LADRAM BAY
N
0   400 YARDS
HIGH PEAK 449'
SEA VIEW FARM
BIG PICKET ROCK
BUDLEIGH SALTERTON 2 MILES
OTTERTON
LOST WORLD
BONETTI TOWER
THE RAZOR
CARAVAN PARK
TOWER OF BABEL
RIVER OTTER
LADRAM LADY
LADRAM BAY
CHOCOLATE FINGER

Ladram Lady   60ft   Very Difficult   1968
Best approached by boat. Climb the seaward wall for 15 feet to a large ledge. Walk left and scramble up steep mud to the summit.

Chocolate Finger   80ft   Very Severe   1971
Start on the south side of the pinnacle near the second nose.
1   50ft   Follow a series of ledges leading up to the prominent platform at two thirds height.
2   30ft   Climb the wall above easily.

Sandy Bay   GR 036 798

This lies between Exmouth and Budleigh Salterton. On the west side of Straight Point is a double stack close up to the cliff. The northern portion is a natural arch. Traverse from Sandy Bay to the ledge at the base of the pinnacles.

Kamin Number 5   50ft   Very Difficult   1972
This climbs the narrow chimney between the stacks, and though it looks desperate is in fact very easy.
1   50ft   Follow the chimney and then bridge up the final chimney to either summit. Descend by simultaneous abseil over the natural arch on the higher of the two stacks.

The Parson and Clerk   GR 960 747 Sheet 192

The Parson is the large stack adjoining the cliff between Dawlish and Teignmouth. The Clerk, which is just offshore and reached by swimming or by boat, gives a climb of Severe.
   To approach The Parson descend a narrow lane to the sea to the south of the headland formed by the stack. Go through the railway tunnel, which is approximately 400 yards long. Abseil from the embankment to the beach and traverse to the foot of The Parson. Climb the wall on the landward side to a ledge with a rusty iron spike. From there lassoo a similar spike on The Parson proper. Traverse left to the seaward face.

The Parson   140ft   E3   1971
Bold and serious but a classic route demanding a cool head and a skilful use of loose rock.
1   50ft   Climb the seaward arête to large ledges under an enormous overhang.

2   50ft   Traverse right to the Brown Spider, a mud slope below a prominient corner, which leads to a saddle. No belay.
3   40ft   Climb the wall above the saddle to he summit. Jump to the mainland.

The Clerk   60ft   Severe   1974
There is a curious hole at two thirds height.
1   40ft   Climb the south-west arête to a shoulder. Thread the hole for a belay.
2   20ft   Climb the arête above to the summit.

Pilchard Cove   GR 843 465

This cliff is situated half-way between Dartmouth and Torcross on the A379, near the village of Strete. The rock is sandstone and the climb takes the prominent groove at the back of the cove. The beach is used by naturists in summer.

Pilchard Groove   120ft   Hard Severe   1979
1   85ft   4b.   Climb the prominent cleaned corner, via thin cracks in the slab, to a stance and nut belays.
2   35ft   4a.   Pull around the arête above the stance to a tottery ledge. Traverse right to block belays, taking care with friable rock.

Steeple Cove   GR 705 637 Sheet 202

This is near Salcombe between Bolt Head and Bolt Tail. Several traverses have been made in this area; there may well be more climbing potential.

The Steeple   80ft   Severe   1970
The wall behind the boulder bridge is climbed, then a traverse right is made onto the seaward face. Very poor rock.

Steeple Slab   300ft   Very Difficult   1982
Approach as for The Steeple. Start below a vague line of weakness roughly in the middle of the grassy slab facing the pinnacle. Climb straight up the slab, with no protection and a poor belay at half-height.

The next stack lies some 325 yards south-east of Soar Mill Cove. Approach by descending an earthy gully directly opposite the stack and then by a boulder-bridge to gain a platform on the seaward face.

Erotica   75ft   Hard Severe   1977
A serious route. Climb an open groove on the right to gain a niche. Move left and climb direct to the summit. Descent is by simultaneous abseil.

The nearby outcrops at Soar Mill Cove and Hazel Tor (GR 698 375) offer a number of climbs and some decent bouldering.

Bolt Tail   GR 667 397

Approach by parking cars in Hope Cove then crossing the mouth of the stream. These two climbs lie on the cliff which lies below the coastguard lookout and the island/rock called Bury Rock. Descent is down a gully just south of some large boulder lying between Bury Rock and the cliff.

Flaked Out   85ft   Very Severe   1970
Start opposite the col on Bury Rock, below a layback crack.
1 50ft 4c.   Climb up to and follow the crack diagonally right until the wall overhangs. Climb past a right-facing bulge and mantelshelf onto a ledge. Continue up to the left to a ledge and belay.
2 35ft 4c.   Traverse left passing a corner and then an overhang to a gully. Climb up to the sharp arête and finish by traversing the slab on the left. Scramble to finish.

Helter   80ft   Severe   1970
Start 30 feet right of the previous route. Climb the slab diagonally right by the easiest line.

Hope Cove   GR 673 397

The next climb lies on the impressive-looking slab some 400 yards west of the village of Hope. Descent is down a path just before the slab.

Hopeful   140ft   Severe   1983
Climb the centre of the slab to a horizontal break, then follow a shallow depression to a grassy groove near the top.

Bigbury Bay   GR 659 434

Between Bantham and Thurlestone, on the east side of the estuary stands a most unusual pinnacle. It can be reached at low to half tide. Approach from Bantham car-park.

Bantham Hand   30ft   Very Severe   1974
Climb the steep slab of the North Face, trending left from the base to a depression in the middle of the face, then go right to the summit ridge.

St. Anchorites Rock   GR 591 473

This isolated rock is situated between Mothecombe and Noss Mayo, it lies on the coastal footpath.

Far from the Madding Crowd   60ft   Hard Severe   1981
Start below the large slabby face on the north side of the rock.
1   60ft   4a.   Climb the slab via cracks to a steep groove, which leads to a 'juggy' finish.

First Ascents

The number of points of aid known to have been used on a first ascent are given in brackets after the names of climbers. (Aid) indicates that the route or a section of it was climbed with continuous aid.

The abbreviations (AL) and (VL) indicate alternate and varied leads respectively. The presence of only one name does not necessarily denote a solo ascent.

THE DEWERSTONE

1935 Sept. 2	**Climbers' Club Original** D. Cox, R. Bere	
	By the Original Finish	
1936 June 27	**Climbers' Club Direct** R. Hodgkin, D. Cox.	
	After pitch 1 they followed what is now the Ordinary. Pitch 2 was climbed by G. Whittaker in September 1950 as part of a Super Direct. The top crack was first climbed direct by J. Deacon in 1959 as part of Globe and Laurel. The Super Direct Start was climbed by B. Page in 1957	
1948 Summer	**Colonel's Arête** J. Moulton (solo)	
1949 Jan. 22	**Route B** K. Lawder, R. Higgins (VL)	
1949 Jan. 28	**Pinnacle Buttress** R. Higgins, K. Lawder (VL)	
1949 Jan. 28	**Pinnacle Chimney** R. Higgins, K. Lawder (VL)	
1949 Jan. 28	**The Tunnel** K. Lawder	
1949 Feb. 5	**Central Groove** J. Simpson	
1949 Feb. 5	**Needle Arête** J. Simpson (solo)	
1949 Feb. 26	**Raven Face** R. Higgins	
1949 April 30	**Reverse Cleft** W. Higgins, R. Higgins (AL)	
1949	**The Admiral's Traverse**	
	This name originally referred to the short traverse on pitch 3 but the name is now used for the complete girdle in recognition of the exploration of the crag done by Admiral Lawder. The pitches were climbed at different times by K. Lawder, G. Whittaker and W. Higgins	
1949	**The High Traverse** K. Lawder, R. Higgins	
1950 June 25	**Agag's Slab** J. Derry	
1950 July 23	**Saint's Niche** J. Goss	
1950 Dec. 9	**Sloppy Gully** R. Smith, J. Goss	
1952 June 1	**Vineyard** W. Dowlen, J. Smith (VL)	
1952 June 1	**Armada** J. Smith, W. Dowlen (VL)	
1957 May 1	**Corner Chimney** B. Page, P. Henry	
1957 Sept.	**Leviathan** T. Patey	
	The direct finish to pitch 1 was climbed by A. McFarlane, D. Ballin 1969	
1958 March	**Scorpion** T. Patey	
1958 April	**Windowsill** T. Patey	
1958 Nov. 4	**In Extremis** T. Patey	
1958 Nov. 17	**Silken Thread** T. Patey	
1959 May	**Spider's Web** T. Patey, B. Page, P. Henry	
	The present finish was added by J. Jones	
1959 Sept. 30	**Globe and Laurel** J. Deacon, S. Jarvis, V. Stevenson (3pts.)	
1960 July	**La Bête Noire** R. Griffith, M. Rabley (1pt.)	
	First free ascent in 1977 by P. O'Sullivan, C. George	
1960 Aug.	**Babylon** M. Rabley, B. Shackleton	
1962 Jan.	**Valhalla Wall** M. Rabley, B. Shackleton (AL)	
1962 May 19	**Inkspots Hangover** D. Bassett, J. Barry	
1962 Dec.	**Gideon** M. Rabley, J. Jones (Aid)	
	Climbed free in 1969 by L. Benstead, D. Morrod	
1962	**Cretin's Cavort** M. Rabley	

1963	**Vala** B. Shackleton, R. Mellor
1963	**Cornish Reprieve** R. Mellor, R. Moulton (1pt.)
1964	**Knucklecracker** B. Shackleton
1964	**Camel** B. Shackleton, J. Jones (AL)
1964	**Yogi** J. Jones, B. Shackleton (1pt.)
	First free ascent by P. O'Sullivan, C. George in 1977
1964	**Mango Corner** J. Jones, B. Shackleton
1964 Nov.	**Cyclops** F. Cannings, B. Shackleton (AL)
1965	**Beeline** B. Shackleton, R. Hemes
1968 June 13	**Exaltation** P. Leedel, M. Chambers
1968 Aug. 3	**Scimitar** P. Littlejohn, J. Fowler
1969 April 19	**Randy** I. Duckworth, R. Ward, R. Watson
1969 April 19	**Dangler** L. Benstead, D. Morrod
1969 April 27	**Bolshevik** L. Benstead, D. Morrod
1969 May 14	**Imperialist** L. Benstead, D. Morrod
1969 Aug. 28	**Goblin** B. Hocken, P. Gross
1969 Sept. 14	**Fruitflancase** A. McFarlane, D. Ball (VL)
1969 Dec. 27	**Tarantula** D. Ball, A. McFarlane
1970	**The Crow Buttress Routes** P. Williams, J. Baker, P. Crossley and P. Gross
1976 July 4	**Nibelung** P. O'Sullivan, A. Pearson
	The 2nd pitch was added in 1979 by P. O'Sullivan and S. Bell
1976 Sept. 4	**The Stitch** P. O'Sullivan, D. Blackler
1976 Sept. 4	**The Winnet** P. O'Sullivan, S. Cook, D. Blackler, A. Pearson
1977 Oct.	**The Echo** P. O'Sullivan, C. George
1978 June 21	**Shades of Green** P. O'Sullivan, C. George
1978 Aug. 16	**Lateral Thinking** P. O'Sullivan, C. George
1978 Sept. 16	**Energy Crisis** P. O'Sullivan, C. George
	Previously climbed with aid as a direct start to Gideon
1979 Jan. 27	**Extendable Arms** P. O'Sullivan
1979 April 8	**Black Widow** R. Bennett, M. Dunning
1979 July 8	**Dragon Song** S. Bell, P. O'Sullivan
1979 July 8	**The Apparition** P. O'Sullivan, S. Bell
1979 July 10	**Final Touch** P. O'Sullivan, S. Bell
1979	**Wobbling Wall** J. Maund
1980	**Noddy** A. Cotter, S. Deeming
1981	**Cleopatra** D. Thomas, N. Hancock
1981	**Asp** N. Hancock, D. Thomas
1981	**Shelob** D. Thomas, N. Hancock
1981	**Boris** D. Thomas, N. Hancock
1981	**Back to Nature** J. Wyatt, N. Hancock

THE DARTMOOR TORS

1946 May 18	**Aramis** A. Moulam
1949	**Raven Gully** W. Higgins, R. Higgins
1952 Jan. 8	**Canis** A. Moulam
1954 July	**Cantilever Direct** J. Denton
1954 Aug. 16	**Cantilever Crack** J. Denton
1954 Aug. 16	**North Face Chimney** J. Denton, J. Denton
1954 Aug. 16	**Suspension Flake** G. Sutton
1954 Aug. 26	**Sheep May Safely Graze** G. Sutton
1955 Sept. 18	**Letterbox Wall** J. Denton
1955 Oct.	**Ann** G. Sutton, Mrs A. Sutton
	This was later combined with Vandal which was led by T. Patey in July 1959
1955 Nov.	**Honeymoon Corner** G. Sutton, Mrs A. Sutton
1958 Sept. 8	**Green Beret** T. Patey
	First pitch added by P. O'Sullivan, A. Cloquet, M. Wilson in 1979
1959 June	**Commando Crack** J. Deacon, T. Patey, V. Stevenson
1959	**Oak Tree Zig Zag** A. Borwick

1959	**Central Buttress** (Bench Tor) A. Borwick
1960 Easter	**The Original Route** (Eagle Rock) C. Fishwick, G. Seale
1960 Easter	**Main Gully** (Eagle Rock) C. Fishwick, G. Seale
1960 June 30	**Outward Bound** T. Patey
1960 July	**Right-hand Chimney** (Eagle Rock) C. Fishwick
1961 May 14	**Ivy Wall** B. Biven, P. Biven, C. Fishwick
	The right-hand variation was climbed by F. Cannings is 1964
1961 May	**Black Jam Crack** P. Biven, C. Fishwick
1961 May	**Eagle's Nest** P. Biven, C. Fishwick
1961 Aug.	**Aviation** D. Bassett, H. Cornish
1961	**Hangover** J. Barry
1961	**Haggis** R. Shaw
1964	**Superdirect** (Haytor) F. Cannings, P. Badcock
1964 Aug. 9	**Interrogation** F. Cannings, P. Badcock (6pts.)
	The original aid was eliminated and the Direct Start added by P.
	Littlejohn in 1971. The point of aid on the Direct Start was eliminated
	by M. Fowler in 1980
1964 Oct. 25	**Low Man Girdle** F. Cannings, P. Badcock (Aid)
	First free ascent by M. Fowler in 1980
1965 May	**Three Steps** R. Binns
1965 June	**Lime Street** R. Widdows, B. Shackleton
1965 June	**Oblomov** B. Shackleton, R. Widdows
1967 March 18	**Raven Wing** F. Cannings, P. Biven
1967 April	**Levitation** A. Powling, P. Littlejohn
	The Direct Start was climbed by P. Littlejohn, S. Jones in 1968
1967 May 29	**Tenterhooks** P. Littlejohn, S. Jones
1967 May 29	**Swan Lake** P. Littlejohn, S. Jones
1969 June 7	**Plektron** P. Littlejohn, J. Fowler
1970 May 2	**Screw** E. Grindley, J. Fowler
1971 May 1	**The Flier** P. Littlejohn
1971 May 14	**Rhinoceros** P. Littlejohn, S. Whimster
1974	**Senior's Wall** I. Peters, D. Garner
1974	**Ash Chimney** I. Peters
1974	**Trembling Wall** I. Peters, D. Garner
1974	**Widecombe Wall** K. Darbyshire
1976 April 23	**Hostile Witness** P. Littlejohn, D. Garner
1976 July 6	**Stepladder, Wicked** P. Littlejohn, D. Garner
1976 July 29	**Rockface** P. Littlejohn, I. Peters
1976 July 29	**Fogginard** P. Littlejohn, I. Peters
1976	**D'Artagnan** P. Littlejohn (solo)
1978 July 4	**Brief Encounter** S. Cardy, A. Clarke
	First Winter Ascent B. Woodley December 1981
1978 Sept. 21	**Feasibility Study** P. O'Sullivan, C. George, A. Cotter
	Pitch 2 added in February 1979 by P. O'Sullivan, M. Wilson
1979 May 20	**Igneous Pig** S. Bell, J. Grubb
1979 July 7	**Rough Diamond** P. Littlejohn, P. O'Sullivan
1979 Aug. 17	**Xmandifer** N. Crowhurst, Mrs S. Crowhurst
	Direct Finish added by A. Winfield, J. Pym in 1983
1979 Sept. 30	**Solus** S. Bell, R. Mear
1979	**Torture** R. Harrison, J. Edwards
1980 April	**The Eyrie** P. O'Sullivan
1980 April	**Legal Aid** P. O'Sullivan, R. Mear
1980	**Docker's Dillema** P. Dawson
1980	**Don't Stop Now** P. Dawson
1980	**Black Jam Arête** E. Holt, D. Thomas, N. Hancock
1981 June	**Monarchist** I. Peters, D. Sargeant
1981 June	**Anarchist** I. Peters, A. Clark
1982 July	**Dehydration** B. Woodley, K. Phillips
1982	**Crunchy Toad** S. Lewis, M. Lynden, C. Jones, M. Fowler
1983	**The Diamond Sky** P. Bull

1983 April	**Hob Hound** B. Woodley, M. Parry
1983 June	**Jazoo** C. Nicholson (solo)
1983 June	**The Saversnake** B. Woodley, C. Nicholson
1983 June	**A Fall of Moondust** C. Nicholson, B. Woodley
1983 Sept.	**Le Dernier Cri** B. Woodley, A. Whyte, M. Parry
1983 Oct. 4	**Rough Justice** P. Bull
	The direct start, Direct Justice, was climbed by P. Bull on 18 May 1985
1983 Oct. 16	**Saturday Night Finger** A. Winfield, M. Lane
1984 April 14	**Spear of Destiny** A. Winfield, R. Stowell
1984 June	**Hydraulic Arête** P. O'Sullivan, I. Thomas
1984 Aug. 11	**Bloodshot** A. Grieve, N. Hancock
1984 Oct. 21	**Aerobic Wall** P. O'Sullivan, M. Dunning
1984	**The Fair** B. Woodley, A. Whyte
1984	**Scrumpy Special** B. Woodley, A. Whyte
1984	**Little Prow** I. Peters (solo)
1985 May 8	**Two Way Stretch** N. Hancock, P. Saunders
1985 May 8	**Glass Bead Game** C. Nicholson, M. Courtier
1985 May 18	**Blood Lust** N. Hancock
1985 June 1	**Old Friends** P. O'Sullivan, J. Grice
1985 June 6	**Republican** I. Peters, P. O'Sullivan, D. Butterrick

MORWELL

1958 Sept.	**Salvationist** T. Patey
1958 Nov. 8	**Spinal Column** T. Patey
1958 Nove 9	**Perfecto** T. Patey
1958 Nov. 16	**Pine Top** T. Patey
1958 Dec.	**Thor** T. Patey, E. Sloin (1 pt.)
	The aid point was eliminated by P. O'Sullivan and B. Rossiter in 1979
1958 Dec.	**Cerebus** T. Patey, E. Sloin
1958 Dec.	**Overhanging Crack** T. Patey, E. Sloin
1958 Dec.	**Tiptoe** T. Patey, E. Sloin
1959 Jan	**The Cleaver** T. Patey
1959 June	**Ultramontane** J. Deacon, T. Patey, V. Stevenson
1978 Aug. 8	**Vacancy at the Vatican** P. O'Sullivan, T. Carter
1978 Aug. 24	**Limping Home** P. O'Sullivan, T. Carter
1978 Aug. 24	**Divine Inspiration** P. O'Sullivan, T. Carter
1979 Jan. 3	**Impertinent Robin** P. O'Sullivan, J. Maund, M. Wilson
1979 Jan. 3	**Quiet River** P. O'Sullivan, M. Northcott, J. Maund
1979 Jan. 3	**Maybe Tomorrow** P. O'Sullivan, J. Maund
1979 Jan. 3	**Aerial Ballet** P. O'Sullivan, J. Maund
1979 Feb. 2	**The Quickening Pulse** P. O'Sullivan, B. Rossiter
1979 Feb. 2	**Odin Your Tea's Ready** B. Rossiter, P. O'Sullivan
1979 Feb. 17	**Palace of Skulls** P. O'Sullivan, M. Wilson
1979 Feb. 17	**Love is like Anthrax** P. O'Sullivan, M. Wilson
1979 Feb. 17	**Haunted People** P. O'Sullivan, M. Wilson
1979 Feb. 20	**Cold Grief** P. O'Sullivan, M. Dunning
1979 March 31	**Damaged Goods** P. O'Sullivan, M. Wilson
1979 May 5	**Daylight Saving** P. O'Sullivan, M. Wilson
1979 Oct. 4	**Thought Process** P. O'Sullivan, R. Perriment

PLYMOUTH LIMESTONE

1969-71	**Mac's Route, Brewery Arête, Diamond Lil** A. McFarlane, D. Ball
1977	**Strictly Private, Long Slide, Lonely Hold** P. O'Sullivan, A. Cotter
1979	**Hot Fun** P. O'Sullivan, A. Cotter, H. Cripps
1980	**Traffic Jam, Traffic Lights, Mayflower, Drake's Circus, Cash Investments, Night Club** D. Nicholls
1981	**Brec to the Vag** D. Nicholls
1983	**Charlie Don't Surf, Suburbia, Depression, Slippin' and a Sliding** P. O'Sullivan, B. Rossiter, S. Deeming

CHUDLEIGH
1923	**Wogs** I. Prowse	
1960	**Sarcophagus** T. Patey	
1960	**Chudleigh Overhang** T. Patey (1pt.)	

*He traversed off left after pitch 1 and the modern finish was added by
F. Cannings in 1965. Free ascent in 1961 by P. Biven*

1960 July   **Barn Owl Crack**   T. Patey, R. Grant, S. Bemrose
1960   **Scar**   N. Hannaby, T. Patey

Pitch 1 added in 1962 by F. Cannings. Direct Finish in 1966 by P. Biven

1960 Sept.   **Lute**   N. Hannaby, E. Rayson
1960 Nov.   **Slot**   N. Hannaby
1960 Nov.   **Inkerman Groove**   E. Rayson, N. Hannaby

Direct variation by A. McFarlane, A. Pearson, 18 September 1971

1960 Nov.   **Guy Fawkes Crack**   N. Hannaby, E. Rayson
1961 Jan.   **Reek**   E. Rayson, B. Waistell

*Probably **Spearhead** at the same time*

1961 March **Machete Wall**   E. Rayson
1961 March **Sisyphus**   T. Patey, J. Braven
1961   **Brer Fox**   R. Moodie, R. Gammage
1961   **Brer Rabbit**   R. Moodie, R. Gammage
1961   **The Squirrel**   J. Braven, R. Gammage
1961 Aug.   **Never On Sunday**   D. Bassett, A. Allen

Leap Year Finish by F. Cannings in 1964

1961 Summer **Great Western**   N. Hannaby, E. Rayson
1962 Summer **Combined Ops**   P. Biven, B. Biven, C. Fishwick, J. Braven
1962 Summer **Oesophagus**   B. Biven, J. Braven
1962 Summer **Stalactite**   P. Biven, J. Braven
1962   **South Face** and **Eastern Girdles**   P. Biven, J. Braven
1962 Oct.   **The Fly**   P. Biven, J. Braven
1963 March **Tropic of Capricorn**   P. Biven, J. Braven
1963 March **The Notch**   F. Cannings, D. Morrod, J. Braven
1963 April   **Tropic of Cancer**   F. Cannings
1963 April   **Ben Gunn**   F. Cannings, D. Rainford
1963 Dec.   **Dripdry**   F. Cannings, D. Rainford (Aid)

*Pitch 2 added by B. Houseley, J. Neely in 1966. Pitch 1 free by P.
Littlejohn in 1982*

1964 Feb.   **Green Mantle**   J. Brooks, R. Cockran

Alternative start also in February 1964 by J. & R. Brooks

1964 Feb.   **Smoke Gets In Your Eyes**   F. Cannings (Aid)

   $*Free ascent by P. Leedel in February 1971*

1964 Feb.   **Nexus**   P. Biven, D. Horley
1964 March **Sexus**   P. Biven, D. Horley
1964 April   **Plexus**   P. Biven, D. Horley
1964 April   **The Dial**   F. Cannings, A. Thompson
1964 May   **Thornifixion**   P. Biven, D. Horley

Rosy Exit by P. Littlejohn in 1966

1964 Oct.   **Colossus**   P. Biven, D. Horley, W. Reilly, P. Raven
1964 Nov.   **The Spider**   F. Cannings, P. Biven
1965 Feb.   **Gagool Original**   I. McMorrin, W. Reilly

*Variation climbed in 1965 by F. Cannings, A. Thompson. Direct Start
by P. Littlejohn (solo) in 1971*

1965 Feb.   **Sickle**   P. Biven, P. Raven
1965 March **Nimrod**   F. Cannings, B. Housley
1965 April   **Titan, Ivy League**   F. Cannings, F. Stebbings

*Pitch 3 of Titan was climbed free in 1984 by C. Nicholson and named
Pig's Ear*

1965 June   **Prometheus**   P. Biven, F. Cannings (VL)
1965 June   **Scorpion**   F. Cannings, P. Biven
1965 June   **Andromeda**   P. Biven, D. Horley

Direct in 1965 by C. Bonington, P. Biven

1965 June	**Hammer**	B. Shackleton
1965 Sept.	**Cygnus**	P. Biven, F. Cannings
1965 Sept.	**The Track**	F. Cannings, P. Biven
		Variation by E. Grindley in October 1970
1965 Oct	**Gemini I**	F. Cannings, P. Biven
1965 Oct. 10	**Gemini II**	P. Biven, J. Braven, A. Clarke
1965 Oct. 10	**Orion**	B. Shackleton, R. Moulton (AL), P. Biven
1965 Oct. 10	**Little Subtleties**	S. Dawson, L. Elton
1965 Oct. 17	**Rock House Corner**	B. Shackleton
1965 Nov. 21	**Leo**	G. Lowe, M. Taylor (Aid)
1965 Dec. 26	**Highway '65**	F. Cannings, D. Walls
1965 Dec. 27	**Central Pillar**	F. Cannings, P. Biven
1966 Feb. 20	**Obstreperous**	D. Rainford, E. Housley (Aid)
1966 Feb. 27	**Tantalus**	A. Powling, J. Neely (2pts.)
		Pitch 1 added 14 April 1979 by B. Wilkinson, A. Gallagher
1966 March 5	**Route '66**	S. Dawson, L. Elton
1966 March 20	**Concerto**	F. Cannings, A. Powling (3pts.)
		First free ascent S. Bell 23rd March 1979
1966 April	**White Edge**	P. Biven, I. McMorrin (AL)
1966 April	**Tar Baby**	S. Dawson, P. Butler
1966 May 1	**Panga**	I. McMorrin, P. Biven (2pts.)
		First free ascent 27 June 1979 by S. Bell, B. Woodley
1966 May 14	**Black Death**	D. Rainford, E. Phillips (Aid)
		Climbed with 1 point of aid by K. Buckley, P. Dawson in 1980 and free by P. Littlejohn in 1982
1966 May	**Bolero**	A. Powling, P. Littlejohn, J. Neely
1966 June	**East Gully Wall**	P. Biven, J. Braven
1966 July	**Perseus**	I. McMorrin, P. Biven
		$*Direct Finish added by E. Grindley in 1970*
1966 Aug.	**Hansel**	J. Neely, S. Dawson
1966 Aug.	**Gretel**	S. Dawson, J. Neely
1966 Sept. 26	**Diana**	P. Biven, I. McMorrin
1966 Sept. 26	**Grey Wall Eliminate**	F. Cannings, A. Powling
1966 Sept. 26	**Garden Wall Eliminate**	F. Cannings, P. Biven (AL)
1966 Sept.	**Nemesis**	P. Littlejohn, S. Dawson (1pt.)
1967 April 9	**Yggdrasel**	S. Dawson, P. Littlejohn
1967 April	**West End**	P. Littlejohn, S. Dawson, J. Hammond
1967 April	**Crescendo**	J. Taylor
1967 April	**Barn Owl Variant**	J. Neely, A. Powling
1967 June	**Ancient Mariner**	P. Littlejohn, R. Littlejohn
1967 July	**Two Stroke Banana**	P. Littlejohn, S. Dawson
1968 Feb. 9	**Penny Lane**	P. Littlejohn, J. Hammond (1pt.)
		Climbed free 31 March 1979 by S. Bell, J. Grubb
1968 March 9	**The Spy**	P. Littlejohn, J. Hammond (1pt.)
		Climber free by E. Hart in early 1970's
1968 June 30	**Seguidilla**	P. Littlejohn, E. Grindley
1968 June 30	**Twang**	P. Littlejohn, E. Grindley (AL)
1970 Nove. 15	**The Equation**	P. Littlejohn, C. Wand-Tetley. (2pts.)
		Climbed free by P. Newman, S. Bell October 1978
1971 Sept. 2	**Combat**	P. Littlejohn, S. Jones
1978 Oct.	**Hot Ice**	K. Buckley (solo)
1979 May 27	**Saturn Five**	S. Bell, J. Grubb
1979 Sept. 9	**Gagool Direct**	S. Bell, R. Mear
1979 Nov. 8	**Farewell to Arms**	I. Parsons, R. Mear
1980	**Charlie Chaplin Walks on Air**	P. Dawson et al
		Previously climbed as the Direct Start to Leo
1983 April	**Pigs Might Fly**	C. Nicholson, B. Woodley
1983	**South Face**	R. Greatrick
1984	**Major Tom**	C. Nicholson (unseconded)

1984 April 9	**Tendonitis** D. Cope, B. Frampton
1984 April 23	**Phoenix on Fire** R. Warke (unseconded)
1984 May	**Smokey Joe** N. White, C. Nicholson
1984 July	**Alpha One** R. Warke, P. Warren
1984 July 11	**Sly Boots McCall** N. White, M. Courtier
1984 Aug.	**Before The Storm** R. Warke, R. Meek
1985 April 26	**Ground Control, Space Odyssey** B. Woodley and party

PALACE QUARRY

1967 June 23	**Tremor** P. Littlejohn, J. Taylor
1969 Aug. 23	**Quiver, Zen** P. Littlejohn, S. Jones (VL)
1976 Aug.	**Wild Bunch, Olympia, The Bat** C. Gibson, P. Leedel
1976 Nov.	**Astral Traveller** C. Gibson, S. Bell

BERRY HEAD AREA

1961 Sept. 7	**Red Crack, Thursday Rib** D. Bassett
1961 Sept. 8	**Evening Buttress** D. Bassett
1961 Sept. 11	**Crystal Corner, Hawkin's Climb** A. Allen, L. Message
1961 Sept. 12	**Hawkin's Climb** A. Allen, L. Message
1961 Oct. 13	**Captain's Corner** D. Bassett, A. Allen, L. Message
1961 Oct. 16	**Abbot's Way** D. Bassett
1967 April 30	**The Red Monk** R. Crawshaw, D. Rogers
1967 April 30	**Schizophrenia** I. Staples, S. Dawson (AL)
1967 May 7	**Chastity Corner** P. Littlejohn, D. Rogers, R. Crawshaw
1967 May 7	**Ruddy Corner** R. Crawshaw, D. Rogers, P. Littlejohn
1967 July	**Evening Arête** J. Fowler, F. Stebbings
1967 Aug. 6	**Moonraker** P. Biven, P. Littlejohn (VL)
1967 Sept. 3	**Barbican** F. Cannings, P. Biven (5 pts.) *Final pitch added 1 June 1968 by P. Littlejohn, J. Hammond. First free* *ascent by P. Littlejohn in 1977*
1967 Sept. 9	**Barnacle Traverse** J. Fowler, F. Stebbings
1967 Sept. 9	**Ruddigore** A. Powling, J. Fowler, F. Stebbings
1967 Sept. 23	**Ultimate Trundle** P. Biven, T. Peck
1967 Oct. 3	**Pikadon** P. Biven, F. Cannings (AL)
1967 Dec. 24	**Enterprise** P. Littlejohn, J. Neely
1967 Dec. 31	**Merlin Rocket** P. Littlejohn, A. Powling
1967 Dec. 31	**Magical Mystery Tour I** R. Ballie, J. Cleare
1968 March 31	**Zeta** F. Cannings, P. Biven (AL, 4 pts.) *Climbed free in 1982 by B. Woodley, B. Wilkinson*
1968 March 31	**Magical Mystery Tour III** P. Biven, F. Cannings, A. Thompson
1968 April 5	**Lost Arrow** P. Biven, F. Cannings (AL)
1968 April 6	**Goddess of Gloom** F. Cannings, P. Biven, M. Springett
1968 April 6	**Oggie** J. Fowler, G. Radway, F. Stebbings
1968 April 6	**Neanderthal, Binky** E. Hammond, J. Fowler, F. Stebbings
1968 May 5	**Flying Fifteen, Swashbuckler** P. Littlejohn, J. Hammond
1968 June 2	**Animals Are People** J. Hammond, P. Littlejohn
1968 July	**Ganges** J. Fowler, F. Stebbings
1968 Aug. 21	**Quality Street** J. Taylor, P. Littlejohn (VL)
1968 Oct. 19	**Happy Camper's Crack** P. Littlejohn, J. Fowler
1968	**Magical Mystery Tour II** P. Biven, J. Fowler, P. Littlejohn
1968	**Barnacle Traverse Continuation** P. Biven, F. Cannings
1969 April 4	**Dreadnought** F. Cannings, P. Littlejohn (AL)
1969 April 7	**Seventh Circle** F. Cannings, P. Littlejohn (VL), P. Biven
1969 April 13	**The Hood** P. Littlejohn, F. Cannings (3 pts.) *Climbed free by P. Littlejohn, C. King 28 October 1977*
1969 April 13	**Blood** P. Littlejohn, J. Fowler, F. Cannings
1969 May 11	**Finn** P. Littlejohn

1969 May 26	**The Pinch**	P. Littlejohn, S. Jones (2 pts.)

1969 May 26   **The Pinch**   P. Littlejohn, S. Jones (2 pts.)
Pitch 1 done earlier by J. Fowler. First free ascent in 1983 by P. Littlejohn, A. Penning
1969 June 19   **Bloodhound**   P. Littlejohn, S. Jones
1969 June 19   **High Traverse**   P. Littlejohn, S. Jones (AL)
1969 Sept. 7   **Slipshod**   P. Littlejohn (solo)
1969 Oct.   **Gugu Wack**   J. Hammond, Sue Crosse, J. Fowler
1969   **Magical Mystery Tour IV**   P. Biven, J. Fowler, R. Isherwood (with several rope moves)
The whole of Magical Mystery Tour was climbed free in one solo push by P. Littlejohn in 1982
1970 April 4   **Boo-bah Plost**   J. Hammond, P. Littlejohn (VL)
1970 April 19   **Dust Devil**   P. Biven, S. Jones (2 pts.)
Climbed free by P. O'Sullivan, C. George in 1978
1970 April 19   **Yellow Rurties**   P. Littlejohn, J. Hammond (VL)
1970 May 28   **Cut-throat**   P. Littlejohn, P. Biven, J. Hammond
1970 June 28   **Arncliffe**   E. Grindley, Meg Burrow
1970 Aug. 9   **Fowler's Dolly Mixture**   J. Fowler, Sue Crosse
1970 Aug. 23   **King Crab**   F. Cannings, P. Biven, P. Littlejohn
1970 Sept. 20   **Berry Red Wall**   J. Fowler, Sue Crosse, J. Hammond
1970 Sept.   **Salt**   C. Ross, J. Hammond (VL), S. Willard
1970 Oct. 4   **Melinda**   P. Littlejohn, C. Wand-Tetley
1970 Oct. 18   **Graunching Gilbert**   K. Darbyshire, A. Miller
1970 Oct. 25   **Beggar's Banquet**   E. Grindley, P. Littlejohn (VL)
1970 Nov. 1   **Sloop**   P. Littlejohn
1970 Nov. 1   **Seaworm**   J. Fowler, Sue Fowler
1970 Nov. 3   **Stag Party**   C. Wand-Tetley, A. Miller
1970 Nov. 8   **Home Brew**   C. Gimblett, P. Harper
1970 Dec. 7   **Winterlude**   F. Cannings, P. Biven
1970 Dec. 14   **Paranoid**   E. Grindley, A. Miller
1971 Jan.   **Iron Butterfly**   C. Wand-Tetley, B. Goodman (AL), G. Higginson
1971 March   **Opus Dei**   E. Grindley, A. Miller
1971 March 2   **Curse**   M. Chambers, F. Hayton, N. Gifford. (VL)
1971 May 22   **Rastus**   C. Wand-Tetley, J. Fowler
1972 Aug. 20   **The Quaker**   P. Littlejohn, S. Jones (1 pt.)
Free ascent M. Fowler September 1979
1973 Feb.   **Man Bites Dog**   K. Darbyshire, H. Clarke (1 pt.)
Climbed free in 1983 by B. Wilkinson, B. Woodley
1973 March   **Moving Target**   P. Littlejohn, F. Cannings
1973 Oct.   **Rainbow Bridge**   A. McFarlane, D. Ball (VL, 8 pts.)
Pitches 2, 7, 12 and 13 added and aid reduced to 1pt by P. Littlejohn, K. Darbyshire in 1974
1975 Dec. 21   **Gremlin, Hornet**   P. Littlejohn
1977 Aug. 4   **The Yardarm**   P. Littlejohn, D. Roberts
1977 Dec. 30   **Hot Lips**   P. Littlejohn, E. Hart (AL)
1978 Oct. 5   **Lady of Shame**   P. O'Sullivan, B. Rossiter
1979 March 17   **Cloudburst, Sirocco**   A. Gallagher, B. Wilkinson
1979 March 17   **Jimjam, Squall**   B. Wilkinson, A. Gallagher
1979 March 17   **Broadside**   B. Wilkinson, A. Gallagher
1979 March 30   **Hidden Groove**   B. Wilkinson, A. Gallagher
1979 April 7   **Traversty**   B. Wilkinson, A. Gallagher
1979 May 19   **Rusty Road**   B. Wilkinson, A. Gallagher
1979 July 25   **Relay**   G. Lodge, B. Day
1979 Aug. 19   **Pathos**   P. O'Sullivan, J. Maund
1979 Oct. 6   **Depth Charge**   M. Fowler, A. Strapcans (AL)
1980 Jan. 20   **False Alarms**   P. O'Sullivan, J. Maund (2 pts.)
Free ascent in 1981 by G. Jenkin, K. Marsden
1980 March   **Anti-Matter**   P. O'Sullivan, C. Gibson (AL)
1980 April   **Uncul-Patter**   S. Bell, C. Gibson

1980 May	**Lip Trip** M. Fowler, A. Meyers (AL)
1980 June 21	**Solstice** A. Gallagher, S. Bondi
1980 July 20	**Calcite Diamond** C. Nicholson, A. Gallagher
1980 Oct.	**Bismark** M. Fowler, J. Codding
1981 Jan. 25	**The Long Goodbye** P. O'Sullivan, R. Swinden
1981 April	**Cod** C. Nicholson, A. Gallagher
1981 June	**Izitso** A. Gallagher, P. Way
1981 Summer	**Cod Rock Routes** N. Hearn, M. Stapleton
1982 May 29	**Sidewinder** B. Woodley, B. Wilkinson
1982 Sept.	**Caveman** A. Meyers, M. Fowler (AL)
	The upper reaches had been climbed in 1971 by P. Littlejohn, C.
	Wand-Tetley and named Crocodile
1983 March 3	**Blind Pew, Tied Line** N. White, B. Wilkinson
1983 March 3	**Placebo** B. Wilkinson, N. White
1983 March 3	**Ray Zazorn** N. White (solo)
1983 May 30	**Tough Luck, Good Fortune** T. Penning, P. Littlejohn
1983 Aug.	**Malteaser** K. Phillips, Cath Rolfe
1983 Aug.	**Crunchie** B. Woodley (solo)
1983 Aug.	**Burning Bridges, Sunset Boulevard** B. Woodley, K. Phillips
1983 Aug.	**Sunkiss, All Because** B. Woodley, B. Aplin
1983 Aug.	**Man in Black, Milky Bar Kid** B. Woodley, A. White
1983 Sept.	**Dirt Eater** B. Woodley, I. Day, N. Oxton
1983 Sept. 19	**Douglas Fairbanks Jnr.** P. O'Sullivan, M. Dunning
1984 April 13	**Desparête** B. Woodley, M. Minky
1984 April 17	**Infidel** B. Wilkinson, M. Parry
1984 April	**Semi-Detached, Caius** B. Woodley, S. Lee

DADDYHOLE AREA

1966 May 30	**Central Slabs** P. Littlejohn, S. Jones
1967 May 21	**Mayday** J. Neely, P. Littlejohn (AL)
1967 May 21	**Tree Root** J. Jones, J. Fowler
1967 May 29	**Gates of Eden** S. Dawson, J. Hammond
1967 June 2	**Diamond Rib** P. Biven, C. Fishwick
1967 June 2	**Rubber Soul** P. Biven, C. Fishwick
1967 June 3	**Nest Egg** T. Lindop, E. Phillips (AL)
1967 June 3	**Nardly Stoad's Climb** J. Hammond, Ann Kellow, J. Fowler
1967 June 10	**Last Exit to Torquay** P. Biven, A. Alvarez
1967 June 10	**The Midas Touch** F. Cannings, P. Littlejohn, P. Biven
1967 June 13	**Pinnacle Traverse** P. Biven (solo)
1967 June 17	**Triton** P. Biven, F. Cannings
1967 June 18	**The Pearl** F. Cannings, P. Littlejohn (AL), P. Biven
1967 June 18	**Tobacco Road** F. Cannings, P. Littlejohn, P. Biven
1967 July 8	**The Bead** F. Cannings, F. Stebbings
1967 July 9	**Gargantua** F. Cannings, P. Littlejohn
1967 July 15	**Neptune** P. Biven, F. Cannings, P. Littlejohn
1967 July 15	**The Slithy Tove** F. Cannings (solo)
1967 July 16	**The Mighty Atom** P. Littlejohn, J. Neeely
1967 July 23	**Pantagruel** F. Cannings, P. Littlejohn (AL, 3 pts.)
	First free ascent by P. Littlejohn, E. Hart 22 December 1977
1967 July 26	**Discuss the Thoughts of Chairman Mao** J. Hammond, P. Littlejohn
1967 July 29	**Swing Low** P. Littlejohn, F. Cannings (AL)
1967 July 30	**Readymix** P. Littlejohn, J. Neely, J. Hammond
1967 July 31	**Fandangle** P. Littlejohn, J. Hammond
1967 Aug. 3	**Crinoid** P. Littlejohn, P. Biven
1967 Aug. 20	**Mighty Cheese** J. Fowler, J. Hammond (AL)
1968 Jan. 27	**Romeo and Juliet** J. Neely, E. Phillips (AL)
1968 March 17	**Hermeda** E. Grindley, R. Gibbs, J. Hammond
1968 Dec. 26	**Jeckyll and Hyde** P. Littlejohn, J. Fowler
1969 Jan. 25	**Ramshackle, Eubulus Williams** E. Grindley, G. Higginson, C. Byrne
1969 Jan. 25	**End Crack** E. Grindley, G. Higginson

1969 Feb. 1	**Brass Bound Crack, Sabre Tooth**	E. Grindley, G. Higginson
1969 March 27	**The Meadfoot Girdle**	E. Grindley, G. Higginson (1pt.)

Climbed free 5 August 1979 by P. O'Sullivan

1969 May 25	**Pegs' Progress**	G. Higginson, Deborah Hansen-Bay

Free climbed in 1983 by B. Woodley

1969 June 4	**Caliban**	E. Grindley, T. Lewis, Deborah Hansen-Bay
1969 June 7	**The White Queen**	G. Higginson, E. Grindley, Deborah Hansen-Bay
1969	**The Watchtower**	P. Biven, F. Cannings, M. Springett

Swimming Thunder Hole, which was climbed free by K. Darbyshire, H. Clarke in 1972

1970 Feb. 22	**Median**	P. Biven, E. Grindley, Alison Long, Moira Owens
1976 July 10	**Snakecharmer**	P. Littlejohn, R. Broomhead (1pt.)

Climbed free by P. O'Sullivan, C. George in 1978

1976 Oct. 16	**Revolver**	S. Bell, C. Gibson
1977 May	**Imperial Wall**	C. Gibson, A. Morley
1977 Oct.	**Zuma**	P. Littlejohn, C. King
1978 April 22	**Stratagem**	B. Wilkinson, A. Gallagher
1979 Sept.	**Rocketman**	S. Bell, S. Marriot
1979 Nov. 18	**Demeter**	A. Gallagher
1980 March	**Grand Slam**	P. O'Sullivan, C. Gibson
1980 July	**Mass Murderer**	P. Dunwell, D. Lassasso
1980 July	**Liason with Lenin**	B. Woodley, M. Glaister, J. Brooks
1981 May 17	**Vista**	A. Gallagher, R. Thorn
1981 May 25	**Buzby**	C. Nicholson, A. Gallagher
1981 May 31	**Third Time Lucky**	S. Woollard, A. Holborn
1983 Jan.	**Megatarts**	N. White (solo)
1983 Jan.	**Praline, Saline**	N. White, M. Courtier
1983 Feb. 5	**Aquiline**	N. White, M. Courtier
1983 Feb. 26	**Jericho**	P. Bull, N. Green
1983 May	**Prime Time, Splash Down**	P. Bull (solo)
1983 May	**Back Brain Stimulator**	A. Winfield (solo)
1983 June	**Bird Scarer, Total Control**	P. Bull, N. Green
1983 July 3	**Flashdance**	P. Littlejohn, T. Penning, P. Cresswell
1983 July 3	**Blinding Flash**	P. Littlejohn, T. Penning
1984 April 2	**Date with the Devil, Devil's Alternative**	N. White, C. Nicholson
1984 April 2	**Clotted Cream**	C. Nicholson, N. White, M. Courtier

*Previously climbed as an aid route, named **Rainyday** by E. Grindley, C. Bryne.*

1984 April 2	**Blue Monday**	C. Nicholson, N. White
1984 April 11	**Mukdah's Wall**	B. Woodley, K. Phillips

LONG QUARRY AREA

1962	**The Long Traverse**	Quarry Pinnacle J. Worsley
1964	**The Grey Tower, The Ridge**	P. Biven and party
1967 June 9	**Love Not War**	J. Hammond, T. Lindop *by original finish*

Present finish added by J. Neely 18 June 1967

1967 July 25	**Coup de Grâce**	P. Littlejohn, B. Housley
1967 Aug. 12	**Osram**	P. Littlejohn, J. Neely
1967 Oct. 1	**Quantum of Solace**	J. Neely, J. Hammond (AL)
1967 Nov. 5	**St Gregory the Wonder Worker**	M. Springett, P. Biven (AL)
1968 Jan. 27	**Acheron**	P. Littlejohn, E. Grindley, J. Taylor
1968 March 30	**The Cope**	F. Cannings, A. Thompson
1968 March 30	**Incubus**	P. Littlejohn, P. Biven (AL)
1968 March 30	**The Mitre**	F. Cannings, P. Biven, P. Littlejohn (1pt.)

Modern finish added 5 January 1969 by P. Littlejohn, J. Hammond, and start climbed free 22 September 1979 by S. Bell, B. Woodley

1968 April 20	**Crooked Man**	E. Grindley, R. Gibbs, P. Littlejohn
1968 May 18	**Ichor**	P. Littlejohn, J. Hammond
1968 May 18	**Krapp's Last Fake**	J. Hammond, P. Littlejohn

1968 June 3	**Jumping Jack Flash** E. Grindley, P. Christie	
	Alternative start in June 1969 by J. Fowler, Sue Crosse, G. Higginson	
1968 June 9	**High and Dry** E. Grindley, P. Littlejohn (AL)	
1968 June 16	**Grip Type Thynne** P. Littlejohn, J. Hammond, J. Fowler	
1968 June 21	**Epoc, Gut Bucket** E. Grindley, J. Fowler	
1968 June 23	**Lethe** E. Grindley, J. Fowler	
	Right-hand finish by S. Woollard in 1981	
1968 June 29	**Fake's Last Krapp** P. Littlejohn, J. Hammond	
1968 Nov. 2	**Era** E. Grindley, G. Higginson	
1968 Dec. 6	**Cocytus** E. Grindley, P. Littlejohn (AL, 2 pts.)	
	Climbed free by P. Littlejohn, D. Garner in 1976	
1968 Dec. 14	**Aornis** E. Grindley, P. Littlejohn	
1968 Dec. 22	**Moonshot** P. Littlejohn, J. Hammond	
1969 Jan. 19	**The Jaywalk** P. Littlejohn, J. Hammond	
1969 Feb. 2	**Tiny Tim** P. Littlejohn, E. Grindley, J. Hammond	
1969 Feb. 5	**Ferocity** E. Grindley, G. Higginson (AL), E. Hammond	
1969 Feb. 14	**Magic Carpet Ride** P. Littlejohn, E. Grindley (VL)	
1969 Feb. 15	**Sacrosanct** P. Littlejohn, E. Grindley, P. Biven	
	Pitch 1 added later by S. Jones	
1969 Feb. 23	**Lynch** P. Littlejohn, E. Grindley	
1969 April 19	**Neophron** P. Littlejohn, S. Jones (2 pts.)	
	Climbed free by S. Bell, J. Grubb in 1979	
1969 May 11	**Little John** E. Grindley, G. Higginson	
1969 May 25	**Snoopy** P. Biven, P. Littlejohn (AL), S. Jones	
1969	**The Kraken** P. Biven, E. Grindley, J. Fowler	
1969 June 8	**The Gilded Turd** P. Littlejohn, J. Hammond (AL), P. Biven, E. Grindley	
1969 June 14	**Iconoclast** P. Littlejohn, E. Grindley	
1969 June 28	**The Magus** P. Littlejohn, E. Grindley (AL), P. Biven, G. Higginson	
1969 June 29	**All That Fall** P. Littlejohn, E. Grindley, G. Higginson	
1969 July	**Safari** (pitches 1-5) P. Littlejohn, P. Biven (VL)	
	Completed November 1969 by P. Littlejohn, E. Grindley	
1969 Sept. 21	**St. Jude** P. Biven, Judie Herbert	
1969 Sept. 21	**Little Wonder** J. Fowler, Sue Crosse	
1969 Sept.	**Cross Route** C. Ross, Sue Crosse, P. Biven	
1969 Sept. 28	**Gilgamesh** I. McMorrin, P. Biven (AL)	
1969 Oct. 11	**The Girdle Turd** E. Grindley, G. Higginson (AL)	
1969 Oct. 18	**Steppenwolf** E. Grindley, and party	
	Direct Finish added by P. Littlejohn, H. Clarke in 1974	
1969 Nov. 1	**Ulysses** P. Littlejohn, E. Grindley	
1969 Nov. 1	**The Odyssey** P. Littlejohn, E. Grindley (AL)	
1969 Nov. 9	**Mars** P. Biven, Alison Chadwick	
1969 Nov.	**Just One More** C. Byrne, M. Tracey (VL)	
1970 April 25	**Incubus Direct** P. Littlejohn, E. Grindley (2 pts.)	
1971 Jan. 9	**Deadline** P. Littlejohn, S. Jones	
1971 Dec. 12	**The Exile** P. Littlejohn, N. Townsend	
1973 Feb.	**Black Ice** P. Littlejohn, K. Darbyshire	
	The start described was added by B. Woodley and the alternative start by S. Bell, R. Mear 9 September 1979	
1973 Oct. 22	**Ruby in the Dust** K. Bentham, C. Gimblett	
1973 Nov. 1	**Band of Rusty Gold** K. Bentham, C. Gimblett	
1973 Nov. 7	**Normal Hero** K. Bentham, C. Gimblett (2 pts.)	
	Climbed free in 1981 by M. Fowler	
1973 Nov. 20	**Transferance** K. Bentham, C. Gimblett	
1975 Nov. 30	**Small Change** P. Littlejohn, D. Garner	
1976 April	**Groove and Slab** P. Littlejohn, D. Garner	
1976 May 29	**Fear of Flying** P. Littlejohn, D. Garner	
1976 July 10	**The Wake** P. Littlejohn, R. Broomhead	
1977 April 16	**Crook Bruce** P. Littlejohn, C. Wand-Tetley	

1978 March 4   **Storm Child, Crêpes Suzettes**   B. Wilkinson, A. Gallagher
1978 March   **Sea Slip, Flambé**   A. Gallagher, B. Wilkinson
1979 April 7   **Cunard Line**   B. Wilkinson, A. Gallagher (AL)
1979 May 25   **Ikon**   P. Littlejohn, P. O'Sullivan
1980 May   **Call to Arms**   S. Monks, E. Hart
                Pitch 2 added by S. Lewis, J. Codding in 1983
1981 June 23   **Weeble**   A. Gallagher, P. Way
1983 Jan 29   **Afterglow**   C. Nicholson
1983 May 29   **Blonde Bombshell**   P. Littlejohn, T. Penning
1983 May 29   **Madness**   (crux pitch only) P. Littlejohn, T. Penning
                Pitches 1 & 2 first climbed by P. Littlejohn, H. Clarke in 1977
1983 Aug.   **The Big 'Y'**   B. Woodley, B. Wilkinson
1984 March 4   **Dumb Blonde**   C. Nicholson, N. White
1984 April 2   **Devonshire Cream**   C. Nicholson, N. White
1984   **Big Jim**   C. Nicholson, I. Day
1984   **American Express**   C. Nicholson, N. White

HAZARD QUARRY
1978 June 6   **Dumnonia**   P. O'Sullivan, C. George, A. Cotter 1st pitch only
                First complete ascent by A. Gallagher, I. Richards in June 1979
1979 June 26   **Twilight**   A. Gallagher, I. Richards
1979 July 3   **Meadow Fly**   A. Gallagher, I. Richards
1979 July 6   **Green Ranger**   A. Gallagher, P. Haworth
1979 July 9   **Haphazard**   A. Gallagher, G. Richards
1979 Sept. 9   **Samurai**   C. Bryant (unseconded)
1979 Oct. 21   **Pastoral**   A. Gallagher

GALMPTON QUARRY
1966 May   **Port Tack**   P. Biven, C. Fishwick
1966 June   **The Main Mast**   F. Cannings, P. Biven
1966 June   **The Ropeway**   P. Biven, F. Cannings
1966 June   **Slipway**   P. Biven, C. Fishwick
1984 March   **Up the Creek**   P. Bull (solo)
1984 March   **The Final Taxi**   P. Bull, N. Tetley

CHIPLEY QUARRY
1983 Oct.   **Isca**   N. Biven, T. Bowdler
1983 Nov.   **Ivy Route**   T. Bowdler, N. Biven
1983 Nov.   **Dalby**   N. Biven (solo)
1983 Nov.   **Doing a Dalby**   T. Bowdler (solo)

TORBRYAN
1980 April   **Famine**   S. Bell, R. Mear, B. Woodley

THE SOUTH COAST
1968   **Ladram Lady**   J. Fowler (solo)
1970   **Flaked Out, Helter**   B. Rossiter, M. Rossiter (VL)
1970   **The Steeple**   K. Darbyshire, J. Fowler, P. Biven
1971 Oct.   **Chocolate Finger**   P. Biven, J. Fowler
1971 Nov.   **Big Picket Rock**   P. Biven, K. Darbyshire, J. Fowler
1971 Nov.   **Lost World**   P. Biven, J. Fowler, A. Onyskievich
1971 Nov.   **Bonetti Tower**   K. Darbyshire, A. Onyskievich, P. Biven
1971   **The Razor**   J. Fowler, A. Onyskievich
1971 Nov.   **Tower of Babel**   J. Fowler, K. Darbyshire, P. Biven
1971   **The Parson**   K. Darbyshire, P. Biven, J. Fowler, S. Nicholls
1972   **Kamin Number 5**   K. Darbyshire, J. Fowler
1974   **The Clerk**   J. Fowler
1974   **Bantham Hand**   J. Fowler, S. Nicholls, C. Gibson
1977 Jan. 16   **Erotica**   J. Fowler, S. Fowler, S. Bell
1979 April 2   **Pilchard Groove**   D. Carroll, D. Viggers

1981 July 11	**Far From the Madding Crowd** N. Hancock, A. Grieve
1982 June 12	**Steeple Slab** J. Bebb, N. Hancock (AL), A. Grieve
1983 March	**Hopeful** S. Deeming, P. O'Sullivan, P. Haworth

DEWERSTONE – MAIN CLIFF

(The starts of these routes are obscured by trees)

		Grade
1	Pinnacle Buttress	D
2	Mucky Gully	D
3	Colonel's Arête	VD
4	The High Traverse	VD
5	Inkspots Hangover	HVS
6	Vineyard	HS
7	Leviathan	VS
8	Vala	HVS
9	Central Groove	HS
10	Scimiter	HVS
11	Fruitflancase	HVS
12	Gideon	E1
13	Climbers' Club Direct	HVS
14	Climbers' Club Ordinary	VS
15	Globe and Laurel	HVS
16	Bee line	VS
17	Route B	VD

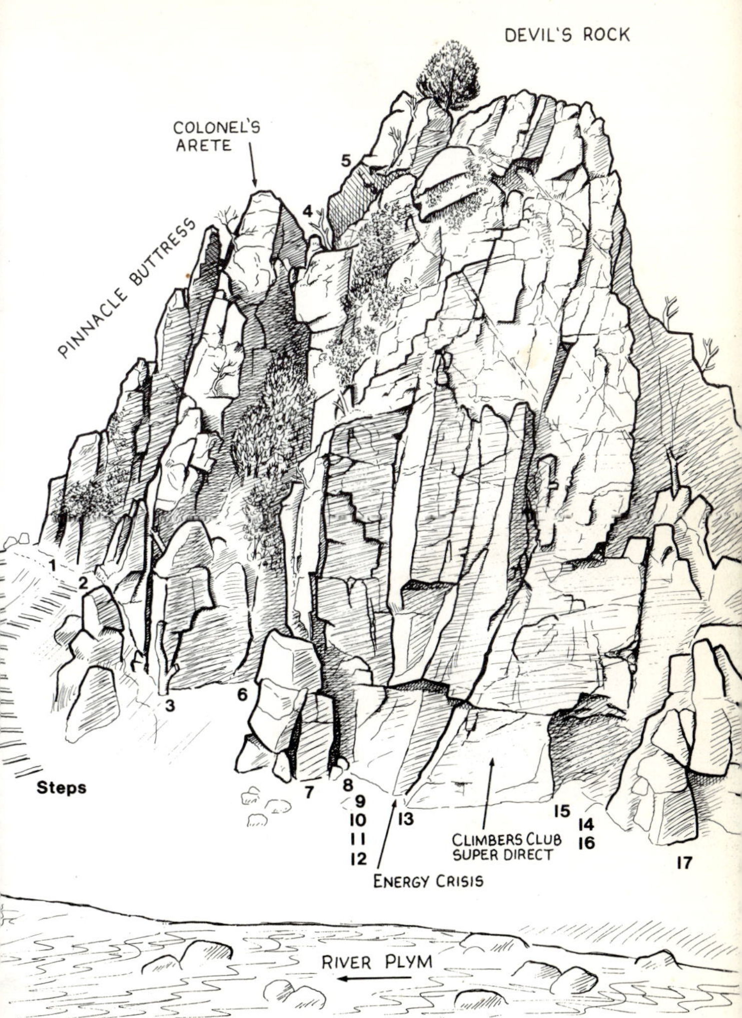

DEWERSTONE - MAIN CLIFF

The trees have been excluded from this drawing in order to show the starts of the routes.

THE DEWERSTONE – NEEDLE BUTTRESS & RAVEN BUTTRESS

		Grade
1	Portal	S
2	Needle Arête	VD
3	Camel	S
4	Cyclops	HVS
5	Yogi	HVS
6	Raven Face	VD
7	Valhalla Wall	HVS
8	Fly on the Wall	HS
9	Imperialist	HVS
10	Silken Thread	VS
11	Tarantula	HVS
12	Spider's Web	HVS

(The starts of these routes are obscured by trees)

	Grade					
1 Play Crack	D	7 Mushroom Wall	VS	14 Sheltered Crack	VD
2 Workers' Wall	HS	8 Omega Crack	VD	15 Windy Corner	M
3 Crack & Chimney	S	9 Burdock	HS	16 Snapdragon	VD
4 Wind Wall	HVS	10 Overhang Crack	S	17 Wallflower Route	VD
5 Slab Route	D	11 Dandelion	S	18 Bracket Wall	VD
6 Slanting Crack	S	12 Barking Crack	VD	19 Yogi Wall	VD
		13 Sheltered Wall	E1	20 The Mantelshelf	D

HAYTOR – NORTH FACE AND NORTH WEST FACE

		Grade
1	Canis	HS
2	East Chimney	M
3	The Diamond Sky	E2
4	Vandal & Ann	HVS
5	Central Chimney	D
6	Bridle Piton Slab	D
7	West Chimney	D
8	North Face Chimney	HS
9	Rough Justice	E4
10	Rough Diamond	E3
11	Cobleigh's Chimney	VD
12	Grey Mare's Groove	D
13	Letterbox Wall	VS

HAYTOR – WEST FACE

		Grade						
12	Grey Mare's Groove	D	15	Hangover	HVS	19	Haggis	VS
13	Letterbox Wall	VS	16	Zig Zag	D	20	Athos	VD
14	Don't Stop Now	E1	17	Bulging Wall	VD	21	D'artagnan	HVS
			18	The Step Across	D	22	Aramis	HS

HAYTOR – LOW MAN

		Grade
1	Screw	VS
2	Honeymoon Corner	S
3	Outward Bound	HVS
4	The Flier	HVS
5	Raven Wing	VS
6	Raven Gully	S
6a	·· ·· Direct Finish	VS
7	Interrogation	E3
8	Aviation	E1
9	Igneous Pig	E3
10	Rhinoceros	E3
11	Levitation Direct Start (Levitation HS)	HVS
12	The Low Man Girdle	E3
13	Dehydration	E2

DURL HEAD

		Grade
1	Man Bites Dog	E2
2	Berry Red Wall	VS
3	Fowlers Dolly Mixture	HS
4	Lady of Shame	E1

CRADLE ROCK BUTTRESS

		Grade
1	Sidewinder	HVS
2	Zeta	HVS
3	Finn	HVS
4	The Pinch	E4
5	Ganges	HS

TELEGRAPH HOLE QUARRY

		Grade
1	Nardly Stoad's Climb	S
2	The Slithy Tove	HVD
3	Bird Scarer	E4
4	Blinding Flash	E4
5	Flashdance	E2
6	Crinoid	HVS
7	The Midas Touch	HVS
8	Liaison with Lenin	HVS
9	Discuss the Thoughts of Chairman Mao	VS
10	Jericho	VS
11	Swing Low	S
12	The Mighty Atom	E1
B	Buzby	E2

OLD REDOUBT

		Grade		
1	Anti-matter	VS	5	Melinda
2	The Long Goodbye	E1	6	Pikadon
3	King Crab	HVS	7	Goddess of Gloom
4	False Alarms	E3	8	The Quaker
			9	Moonraker
			10	The Hood

VS	11 Dreadnought	E3
VS	12 Caveman	E5
VS	13 Barbican (finish)	E3
3	14 The Yardarm	E3
VS	15 Sloop	HVS
3	16 Ultimate Trundle	VD

DADDYHOLE MAIN CLIFF

		Grade
1	Caliban	HVS
2	Pinnacle Traverse	S
3	Tobacco Road	VS
4	Rocket Man	E3
5	Snakecharmer	E3
6	Pantagruel	E4
7	Readymix	HVS
8	Gargantua	E1
9	Gates of Eden	HS
10	Last Exit to Torquay	HVS
11	Zuma	E4
12	Triton	VS
13	Neptune	VS
14	The Bead	VS
15	Fandangle	HVS
16	The Pearl	HS
17	Mukdah's Wall	E4

MEADFOOT QUARRY

		Grade
1	Central Slabs	VD
2	Diamond Rib	HS
3	Mayday	VD
4	Third Time Lucky	HVS
5	Demeter	E1
6	Median	HVS
7	Revolver	HVS
8	Rubber Soul	HVS
9	Nest Egg	S
10	Tree Root	VD
11	Peg's Progress	E2
12	Clotted Cream	E4
13	Hermeda	VS
14	Malingerer	VD

ANSTEY'S COVE

		Grade
1	The Mitre	E2
2	The Cape	S
3	Eva	VS
4	Devonshire Cream	E5
5	Ferocity	A2
6	St Gregory the Wonder Worker	S
7	Little Wonder	VD
8	Weeble	HVS
9	Moonshoot	E1
10	St Jude	S
11	Aornis	S
12	American Express	E4
13	Cocytus	E2
14	Blonde Bombshell	E5
15	Groove and Slab	E1
16	Acheron	HVS
17	Lethe (R.h. finish)	VS
18	Gut Bucket	MS

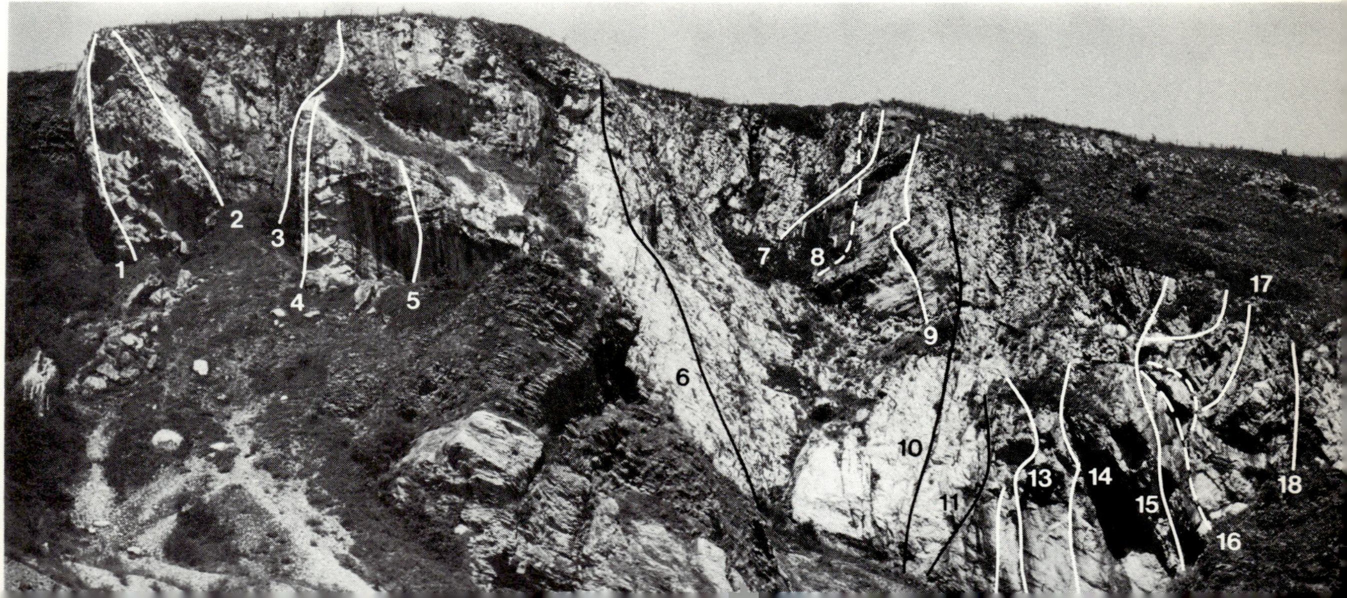

SANCTUARY WALL

1 Madness
2 Sacrosanct

Grade
E5
HVS

3 Call to Arms
4 Incubus Direct
5 Incubus
QP Quarry Pinnacle

E4
E3
HVS

LONG QUARRY POINT

No.	Route	Grade
1	The Ridge	VD
2	Ikon	E2
3	Ichor	E2
4	The Big 'Y'	E2
5	Cross Route	S
6	The Magus	HVS
7	The Gilded Turd	HVS
8	Osram	VS
9	Ulysses	E2
10	Normal Hero	E3
11	Ruby in the Dust	VS
12	Black Ice	E3
13	Grip Type Thynne	E1
14	Coup de Grace	VS
15	Safari	HVS
16	Love Not War	HVD

Index

Rescue Notes

TORBAY
The responsibility for cliff rescue in Devon falls with the Fire Brigade, who liaise with the Coastguard Service for information on the nature of the cliffs in question. In the event of an accident clearly state the exact place and give any information which might affect the method of rescue. For example, if someone is injured at sea level, then it may be decided that evacuation by lifeboat is the most practical form of rescue.

The coastguards themselves would be grateful if climbers could contact them prior to visiting a cliff so that the accidental calling out of the rescue services by, for example a tourist or a fisherman can be avoided. For those climbing at Berry Head, a personal visit to the coastguard station is recommended, or else information can be left at the following number, Brixham (08045) 58292.

DARTMOOR
All rescues on Dartmoor are under the jurisdiction of the police, who co-opt the Dartmoor Rescue Group for assistance. In the event of an accident it is essential that the exact six figure grid reference is given to the Emergency Service. They will then decide if it is necessary to use the police helicopter. Every cliff described in the guide-book is given a grid reference after the title of each cliff.

Appendix of New Routes

CHUDLEIGH

Mortality Crisis   120ft   E4/4, 6b
Climb to the niche on Black Death, good peg. Step out left and climb steeply to another peg, then move up to the break passing another peg, hard to clip. Move out left to the bottom of a steep groove. Dynamic moves lead to good holds and a peg. Finish direct and climb through vegetation to belay as for Black Death.
First ascent: N. White, P. Bull 30.6.1985.

DARTMOOR

GREAT LINKS TOR   GR 551 867
A remote tor shich is reached by a rough track which leads onto the moor from the Tavistock to Okehampton road at the Fox and Hounds public house. The tor offers short technical routes and a wealth of high quality boulder problems and is well worth the effort of a visit.

The rock masses comprising the tor, run in line from west to east, the most westerly block has a trig point on it and the climbing is on the next block east which is joined to the most westerly block by a rocky saddle. The south face is marked by an undercut wall with two obvious overhanging cracks running through it.

Great Flake   25ftVery Severe, 4c
The obvious overhung crack at the left-hand end, starting from a V-shaped niche.
First ascent: I. Peters (solo) 18.7.1985.

Lynx   30ft   Very Severe, 4c
The next crack right, harder than it looks.
First ascent: J. Barker, P. O'Sullivan 30.6.1985.

The next route is the finest overhang pitch on the moor and is an exacting route. The first ascent was made over 3 days and it still awaits an 'on sight' lead. Protection is difficult to arrange and an abseil inspection is recommended.

The Missing Link   30ft   XS, 6a
Climb the fiercely overhanging wall further right of the last route at its widest point.
First ascent: P. O'Sullivan, J. Barker 18.7.1985.

NORTH FACE
Tenuous Link   40ft   Very Severe, 5b
At the highest point of the wall there is a short groove at half height. Climb to this then exit along the obvious line to the right to gain the summit.
First ascent: P. O'Sullivan, J. Barber 30.6.1985.

HAYTOR
Little Gem   25ft   E2, 5a/b
Climb the wall right of Vandal and Ann, trending right, the first move is the crux.
First ascent: P. Bull 18.5.1985.

HOUND TOR
Kistvaen Corner   E3, 6b
Now led. Easier for a tall person.
First ascent: P. O'Sullivan, I. Peters 25.7.1985.

Fogou   30ft   Hard Very Severe, 5a
Climb the obvious overhanging corner right of Kistvaen Corner direct.
First ascent: J. Peters, P. O'Sullivan 25.7.1985.

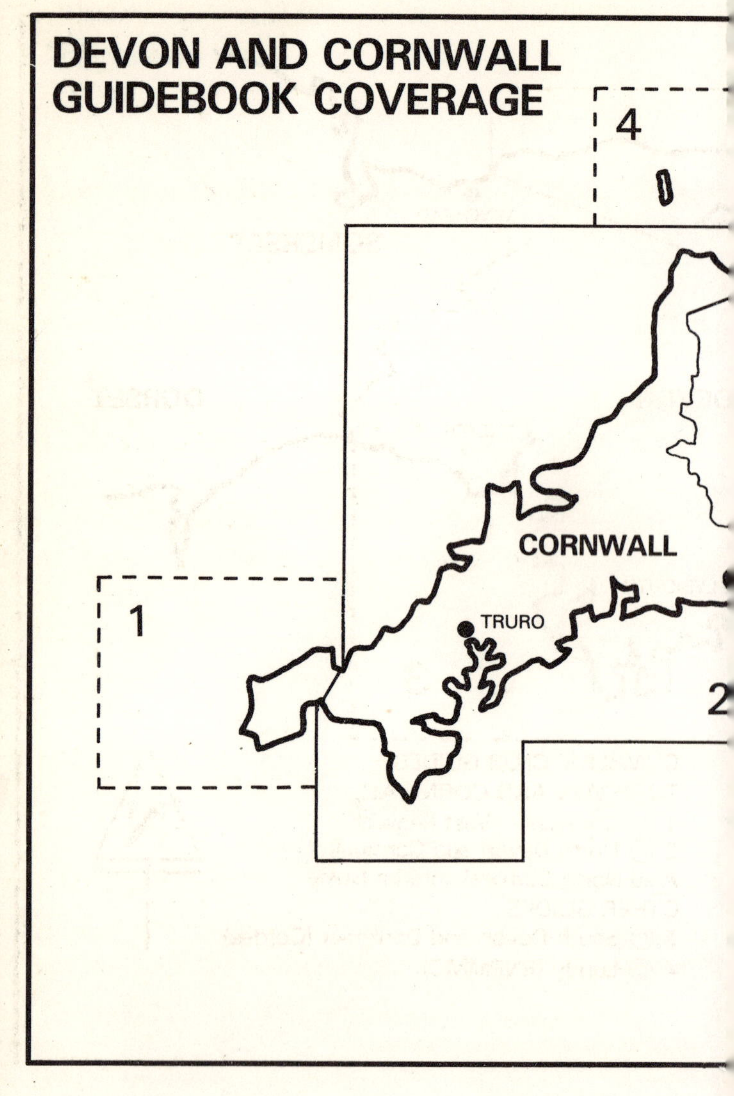

DEVON AND CORNWALL
GUIDEBOOK COVERAGE
4
1
CORNWALL
TRURO
2